ULTIMATE SPEED

The Fast Life and Extreme Cars of Racing Legend

Craig Breedlove

SAMUEL HAWLEY

CHICAGO
REVIEW
PRESS

Published by Chicago Review Press Incorporated
814 North Franklin Street
Chicago, Illinois 60610
ISBN 978-1-64160-020-0

Library of Congress Cataloging-in-Publication Data
Names: Hawley, Samuel Jay, 1960– author.
Title: Ultimate speed : the fast life and extreme cars of racing legend Craig
    Breedlove / Samuel Hawley.
Description: Chicago, Illinois : Chicago Review Press, Incorporated, [2019] |
    Includes bibliographical references and index.
Identifiers: LCCN 2018021891| ISBN 9781641600200 (cloth edition) | ISBN
    9781641600200 (pdf edition) | ISBN 9781641600231 (epub edition) | ISBN
    9781641600224 (kindle edition)
Subjects: LCSH: Breedlove, Craig. | Automobiles, Racing—Speed
    records—History—20th century. | Automobile racing drivers—United
    States—Biography.
Classification: LCC GV1032.B74 H38 2019 | DDC 796.72092 [B] —dc23 LC
    record available at https://lccn.loc.gov/2018021891

Typesetter: Nord Compo

Printed in the United States of America
5 4 3 2 1

CONTENTS

FOREWORD
by Craig Breedlove

THE QUEST FOR THE UNLIMITED LAND SPEED RECORD is just about the most exclusive sport in the world. Only eight people have succeeded in officially breaking the mark in the past eighty years. I'm one of them. I set the ultimate record five times in the 1960s and was the first to drive 400, 500, and 600 miles an hour.

Why are there so few of us? Because traveling at jet airplane speeds on the ground is hard. It takes years of effort to design and build a record-breaker. I'm talking total commitment. It will consume you, put you into debt, and turn your life upside down. And then, when you're finally ready to run, you have to bet everything on your machine and on your skill as a driver. Going into the measured mile, you literally have every bit of your skin in the game. If there is any flaw in your car, or in you, the land speed record will find it. And it will punish you for it. At 500-plus miles an hour, that can be very scary. It's almost a spiritual thing, those few seconds going through the clocks out on the desert, testing your machine and testing yourself. I guess you could call it the ultimate ethic. Setting this record can cost you your life.

This book tells the true story of my life. I first got to know the author, Samuel Hawley, back in 2009, when he interviewed me for an earlier book he was writing about the land speed record in the 1960s. Sam ended up writing a fantastic book, *Speed Duel*. It was the best thing I'd ever read about my rivalry with Art Arfons for the land speed record. Several years later, when I started thinking again about getting my biography written, I asked Sam if he'd like to do it. He said yes.

I'm really pleased with the book Sam has written. *Ultimate Speed* is a great read. It's creditable, it's accurate, it's exciting, and the research behind it is phenomenal. In addition to conducting many hours' worth of interviews with me over the phone and in person, Sam tracked down dozens of people who've been involved in my life, some of whom I'd totally lost touch with. He has dug down deeper into my life than I could have imagined, and not just into my life, but into the whole *Spirit of America* story. That's what I really like about this book, that it includes so many of the people who made *Spirit of America* happen and who have been so important to me.

So here it is: the story of my life, with all the highs and lows, warts and all. Better do up your seatbelts, because the ride is going to get bumpy.

PROLOGUE

A LEADEN SKY HUNG OVER the Bonneville Salt Flats in northwestern Utah, rain drizzling down on the two hundred square miles of white desert. It was November 15, 1965, extraordinarily late in the year for an attempt on the world land speed record, well into the off-season when the salt became flooded. A needle-nosed race car nevertheless sat out here on this chilly morning, sheltered from the weather by a red and white awning. "Spirit of America" was painted on its side and, on the ten-foot-high tailfin, sweeping backward, an American flag. And at the back: the business-end of a jet engine, capable of generating 15,000 pounds of thrust in full afterburner. That was something like 30,000 horsepower, nearly double the juice of the entire field in the Indianapolis 500 earlier that year.

The car's designer and driver, twenty-eight-year-old Californian Craig Breedlove, had been out here waiting since dawn. He hadn't eaten breakfast. He never did before a record attempt. He wanted to keep his stomach empty in case he crashed and had to be rushed to the hospital to be pieced back together. He wasn't thinking of food, however. He was focused on the weather and on what he had to do if it cleared. All he needed was an hour, just one hour, to beat the record set the week before by his archrival Art Arfons. One run down the course and one run back, completed within sixty minutes, the average of the two to exceed Art's 576 mph mark by at least 1 percent. That's how the game of land speed racing was played.

Eight thirty. The drizzle subsided. The air grew still.

Craig turned to *Spirit of America* crew chief Nye Frank. "Let's get it running."

The crew got the battle-scarred racer positioned and ready. They had been here on the salt, off and on, for nearly four weeks, and it showed. Craig's name, painted beneath the cockpit, had been mostly cut away during repair work after the air duct was damaged. Bent body panels had been punched with louvers to relieve the aerodynamic pressure that had alternately sucked them up and squashed them down from the frame. Stabilizing vanes had been welded over the rear wheels and larger fins installed at the center after it was discovered that the front wheels were lifting up off the ground at high speed, that the car was in effect doing a wheelie. That experience had been terrifying.

Craig climbed into the cockpit. Helmet on. Harness on. Air mask snapped into place. Canopy lowered and locked.

He signaled to Nye, twirling his index finger. *Start the engine.*

The start cart attached by an umbilical cord to the side of the racer began turning the compressor inside the J-79 jet engine, spinning it faster and faster. Craig threw a switch inside the cockpit. *Ignition.* Gasoline injected into the compressor hit the pilot light and combusted. The jet whined louder, the pitch steadily rising. *Advance throttle.* The whine rose to a howl.

The J-79 was running on its own now. The start cart was disconnected and towed out of the way. Craig turned off the ignition switch and further advanced the throttle. The howl rose to a shriek that he could feel in his bones.

Hands locked on the steering yoke. He gazed down the black line marking the center of the graded track, the end beyond sight beneath the curve of the Earth.

This was it. This was the opportunity he wanted. This was the hour he feared.

He released the brake. *Spirit of America* took off down the course.

In the 120-year history of land speed racing, no name looms larger than that of Craig Breedlove. He is the preeminent living legend in this, the world's most dangerous sport. A Los Angeles hot-rodder with a high school education, meager resources, a superlative work ethic, and tremendous ambition, he burst onto the scene in the early 1960s with a three-wheeled racer he dubbed *Spirit of America*. It was not powered by an internal combustion engine like the British machines that had dominated the preceding era, driven by land speed icons like Malcolm Campbell, Henry Segrave, George Eyston, and John Cobb. Craig's *Spirit* instead used the less complicated and vastly greater power of a jet. It would take him to a record of 407.45 mph on the Bonneville Salt Flats in 1963 and from there into a speed rivalry with Art Arfons and a beast called *Green Monster*. Over the next two years Craig and Art would trade the land speed record (LSR) back and forth in a series of white-knuckle rides and experience some of the most spectacular crashes in motorsport history, Craig wrecking his original *Spirit* and building a replacement, *Spirit of America–Sonic I*, along the way. When it was all over he had broken the record five times and become the first person to drive 400, 500, and 600 mph.

And that's not the end of the story. In the 1970s Craig would turn from jets to rockets and set an acceleration record at Bonneville that stands to this day. He would suffer financial ruin and repeated heartache in marriage, then would pick himself up and start over again. And he would build a new jet car, *Spirit of America–Sonic Arrow*, and return to land speed competition in the 1990s. His goal this time: first to 650 mph, then to 700, then to Mach 1.

What follows is Craig Breedlove's life story. It is based primarily on the many hours of interviews that I conducted with Craig and his family, friends, and associates. It is an inspiring true story of ingenuity, perseverance, and daring—of what one man with a big dream and boundless drive can achieve.

––––––––––

The speedometer was sweeping through the 200s when *Spirit of America* passed the first mile marker. This was the speed range where the racer started violently shaking, like Craig was driving over a field of ruts. He hung on, clenching his stomach muscles, steadying his guts. He had been through this many times before.

300 mph. The shaking subsided. The ride smoothed out. A second mile marker swept past, this time more of a blur. Shafts of sunlight were breaking through the clouds up ahead. The salt was looking almost sacred, like the inside of a cathedral.

400 mph. A new sensation now, slippery, like Craig was driving on ice. This was where a high-speed run got truly intense, the racer going so fast that the wheels started skimming the surface, maintaining only tenuous contact, the car barely under control.

500 mph. *Spirit* was drifting from the black line. Craig turned the steering yoke to ease back to center. Nothing. He turned the yoke farther. Finally a sluggish response.

550 mph. Another marker, barely seen, whipped by, and with it the timing lights. Craig was now in the measured mile.

575 mph. Drifting again, the black line veering. Craig tried to correct. Nothing. He turned the yoke all the way over. Still nothing.

He knew what that meant. His front wheels were up off the ground. *Spirit of America* was about to fly.

1

IGNITER

Ten-year-old Craig Bowman was flying.

He was going round and round in a circle, hanging on to the handle connected to the seventy-five-foot wires running to his model airplane. He took it around a few times at head level, the two-stroke engine that had nicked his finger so many times buzzing like an angry bee. Then, with a twist of the wrist that elevated the wing flaps, he sent it soaring in a series of inside loops that elicited "oohs" and "aahs" from the crowd gathering in the parking lot at Hughes Aircraft, not far from Craig's home in West Los Angeles. Next came a wingover, flipping the plane upside down for a few turns, then a few more loops, outside ones this time, bringing the plane swooping down so close to the asphalt that it looked sure to crash.

Fortunately it didn't. For this was a magnificent handcrafted model that young Craig was flying, every bit as impressive as the ones built by the grown men competing in the stunt flying contest. It was big too, with a five-foot wingspan—quite a bit bigger in fact than Craig Bowman, who was not much more than four feet tall and weighed barely seventy pounds. "I was so small," Craig remembers with a laugh, "that the airplane would damn near lift me off the ground when I did wingovers. I'd be leaning back in about a 45 degree angle just to fly it around in a circle."

This was where it all began—with model airplanes and Craig's membership in a club called the Sky Kings. It was here that Craig first learned about engines, little two-stroke jobs that ran on alcohol and nitromethane and castor oil for lubricant. It was here that he first learned about design and aerodynamics, for these were no mere kits he was assembling, but customized aircraft that he developed himself. It was here that he first acquired fabrication skills of a high standard, using an X-Acto knife to cut out balsa wood parts by hand, gluing silkspan onto the wing spars, doping it, and applying a flawless lacquer finish. It was here that he first showed the all-consuming drive and intensity that later characterized his approach to land speed racing. It all started here, when he was ten years old, competing in model airplane contests against older kids and adults. Seventy years later Craig's hand still bears traces of the nicks he got turning over the propeller to start up his flying machines.

The year was 1947. Craig was living with his mother Portia and his new stepdad Ken Bowman at 3940 Marcasel Avenue, a stuccoed bungalow in the Mar Vista neighborhood of West L.A. He did his model-building out back, in a shed where Portia had raised chickens and rabbits during the war. He had started with boats, then switched to airplanes with the encouragement of Ed Rourke, a gentle soul who lived across the street. Ed, a Hughes Aircraft employee and model plane hobbyist, had plenty of time to help Craig, for he was on sick leave with tuberculosis. It was Ed who got Craig involved in the Sky Kings and taught him the basics of building and flying his own U-Control planes.

Ed died shortly thereafter. It hit Craig hard. He had already lost his father to divorce and he felt unwanted by his stepdad, so Ed's attention had been important to him and losing it hurt. He would subsequently latch on to another neighbor, Loyola University student Jack Stafford, the second in a long line of older male role models who would mentor Craig during his formative years.

Jack took Craig to a more advanced level of model airplane building. It was a steep learning curve littered with numerous crashed models on the playing field at Venice High School where Craig practiced. But he learned. Then he innovated. He built drop-away landing gear to make his planes more streamlined and faster in flight, gluing skis to the underside of the fuselage so he could belly-land them without damage. To keep the propeller from breaking off, he figured out how to make it stop in a horizontal position as the plane glided in. And all the while he dug deeper into aerodynamics, studying books and attending weekly meetings in the cafeteria at Hughes, where the Sky Kings club screened films on aircraft design. Craig liked a good Western or spy thriller as much as the next kid, but an educational film on how to balance center of lift with the center of gravity—now *that* was exciting!

"That's where I learned about aerodynamics," says Craig. "It's how I got my education. It was very grassroots, basic stuff. I learned because I was really interested in it. I had some world-class airplanes that I had designed and built myself, really good flying airplanes. They were models, but there's really nothing different from building a model airplane to building the real thing."

And then, one day in 1949, when Craig was twelve, a vision of mechanical splendor appeared across the street in the Rourkes' driveway. It was an old jalopy, hood up, guts laid bare, parts strewn about. Ed Rourke's son Roger was working on the thing with his buddies.

Craig wandered over, intrigued. He asked seventeen-year-old Roger, who had grease smeared up to his elbows, what he was doing.

"Building a hot rod. Stay out of the way."

Craig stood back and watched for a while. The complexity of the machinery, so many intricate parts . . . it made his model airplanes look like kid stuff.

He turned back to Roger. "Can I help?"

Like so many other Californians at the time, Craig's family did not have deep ancestral roots in the state. His father, Norman Lloyd Breedlove, had been born in 1906 in Louisville, Kentucky, to Gorman Breedlove and Florence Vanmeter. Gorman contracted tuberculosis in his early thirties and moved his young family out to the West Coast in the hope that the climate would help him recover. It didn't. He died in Los Angeles in 1918, leaving Florence a widow and twelve-year-old Norm without a dad.

Florence went on to achieve success as a seamstress, opening her own shop and making gowns for movie stars like Joan Crawford and Anna May Wong. Norm, meanwhile, chafed under Florence's new husband, his new stepdad, whom he deeply disliked. He seized his independence as soon as he finished school, getting a job in a bank, then in the Hollywood studio system as a special effects technician. It would be here, working on everything from Tarzan movies to John Wayne pictures, that Norm would spend the rest of his life.

It was also here, at RKO Radio Pictures, that he met Craig's mother, a gorgeous young redhead named Portia Champion. Portia had been born in Alberta in 1913 to immigrant parents, Welsh stonemason Ernest Champion and his Irish wife Sarah Craig, who met on the ship to Canada. They married and settled in Edmonton, where Ernest built a successful construction business and a house called Craigmont. Seeking pastures that were greener still, the family moved to California when Portia was a child. She was a twenty-year-old dancer dreaming of Hollywood stardom when Norm first met her, one of the bevy of beauties in the musicals then all the rage. That vivacious looker in the chorus line backing up Fred Astaire and Ginger Rogers in *Flying Down to Rio* and *The Gay Divorcee*? The one with the great legs and a face like Bette Davis? That was Portia. She was never "discovered," never even got a screen credit. But Norm certainly noticed. They were married in 1934. The only child they would have together, Norman Craig Breedlove, was born on March 23, 1937. They took to using his middle name to distinguish him from his father.

Craig's earliest memories of home are of the little stuccoed bungalow that Norm built on Marcasel Avenue. The pictures that survive show a happy childhood: four-year-old Craig and his parents on the front step with the family's two dachshunds, Hans and Gretchen; five-year-old Craig laughing at a birthday party; eight-year-old Craig with family and friends at Newport Beach, enjoying a weekend at the seaside cabin Norm built. But there were dark moments too, for Craig's dad had a temper. Cut Norm off on the road or give him the finger and he was apt to run you down, drag you out of your car, and punch you in the face. And you definitely didn't want to hit on his wife, even if Portia was flirting, which she sometimes did. Norm wasn't a big guy, but he'd take a swing at you just the same.

"I can remember my dad getting out of the car and just decking somebody when I was a kid," Craig remembers. "He used to beat the shit out of me too, when I was really little. He'd smack me, give me a bloody nose, split my lip. If I used one of his tools and didn't put it back, or if I was out playing and I didn't make it home on time and he had to come out and find me, he'd be smacking me in the back of my head all the way home."

Portia hated Norm's violent outbursts. It was a major reason for their divorce in 1944. The sudden departure of his father left a void in Craig's life and, to a seven-year-old boy, felt a lot like rejection. This was why the attention of early mentors like Ed Rourke and Jack Stafford was so important.

Craig and Portia continued to live in the Marcasel house following Norm's departure, as Norm had signed the property over to his ex-wife. Then, in 1946, Portia remarried and a new man moved in. Her second husband, Ken Bowman, formally adopted Craig, making him Craig Bowman. It was a well-intentioned gesture, made in part to disguise the divorce of Craig's parents, which was still considered somewhat shameful back in the 1940s. But it only compounded Craig's insecurity and confused his friends. And then a half sister, Cynthia, was born, adding to Craig's emotional burden the sense that he was just in the way, that he was not wanted—particularly after Cynthia was given his bedroom and he was moved into the den. Norm was upset when Craig told him about it. "I built that house for you and your mom," he groused. "You should have your bedroom." But he kept his peace.

Craig and his stepdad didn't get along. Ken was a bookish type, more interested in reading and classical music than in model airplanes and engines, so the two had little in common. He also had an open dislike for Portia's ex-husband Norm, who frequently took Craig on weekends, leading to further alienation between stepfather and stepson. There was no open warfare, just a rift that developed between them, Craig resenting Ken's authority and convinced Ken wanted him gone, Ken seeing Craig as troublesome and rebellious. As Craig grew older, turning eleven, then twelve, his carefree childhood exuberance faded away and he became shy, withdrawn, a loner. The chicken coop out back, which served as his model-making workshop, became his refuge.

Roger Rourke and his friends working on the jalopy across the street were members of a local hot rod club called the Igniters, one of hundreds of such groups then springing up across the country and particularly in Southern California. The craze had begun with the millions of veterans returning to civilian life after the life-changing experience of World War II. Seeking to recapture something of the excitement of combat, they started souping up and racing used cars that were then flooding the market, unloaded by consumers eager to buy the new cars that Detroit was at last producing again after the long wartime hiatus. Building a hot rod was something an average Joe could afford. It required hard work and mechanical ingenuity and artistry too. It was a chance to enjoy some camaraderie with your buddies, building a machine together, speaking the language of engines, figuring things out. And racing your creation could give you a pretty good adrenaline kick, maybe not as intense as dodging bullets, but certainly more fun.

Craig, only twelve, was too young to join the Igniters, most of whom were in their late teens and twenties. He was eager to help, however, so Roger let him. Sweeping up, sanding off rust, packing grease into bearings—Craig completed every dirty, tedious job he was given with a cheerful diligence that won the guys over. "He was kind of our mascot," remembers Igniters member Doug Sarian. "We'd take him wherever we went. He was just a neat kid. And a fast learner. He was *involved*. When the guys worked on their cars, Craig would be right there with them, working with them, learning as he went. That's all he was concerned about: building cars, working on cars. He was just a good kid."

In the space of a year Craig was talking like a seasoned hot-rodder and was starting to work on a car of his own, a rusty old '34 Ford coupe. He had convinced Ken to kick in the last few bucks to buy it when he couldn't raise the whole seventy-five dollars from saved Christmas money and after-school jobs. "All right," Ken said sternly, "but it's going to represent your birthday present." Ken couldn't understand his stepson's new obsession, but Craig was working hard at it, even studying books on mechanics, so maybe it was a good thing. Besides, he wouldn't be *driving* the car. He was still three years away from even getting a license. He would only be out there in the backyard, tinkering on the machine.

Little did Ken and Portia know that Craig was already driving the streets of L.A. From the den where he slept, it was easy to slip out the back door after his parents thought he was asleep so that he could go cruising with the Igniters. They would hang out at the Clock or Piccadilly Drive-Ins ("A Square Meal on a Round Bun, 25¢"), go street racing on Culver Boulevard out among the fields, make out in the backseat with their girlfriends while Craig did the driving, acting as chauffeur, straining to reach the gas pedal.

The guys in the Igniters would be Craig's older male role models for the next several years, especially Roger Rourke, the group's de facto leader—Roger who couldn't speak a sentence without using a swear word. Some of the others were Marvin Gelbart, Doug Sarian, Carl Cruz, and Lee Ganzer, "Shitty" Schultz and "Hickey" Hickman and Bucky Cole and "Dirty" Tom Brown. They were rambunctious teens always on the lookout for fun . . . and it sometimes took them too far. There was the time, for example, when they decided to get even with Officer Stafford, a local traffic cop who had it in for hot-rodders and was always looking for a reason to bust them. "The guys chained the back of Stafford's motorcycle to a light post or something," Craig remembers, "then one of the guys burned rubber around the corner. Stafford came out and jumped on his bike and took off after him and the chain ran out and it just stopped the bike dead. Sent him flying over the handlebars. Later, it was used in a movie, I think. [George Lucas's *American Graffiti*, where the chained motorcycle became a chained police car.] Well, that was an actual thing that happened. It happened right on the corner of Washington Place and Sepulveda Boulevard, at Piccadilly Drive-In."

And then there was the episode with the firecracker. This was no regular firecracker, but a veritable bomb that Roger made by filling a condom with oxygen and acetylene gas and attaching a fuse. It was set off in the men's toilet in the parking lot restroom at the luckless Piccadilly. *KA-BOOM!* The explosion destroyed the porcelain bowl and sent water geysering up through the women's toilets next door and a drenched and screaming occupant fleeing in a state of undress. Craig was disappointed not to have been there, for the incident was the talk around the neighborhood for weeks. He pleaded with Roger to make him a condom bomb too, just one, so he could see the effect for himself. Roger agreed. Hey, what harm could it do? Craig disappeared down the street with the quivering balloon full of gas.

A muffled explosion was heard a few minutes later. Then Craig returned. "That was the loudest firecracker I've ever heard," he marveled, his eyes still wide. He had set the thing off in a phone booth. It peeled the sides off it like a banana.

In March 1953, as soon as he turned sixteen, Craig went down to the Department of Motor Vehicles and aced the driving exam. He was now a full-fledged member of the Igniters, with a driver's license tucked in his wallet and his very own club plaque, IGNITERS, CULVER CITY, displayed in the back window of his hot rod. For his '34 Ford coupe, after three years of work, was complete. He had finished it at his friend Dick Pollard's house, in a backyard chicken coop that he had converted into a garage, after being evicted from his workshop at home when Ken and Portia started a business growing African violets and needed the space. Craig was glad to get away from the oversight of his stepfather, for while Ken condoned Craig's building a car, he strongly disapproved of the idea of racing—which of course had been Craig's plan all along. The whole point of fabricating a hot rod, after all, was to test it, to push it, to see what it could do. That was the payoff after the thousands of hours of work.

Craig's earliest experience of racing had been as a spectator at street races. For hot-rodders who hung out at the Piccadilly and Clock Drive-Ins, guys like the Igniters, the usual venue was a stretch of Culver Boulevard a few miles west, out among fields where there was no traffic at night. The starting point was the overpass where Culver passed over Lincoln Boulevard. This was where two cars going head to head were flagged off. The end was just before you got to the railroad tracks, a distance someone had measured off as being a quarter mile. Spectators would watch from the Lincoln overpass at the start or from atop boxcars parked on a railway siding down at the end. It was a risky business, racing here at night, even being a spectator, for it was illegal. When the cops showed up, everyone scattered. Craig, home in bed as far as his parents knew, never got caught.

Craig also got a lot of exposure to racing at the drag strips that were just then being established, tagging along with the guys to the track at Fontana and then to Saugus after it opened in 1951. It was at Saugus, in 1952, that he had his first experience of real speed, of actually getting behind the wheel of a dragster and punching it through the quarter. Bill Adair, who had taken a liking to Craig, invited him to tag along to a meet that Saturday morning and help out with Bill's dragster. It was one of the fastest machines at Saugus, a supercharged "fuel" dragster gulping a mixture of alcohol and nitromethane. It therefore came as a shock when Bill, frustrated from having a bad day, tossed Craig his helmet and said, "Go take a ride."

Quivering with excitement, Craig donned Bill's helmet and climbed in.

"Keep it straight and you won't get in trouble," Bill told him. "Get off the accelerator when you get through the lights, and shut the engine off when you get it stopped."

Craig started the engine and pulled up to the start line. Waiting . . . waiting . . .

Green light.

Craig blazed through the clocks at 127 mph, a speed that any driver at Saugus would have been proud of. He did it at fifteen years old. The admiration and respect it earned him—it was addictive. He wanted more.

He never told his parents.

Photos of Craig from this period rarely show him smiling. It was partly shyness but mostly an attempt to look older, for he was still the youngest in the groups he hung out with. He wore jeans and T-shirts like the rest of the guys, slicked his hair back with Wildroot in a style known as the "wave," and tried without success to like smoking. He was on his way to becoming a good-looking young man, James Dean–handsome, the kind of guy girls noticed. But he didn't have a girlfriend. Not yet. He was secretly too afraid of being rejected to ask anyone out.

Craig was now a junior at Venice High School, where he had been since graduating from Betsy Ross Elementary. He was highly intelligent but it didn't show on his report cards. Craig hardly knew it himself. He did well in hands-on classes like machine shop and drafting, where his creative drive found expression, but only the bare minimum in other subjects. This disappointed his parents. They had been hoping Craig would go to college, not become a mechanic, which he now seemed destined to do.

That suited Craig fine. He didn't want to go to college. Cars were his life. If he wasn't working on cars, he was working at part-time jobs to earn money to buy car parts. He was developing a strong, almost relentless work ethic, going back to his first jobs delivering newspapers and trimming hedges, then sanding cars in an auto body shop for fifty cents an hour. He spent a summer working at Van's Muffler Company, where he learned the rudiments of welding at the age of sixteen, then was hired by Bill Cox, owner of Quincy Automotive, to do muffler work, sweep the floor, and drive the parts truck. "I guess I was more attuned than a lot of kids that Bill could have hired," says Craig. "Like when I went to work there, my second or third day, the bathroom was such a gross pigsty, you wouldn't believe it. I mean, you were taking your life in your hands even to walk in there. So I went in and cleaned that bathroom from ceiling to floor—the toilet, the washbasin, everything. The next time Bill walked in there, he said, 'What the hell . . . who did this?' And Harvey Chernik, who worked behind the counter, said, 'It was Craig.' After that I couldn't do anything wrong."

Quincy Automotive wasn't an ordinary garage. It was a speed shop. Bill Cox had opened it after returning home from the war, naming it after a buddy killed in combat. They had planned to open a garage together if they ever got back to L.A. alive. Quincy never made it. By the mid-1950s Quincy's was known to hot-rodders all across Southern California as the place to go for high-performance modifications and to buy specialty parts. It even attracted customers from out of state—like a pair of bootleggers who showed up towing a car behind a beat-up old truck.

"How fast can you make her go?" they wanted to know.

Harvey Chernik eyeballed the car. "How much money you got?"

"Fifteen hundred."

"Well, we can make her go fifteen hundred faster."

The bootleggers nodded. One of them, chewing tobacco, spit a glob on the floor. That set off Harvey. Craig's fastidiousness was rubbing off on the tough ex-marine.

"Spit in the cans, goddamn it! That's what they're for!"

2

THROUGH THE ROOF

THE '32 FORD COUPE BELONGED to Stan Burnhaley, an older guy, a decent automobile bodywork man. He wanted the flathead engine souped up so he took it to Craig, who at age seventeen already had a local reputation for doing good work. Craig boosted the horsepower by boring out the cylinders and installing bigger pistons, and by porting and relieving the combustion chambers to increase the airflow. The rod was rumbling like a barely bridled beast when Stan picked it up—a whole lot of power was now packed under the hood. In fact it scared him a little. The days passed and he couldn't bring himself to floor it, to really open it up like he wanted. Finally he went back to Craig and asked if he'd do the inaugural honors, take the coupe for a test run to see what it could do. Craig, proud of his growing stature as a drag racer, shrugged and said, *Sure.*

Craig didn't know much about Stan's coupe beyond the work he'd done on the engine. And he didn't ask any questions. He had therefore just broken Drag Rule Number One: know your machine before you race it. But it was understandable, for he was just a teenager. He didn't have any conception of how easy it was to get killed.

Craig laughs now as he recalls that night. "That's how stupid I was."

Craig's own coupe, his '34 Ford, was now complete. It was a thing of beauty—pristine blue paint job, supercharged V-8 engine, seats custom reupholstered in Tijuana. "I remember the first time he pulled in with it, and his supercharger was running," recalls high school friend Mike Freebairn. "I mean, it sounded like it was a man-eating lion going by. It was a real screamer."

"Absolutely not," Ken Bowman exploded, horrified when Craig announced that he was taking the coupe to Saugus to race. "You spent about four or five hundred dollars on the engine alone and you're not going to take it up there and ruin it."

"OK, I won't go," Craig glowered. Then he went anyway—and promptly got hooked. He loved how the other guys at the track, most of them older, nodded approvingly as they looked over his car, and how they no longer saw him as a kid but as someone they were competing against. His very first run, on April 18, 1953, four weeks after his sixteenth birthday, was against a mean-looking black Ford. Craig smoked it, earning a bear hug from Bill Adair when he got back to the pits. He beat the next car too, and then the next, a candy-apple bomb dubbed *The Red Baron*. He went home that day with a trophy and proudly showed it to his parents. Ken wasn't happy about being disobeyed but he let it go. At least his headstrong stepson was a winner.

More trophies followed, Craig competing at Saugus or Fontana nearly every weekend. Then he landed his very first sponsor: Quincy Automotive. It wasn't worth much, just a few bucks, his boss Bill Cox donating little things like gaskets and bolts and allowing him to use the shop truck to haul his racer around. But it still made Craig feel important.

Craig had now outgrown the Igniters. He joined another Culver City hot rod group, the Chevaliers, and also a more serious club called the Screwdrivers, part of the Russetta Timing Association. That meant that Craig could compete in RTA-sanctioned events at El Mirage dry lake north of L.A. and in the annual meet known as Speed Week that was held on Utah's Bonneville Salt Flats every August. These were not head-to-head quarter-mile drag races where acceleration was key, but solo tests of ultimate speed where the miles of desert were used to build up speed before making a flying run through the clocks. How fast was your machine? How much nerve did you have as a driver? These were the things Craig wanted to find out.

Craig had made the seven-hundred-mile pilgrimage to Bonneville once before, with Bill Adair for Speed Week in 1953. It was the farthest he had ever traveled from home, camping under the stars for a whole week in heaven with hundreds of hot rods, the most impressive of which were the aluminum-skinned streamliners that some guys were now building. They were a revelation to Craig, a whole new level of design and craftsmanship. In the summer of '54 he returned to the salt flats for Speed Week, this time with his own car, towing it behind Quincy's truck, burning gas that Bill Cox paid for. Craig felt he had arrived in the big leagues.

Craig's plan had been to blow the competition away by installing two supercharged engines in the coupe like in Bill Adair's racer, one to power the front wheels, the other the rear. He was just beginning to install them when a photographer from *Hot Rod* magazine showed up. "A newcomer to Bonneville this year will be Craig Bowman, a member of the Culver City Chevaliers," read the caption under the two published photos. It was the very first media attention Craig ever got, appearing in the September 1954 issue. Unfortunately, someone broke into the chicken coop/garage and stole the rear-engine setup out of the car before Craig had a chance to run it. It was a huge loss, representing months of savings from part-time jobs. The coupe thus went to Bonneville with a single engine, which started choking when Craig got going and managed only 126 mph, placing him well down the list in his category, "C" class coupe. Disappointment—that was part of the game. The solution: Do better. Work harder.

After repairs and modifications, Craig took the coupe to El Mirage dry lake to try again. He wasn't intending to drive this time, for Bonneville had scared him and El Mirage scared him more. "Everybody said it was a tricky course," he recalled in the *Los Angeles Times* in 1965. "So I lined up a guy to drive my car for me. But he was already driving some other cars and the [timing] association told him he couldn't take another one. So I gave it a try myself." This time his machine worked to perfection. Instead it was Craig who almost broke down with a bad case of nerves. He nevertheless blazed off a 141 mph run in practice, beating the course record held by the builder-driver duo of Nick Arias and Don Rackeman—who were suddenly working like mad on their GMC Jimmy to coax out another few miles an hour and put this upstart kid in his place.

They didn't. Craig went out again and did even better, a 144 mph run, then a 148. "I don't care if we put dynamite in that Jimmy," Rackeman finally conceded. "It's not going to go 148." This El Mirage record was a huge confidence builder for Craig. He would experience plenty of pre-run apprehension in the years to follow but never again would he physically shake with fear. From now on he would always be able to keep his nerves under control.

For the time being, however, this didn't help him much with girls. Craig still couldn't bring himself to ask one out. His friends finally helped him break the ice, fixing him up on a blind date with a pretty brunette named Marge Toombs, a fellow Venice High senior. Marge didn't share Craig's obsession with cars but they hit it off just the same. Maybe it was that they were both unhappy at home, Craig feeling like a third wheel to his mom and stepfather, Marge wanting to get away from her mom and her mom's live-in boyfriend, both heavy drinkers.

By early 1955 Craig and Marge were seeing a lot of each other.

———————

They headed west on Culver Boulevard in Stan Burnhaley's '32 Ford, out of the city to the usual spot among the bean and celery fields, the quarter-mile stretch between the Lincoln overpass and the train tracks. There were three of them—Stan, Craig, and Marge—squeezed in the front seat. A few other cars tagged along but none to race against Craig. Craig would be taking a solo run in Stan's coupe.

They arrived at the overpass. Stan and Marge got out and Craig took the wheel. No seatbelt, no helmet. Niceties like that weren't a part of street racing. He started the engine he'd worked on. He gunned it, foot on the brake.

Clutch out. Hit the gas. The coupe took off, leaving behind strips of rubber. It shot down Culver past dark fields, the speedometer needle sweeping past 60, 80, 100, the flathead kicking out horses, doing what Craig had rebuilt it to do.

He was going over a hundred when he flashed past the signpost marking the end of the quarter and hit the train tracks crossing the road. It was like running into a wall, for the coupe's front end was as stiff as a board.

"Stan had put the car together," says Craig, "and had not put shock absorbers on the front. So when I hit those railroad tracks going over a hundred, that thing took two giant leaps and rolled end over end in the middle of Culver Boulevard and threw me through the roof. In the center of the '32 coupe there's a piece of fabric and wood and some chicken wire and stuff that form the top of the car. I went flying through that soft top, came to out in a celery field, a big gash in the top of my head, knocked clean out of my shoes. I was bleeding like a stuck pig and had a really bad concussion."

Marge came running up, frantic, as Craig staggered to his feet. His hair was matted with blood. He was still stunned and glassy-eyed from being knocked out.

Sirens in the distance. Stan had found a phone and called for help. Thinking he was in big trouble, Craig in his confused state had only one thought: *run*.

"I grabbed Marge by the arm and dragged her across these celery fields, trying to ditch the cops. I'm in my bare feet, and the whole time we're stumbling along I keep forgetting what happened. I'd ask Marge, 'Marge, what happened?' And she'd say, 'You were racing the car,' and I'd say, 'Oh yeah . . . oh yeah.' And then five minutes later I'd ask her the same thing, over and over, because I was cuckoo from smashing my head."

Craig dragged Marge all the way back to the Clock Drive-In, where his own car was parked. When they finally got there he got spooked. What if the cops had his car staked out? What if they were waiting to arrest him?

He kept walking, dragging Marge down Venice Boulevard, down past the high school, back to her house. Then he got spooked again and took her to a neighbor's house instead, where she sometimes babysat.

It was the neighbor who phoned Ken Bowman to come and do something about his bloodied and addled stepson. Ken was not happy when he showed up in the family sedan. He drove Craig to Santa Monica Hospital and got his head stitched up.

————————

Thirty years later, in the mid-1980s, Craig went to a chiropractor seeking relief from neck pain that had dogged him throughout his life. It had been manageable when he was younger but was now getting worse. As a first step before attempting treatment, the chiropractor took X-rays and sent them out to be developed.

He phoned Craig up the next day, deeply concerned. "What the hell did you do to your neck?"

"I don't know," Craig said. "It just hurts."

"Well, you've got a double compression fracture in vertebrae five, six, and seven."

It took Craig a few minutes to think back to that crash on Culver Boulevard in 1955. It had done a whole lot more than put a gash in his head. He had broken his neck.

Craig's condition was considered inoperable when it was first discovered. He would have to live with a badly healed broken neck for another decade and more, getting by on ibuprofen to ease the discomfort. Finally the pain became so bad that an operation was deemed necessary despite the risks. It was gruesome—the surgeons went in through his throat—but ultimately successful. Craig walks around today with three of his neck vertebrae fused together with a titanium plate.

"That crash was actually a good thing," he says, looking back, "because it slowed me down. It made me respect those things [race cars]. I didn't think I was invincible anymore."

————————

Craig graduated from high school in 1955, the gash on his head from the crash only just healed. Later that summer Marge came to him with big news: she was pregnant. Going from first base to rounding third with his new girlfriend had had consequences. Getting an abortion was not an option, not back in the 1950s. Neither was having the child out of wedlock. That left only one thing to do. Craig and Marge, both eighteen years old, drove to Yuma, Arizona, where no license was required, and got married on September 12, 1955.

That was the last straw for Craig's parents. They made it clear that it was time for him to move out. As he puts it, "I was basically shown the door." He and Marge rented an apartment and they both started working full time and saving to buy a house, Marge getting a job at Coast Federal Savings and Loan in downtown L.A. "We'd been in the apartment maybe four months when we bought the house on Venice Boulevard," Marge remembers, "this little one-bedroom house for $6,000. It was awful! It didn't have a garage. That was the first thing Craig did, was he built a garage so he could put his car in there."

This would be where their first child, daughter Chris, would be born in 1956, followed in quick succession by son Norman in 1957 and daughter Dawn in 1958. To squeeze them all in, Craig walled in the porch to make a tiny second bedroom for the kids, barely five by eight feet. He also fenced in the front yard to give them a place to play that was safe from the traffic whizzing by on Venice, using wood from dismantled sets that his dad Norm hauled over from the MGM studio lot where he was now working. For Craig, these years were a headlong rush into adulthood and the start of a lifelong struggle—a losing struggle—to balance the needs of family with racing.

Craig worked hard to support his young family. Faced with the sudden need for more money, he left Quincy's for a better-paying job at Bill Murphy Buick as assistant manager of the new car get-ready department. New cars back then weren't ready for delivery to customers when they arrived at a dealership direct from the factory. It was up to the dealer to tune up the engine and align the front wheels, to fix paint chips and apply underseal if it had been ordered, and to install whatever accessories the customer wanted. At Bill Murphy Buick, a major dealership selling five-hundred-plus cars a month, this required moving each vehicle through a series of departments and garages scattered over a couple square miles of L.A. It was a hugely disorganized system in which cars were constantly going missing and where customers had to wait when they came in to pick up a new car while staff phoned around to the different departments to find it.

Craig saw the problem right away. And he saw a solution, which he explained to the department manager and got permission to try. "I went out and bought two sheets of plywood," he says, "and painted them with blackboard paint and white stripes for different categories, balance, underseal, whatever, all the places the cars had to go. Then I came up with a procedure where the mechanic would sign in next to the customer's name and the model of the car, then he'd cross out his name after he'd finished working on the car, so I knew when the car was done and ready to go to the next category, and I would assign the next guy to that car."

One of the bosses there at the dealership was racing legend Sam Hanks, a friend of Bill Murphy's. Craig had seen Sam race back when he was a kid, when his Uncle Ruzzy, Portia's brother, took him to the midget auto races on a board track at the L.A. Memorial Coliseum. Their paths were about to cross again.

"Anyway, I organized the whole thing," Craig continues. "And then Sam Hanks sees this big chart I had up there, with all the cars labeled and everything organized, and he says, 'What the hell is this?' I explained it to him and he was blown away. From that day on, Sam took me under his wing. He was about forty then and I was eighteen."

It was Sam who introduced Craig to the world of professional racing. He took Craig to the track and let him hang out in the pits alongside up-and-comers like Carroll Shelby and Dan Gurney, and gave him an inside look at the Indianapolis 500 car being built by Sandy Belond in Quincy Epperly's shop in Gardena, the one Sam would drive to victory at Indy in 1957. For Craig, it was an up-close look at a whole new level of high-performance racing. This, he knew, was what he wanted for himself. This was where he had to be.

But how? Working full time to support his family left Craig little time and no money to pursue his dreams. He confided his problem to Sam, asking him how he managed to balance his passion for racing with the needs of family. Sam gave him some tough, adult advice. "Get your financial situation worked out," he said. "Make sure your family is taken care of, *then* go racing."

Craig tried. He parked his coupe and concentrated on work, earning a promotion to manager of the new car get-ready department. But the demands at home seemed endless, consuming all the extra money he made and all his free time. At this rate, following Sam's advice, he would be middle aged and past it before he ever got to go racing. Giving the sport the attention Craig felt it deserved, however, meant devoting evenings and weekends and a sizable sum of money to his car—and that meant neglecting Marge and the kids.

It was at this crossroad in his life that Craig made the decision to reclaim his name. He had been growing closer to his real dad since moving out on his own and getting married and starting a family. Norm, wanting to do what he could, bought Craig and Marge a set of furniture and a washing machine for their little house and helped fence in the yard and build the bedroom for the kids. He also tried, without success, to get Craig a job as an assistant cameraman at Goldwyn Studios. "I have really fond memories of my dad helping us out like that," Craig remembers. "It really brought me close to him. I loved him. He was a generous guy. He was really good."

In the fall of 1957, around the time Marge gave birth to their second child, christened Norman, Craig jettisoned his adoptive surname Bowman and legally changed his name.

From now on he would be known as Craig Breedlove.

3

BELLY TANK RACER

It was 1958 and Craig and Marge's Venice Boulevard house was bursting at the seams. With a third child on the way they needed more space. Craig's dad Norm once again helped them out. He bought the place and Craig used the money as a down payment on a larger three-bedroom home in the up-and-coming Orange County suburb of Costa Mesa, where decent properties could still be had for a good price. It was too far for Craig to commute to Douglas Aircraft, where he was now working, so for the time being he stayed on in the old house with his dad and spent weekends at Costa Mesa with Marge and the kids.

The new job at Douglas, in the Materials and Process Engineering Department, paid almost double what Craig had been making at Bill Murphy Buick. That's why he made the move. The work was more interesting too. Devouring every structural engineering book he could find, he developed a more reliable method for testing aircraft parts at high temperature and under load to see when they would fail, solving a problem the department had been having with inconsistent results. It could have been the start of a promising career, but it wasn't what Craig really wanted. He wanted to *race*.

A possible solution presented itself in the form of a newspaper ad announcing five new openings in the Costa Mesa Fire Department. The job seemed perfect. It paid well, $4,500 a year, so Craig could continue to meet the needs of his family. It was in Costa Mesa, so he could live at home. And best of all, the twenty-four-hour shifts meant lots of time off—time he could devote to racing and working on cars.

More than five hundred applicants showed up to write the exam. Craig, with a crummy high school diploma in industrial arts, figured he didn't stand a chance. He struggled through the two-hour test, a US Army intelligence exam, the questions getting tougher as he went along. Guys started turning in their papers and leaving after forty minutes, when Craig was not even halfway through. How did they finish so fast? Now he was certain it was utterly hopeless. He kept plugging away for the whole two hours, then went home feeling dejected, convinced that he would never hear from the fire department again.

Much to his surprise, he was called back in for the second round, a test of physical strength and agility, and then for the third round, an interview. And then, wonder of wonders, he was offered a job. "Want to know how you did?" the fire chief said when Craig went in to accept. "On the intelligence test you were number two. You were seventeenth on the physical test, and first in the oral interview. You're the first guy being hired." Craig couldn't believe it. "I about fell over," he says.

Craig had long had a secret feeling that he was somehow different, that he was meant to do something big. He never really allowed himself to believe it, however. Didn't most kids feel that way, until they grew up and confronted the reality that they were just average, no different from anyone else? And yet here in the fire department exam, for the first time in Craig's life, was evidence that he really was different. He had been second out of five hundred guys on the intelligence test. That meant he was smart! And he had been first in the interview. That meant these people had been impressed with what he had to say. For Craig, this was a revelation, a turning point in his life. It helped him to push aside his self-doubt and see himself as somebody who might really be able to do something *big*.

After joining the fire department, Craig returned to racing in a more serious way. He started working on his coupe again, modifying it and improving the craftsmanship until it was a thing of beauty, the kind of hot rod that made other guys drool. He also began studying up on aerodynamics, that old subject that had so interested him back when he was a kid making model airplanes. His interest now wasn't the airflow around airplanes, but around cars—in particular, what was the optimal design for a vehicle capable of breaking the world land speed record? In his idle hours at the firehouse, when Craig wasn't working on the coupe in the parking lot outside, he was in the day room poring over engineering books and making far-out sketches of racers. When the other guys asked him what he was doing, he didn't say much. In the back of his mind, however, an idea was forming.

Marge wasn't happy about Craig's renewed obsession with racing. She felt it was driving them apart. In an attempt to appease her, Craig agreed to be baptized into her faith, Mormonism, and to have the kids baptized too. "It seemed like a good idea at the time, and it was what she wanted," he says. The baptisms were performed by Mormon bishop Ed Perkins, owner of a specialty nuts and bolts manufacturing outfit called the Perkins Machine Company.

It was Ed, perhaps not coincidentally, who became Craig's next sponsor, kicking in a few bucks to help him run the coupe at the drag strips. He would also back Craig's next project, a belly tank racer.

The belly tank racer, otherwise known as a "lakester," was first developed in the late 1940s as a streamlined speed machine that hot-rodders could build on the cheap. It used an aircraft drop tank for the car's body, the kind that was attached under the fuselage of planes like the P-38 fighter to carry extra fuel for longer missions. With military surplus equipment flooding the market after the war, a drop tank could be picked up for less than fifty bucks. It had a perfect torpedo shape for building a lightweight, low-drag race car, one capable of pushing past 200 mph at El Mirage or on the Bonneville Salt Flats. The trick was to cram an engine and cockpit and everything else into a space not much bigger than a coffin. It helped if the driver wasn't too big. Craig, at five foot eight and 150 pounds, would fit in nicely, like a hand in a glove.

It was Craig's old Igniters buddy Roger Rourke and Roger's younger brother Gene who started the project, acquiring a drop tank and an

Oldsmobile V-8 engine. Craig then came on board to help build the machine and serve as the driver. It seemed a perfect intermediary step toward building and driving a racer for the land speed record . . . if one were to ever seriously undertake such a thing. He assured Marge that this new project would take only a couple evenings a week, but it inevitably came to consume much more of his time. Between it and the fire department and a side job pouring concrete to help pay the bills, Craig had little time left over for her and the kids.

When the belly tank racer was finished, Craig invited Marge to come along to Bonneville for Speed Week to watch him compete. Maybe if he could get her more involved she would be more understanding. Marge at the time was pregnant with their third child, Dawn. They took one-year-old Norm with them and left Chris, then two, with Marge's parents. The drive out to Bonneville in Craig's pickup, hot wind blowing through the windows, lakester on the trailer behind, took two days.

Craig found the racer to be a real handful out on the salt flats. "You drove it lying on your back," he says, "your head and upper back hunched forward so that you could see out the canopy between your knees. And you were way up in the nose, so you didn't have a lot of feel for the back end when it started to fishtail and slide. You had to be pretty attuned to minor movements to drive it. It took a real knack." Part of the problem was that the racer, with its rear-mounted engine, was tail heavy. Craig discovered the effect this had on his first run, a preliminary pass to qualify for an attempt on the "A" class lakester record. Roger, driving the truck, pushed the racer to 60 mph—the lakester was so highly geared it needed a push start—then signaled Craig with a honk of the horn to take off. As Craig shot ahead and got up past 200 mph, he could feel the back end trying to swing around, as if the car wanted to go sideways. It took all his concentration to keep going straight.

Craig hit 234 mph on that qualifying run, faster than the record. When he started to slow down, the clutch exploded. It was an off-the-shelf, cast-iron truck clutch, not intended for a supercharged engine and speeds over 200 mph, and it just couldn't take it. Roger worked all night welding the shattered pieces back together only for the clutch to blow apart again the next day. In a last-ditch effort to get the racer running again so they could grab the record, Craig drove to Salt Lake City and spent all the money they had on a replacement truck clutch. But it didn't work either, slipping and then burning out before Craig got to 200.

That was it for the belly tank racer that year. Speed Week was over and Craig and the Rourkes were now stranded, two days' drive from L.A. without money even for gas. Marge laughs about it now, but at the time, with a broke husband and a crying baby and heavily pregnant, it didn't seem funny. Fortunately, Ed Perkins was at Bonneville too and bailed them out. Impressed with the effort the guys had made, he gave them money for a meal and a motel and gas to get home.

Craig pulled out of the project not long after that due to a disagreement with Roger Rourke over the racer's design. "Belly tank racers were basically unstable with the engine in the back. They needed a tailfin to stabilize them, to get more of the aerodynamic center of pressure to the back. And that was where I got into a dispute with Roger. I wanted to decamber the rear wheels and put a fin on the tail and Roger, he just thought doing all of that work was unnecessary. He was a great machinist, a good mechanical guy, but he didn't know much about aerodynamics. So I said, 'Well, either we make the changes or you can find somebody else to drive it. Because this thing is just too dangerous like it is.'"

The Rourkes went on alone, leaving the belly tank racer unchanged. When they ran the machine again a few months later, six-foot-tall Roger did the driving himself, his knees pressed against the windshield when Gene got the canopy on. In the run down the desert, the back end came out from under him just like Craig said and the racer started tumbling end over end at over 200 mph. It was utterly destroyed, reduced to a tangle of wreckage with Roger trapped inside, terrified that the alcohol fuel would burst into flames and roast him alive.

"Roger came within a hair's breadth of losing his life," says Craig. "He really, really had a bad crash and it was a miracle that he wasn't more than just banged up. It was a hard way to prove your point."

Early the following year, 1959, Craig's interest in the land speed record grew from an abstract study of design into a burning ambition. It was partly due to inspiration from a fellow hot-rodder and drag racer named Mickey Thompson, nine years Craig's senior. Mickey had been at Bonneville with Craig during Speed Week in '58, running a two-engine streamliner to a two-way average of 266 mph and hitting a top speed of 294. And he was just getting started. Back at his garage in L.A., he started building a new car, a land speed racer, equipped with four engines churning out 2,000 horsepower.

Anybody who knew anything about the history of land speed racing—and Craig had read most of the books—knew that the British had dominated the sport since the early 1920s, first on a stretch of beach in Wales known as Pendine Sands, then at Daytona Beach in Florida, then on the Bonneville Salt Flats. They made the LSR their own by treating it as a national goal and a matter of national pride, like the quest to climb Mount Everest. Their cars were designed by the country's top engineers; financial backing was provided by leading British corporations; the driving was done by the biggest British names in racing, men like Malcolm Campbell, Henry Segrave, and George Eyston, all of whom had won the Grand Prix. This was why the final speed record established by the British, the 394 mph mark set by John Cobb in 1947, seemed so secure—because an entire national undertaking lay behind it. To beat it surely would require a similarly grand effort, a corporate program by a major car manufacturer perhaps, or some sort of government-supported campaign.

Mickey Thompson had none of this. He was just an average guy, high school education, married, one kid, no money—"just some asshole hot-rodder that worked at the *L.A. Times*, running the color press," as Mickey's car-building partner Fritz Voigt put it. But that didn't stop him from dreaming big. He completed his four-engine car, dubbed *Challenger*, in 1959 and reached a top speed of 362 mph, making him the fastest American on wheels. "Very colonial," Fritz remembered British land speed legend George Eyston commenting as he and Mickey tore a transmission apart out on the Bonneville Salt Flats, working on the tailgate of a truck. "I had to ask one of the Goodyear college guys what he meant by 'colonial,'" said Fritz. "And he said, 'Kind of Okified.'" Okified, huh? Well, these Okies were going to break your British record. How about that?

It was Mickey's example that stirred Craig to action. He made the decision during a shift at the fire department, reading about Mickey and *Challenger* as he whiled away the long, boring hours of sitting and waiting. One of the veterans at the station, Ray, was dozing on the sofa, the fireman's manual open on his lap. Looking over at Ray, Craig suddenly saw an older version of himself—in his fifties, ambition all gone, on his way to retirement without ever leaving his mark. And it bothered him. It felt like a betrayal of the ambition burning inside him, the feeling that he was meant to do something that would be remembered, something that would let him realize his potential, something that would distinguish him.

In that moment in the firehouse, he realized he was on the wrong track. He was pouring his life into trying to be fastest in "C" class coupe and "A" class lakester, esoteric categories that few people appreciated and no one would remember, while Mickey Thompson was doing something of lasting significance. Mickey wasn't working any harder than Craig. He wasn't any more advantaged or any more committed. He just had more audacity, the guts to set his sights on a much higher goal.

Craig looked over at his older coworker, the embodiment of a future he didn't want. "Ray," he said, "I'm going to break the world's land speed record."

Ray didn't take him seriously. Neither did some of Craig's friends. One of them even laughed out loud. He thought it was a joke.

4

THE JET CAR IDEA

WHAT KIND OF CAR SHOULD Craig build to go after the world land speed record? He rejected Mickey Thompson's approach as too mechanically complex, with its four supercharged engines and four transmissions, four clutches, and four synchronized actions every time the machine had to change gears. After the experience of running a single-engine lakester at Bonneville and blowing the clutch, he could well imagine what a nightmare four engines would be. Heck, he had seen it firsthand. "I'll always remember hanging out in Wendover with Mickey Thompson when they were having trouble with *Challenger*," says Craig. "Mickey's partner Fritz was saying, 'Well, this doesn't work,' and Mickey says, 'Goddamn it, Fritz, do *anything*, even if it's wrong!' I'll never forget that. I started to laugh and had to duck out of the shop."

Another idea was to use a much more powerful engine than Mickey's V-8s so that only one would be needed. This was the route Salt Lake City mechanic Athol Graham was taking, shoehorning a massive Allison V-12 out of a P-51 fighter into a streamliner fashioned from a jumbo-sized drop tank off a B-29. Athol would hit 344 mph in his 2,200 hp *City of Salt Lake* in December 1959, becoming the third fastest driver in history after John Cobb and Mickey—a testament to what an average Joe could accomplish with an Allison, very little money, and a whole lot of sweat. Mickey was quietly confident, however, that Athol wasn't going much faster—not in a car with only rear-wheel drive.

Craig initially planned to build a similar sort of streamliner powered by two Allison engines, one driving the front wheels, the other the rear. The Allison V-12 was the most powerful internal combustion engine available at the time on the surplus market and thus an obvious choice for a car needing maximum juice. Using two of them would give him more than twice the horsepower of *Challenger*, plus the all-wheel drive that Athol Graham's racer was lacking. When Craig went looking for a pair of the engines, however, he found that they cost more than he could afford. The demand for them from hydroplane enthusiasts and air racers had driven up the price.

A third option was to break away entirely from the internal combustion engine and to take the novel approach of using a jet. Craig was initially attracted to this idea for the simple reason that it would make it cheaper to build a land speed racer, a jet not requiring a transmission, drive train, gears, or a clutch—all those complex components that make the wheels turn on a traditional car. "The problem," he admits today, "was that I just didn't have enough money to build a wheel-driven car, put the drive line together and everything. Using a jet engine really solved that." The more he thought about it, the more sense a jet made all around. A jet would not only be much more powerful than a pair of Allison V-12s, it would be more reliable, with far fewer moving parts that could fail, and hardier, capable of running on just about any kind of combustible liquid. And finally and most importantly, it would free a racer from the perennial problem of "wheel spin," the tendency of the wheels to lose traction and spin ineffectually when you were trying to accelerate to high speeds. With a jet car, a *thrust* vehicle, wheel spin would be a thing of the past.

Given enough space, a distance of thirty miles for example, the driver of a wheel-driven car might be able to accelerate gradually enough to avoid wheel spin and get up well into the 400 mph range. But no such track existed. The ten-mile-long course at Bonneville was the best thing going. You had to accelerate quickly to have any chance of breaking the record in that limited space, pushing your car hard up to maximum speed but not so hard that your wheels lost traction. It became so difficult when you got up into the high 300s, wheels starting to spin no matter how carefully you applied the gas, that Craig was convinced that the wheel-driven car had nearly reached its speed limit. Mickey Thompson might break Cobb's 394 mph record, perhaps even breach 400. But he would never go much faster than that. Not in *Challenger*. Not in a wheel-driven car.

Yes, a jet car seemed to be the answer. It would be the surest, most cost-effective way to break the land speed record. With a futuristic jet car that he could build on the cheap, Craig would blow the record wide open, scorching past Cobb and leaving Mickey in the dust as he rocketed to 450 mph and beyond. He would make history with a jet car. He would leave a big mark.

Craig wasn't the only person to have this idea in early 1959. A hot-rodding family doctor named Nathan Ostich was at that very moment building an LSR jet car, *Flying Caduceus*, on East Olympic Boulevard right there in L.A., paying for the whole thing out of his own pocket. For Craig this was more motivation. If Ostich could do it, so could he. But he had to get started.

The first thing Craig needed was a jet engine. He looked in military surplus stores but the pickings were slim, just the odd J-35. Then he stumbled on a big lead—in Jesse's Barber Shop, where he stopped for a haircut. His old hot-rodding buddy Mike Freebairn was there and they started talking, catching up on life since graduation. Mike, it turned out, had just gotten out of the Air Force, flying fighters, and knew a lot about jets. What Craig should buy, Mike suggested, was a J-47. It was more powerful than older engines like the J-35, 5,000 pounds of thrust packed into a tube of about the same size and weight. "It's really a more advanced engine," Mike said. "Just figure how much less of the total engine power you would have to use to go the same speed. You wouldn't have to operate at 100 percent power with the 47, and that's an advantage—less strain on the engine." Mike seemed to know what he was talking about. A J-47 made sense to Craig. And, according to Mike, a whole bunch of them were about to hit the market, a mass of engines that the government was unloading out of decommissioned Korean War–vintage planes.

A large consignment turned up shortly thereafter at surplus dealer Airmotive on Alameda Street. Craig went down to take a look. He found a whole sea of J-47s out behind in the back lot, four hundred or more, each one sealed in a big olive drab can. Airmotive's owner Jack Colville was selling them off for scrap.

"What are you getting for an engine?" Craig asked him.

"Oh, we make about five hundred bucks."

That seemed a bit pricey for scrap. But it was a lot less than a pair of Allison V-12s. "If I gave you five hundred, would you be willing to sell an engine to me?"

Jack shrugged. "Sure, we'll set one aside."

That's how Craig got his first jet. Now he needed some money—starting with five hundred bucks. He approached Ed Perkins, who had sponsored the belly tank racer, and laid out his plans to break the land speed record, bringing it back to the United States for the first time in thirty years; how it would be a sure thing with a jet car; how it was a golden opportunity just waiting for someone to grab it; how the time to do it was now.

It was a big, bold, patriotic idea. Ed liked it. *How much do you need?* he asked.

Craig swallowed hard and looked him in the eye. "With $10,000 I could get the design completed, buy the engine, and get enough material to get the thing off the ground and organized to the point that we could interest the big companies in it."

Ed thought for a moment. "OK, you've got it."

Bingo! Craig drove back to Airmotive, bought the J-47 with the up-front money Ed gave him, and hauled it home on a rented trailer. Marge did a slow burn but Craig hardly noticed. He was too busy getting the 47 wheeled into the garage on its dolly and painting lines around it on the floor, figuring out dimensions and layout. The racer would be this long and this wide . . . the wheels would go here . . . the cockpit would go there. "I laid out a design for a four-wheel car," says Craig, remembering those lines on the floor. "It was very similar to Art Arfons's later car, the *Green Monster*."

Craig drew up some plans for his four-wheel jet car and fired off a letter of inquiry to the Fédération Internationale de l'Automobile in Paris, the sanctioning body for the land speed record. The response was disappointing. The FIA had just created a new jet-powered class to accommodate a racer called *Bluebird* being built by Malcolm Campbell's son Donald. But it had imposed a huge stipulation: at least 60 percent of the jet's power had to be delivered through the wheels rather than as pure thrust. This robbed the jet car idea of almost all its appeal, for to build such a vehicle would be vastly complicated and hugely expensive—as Donald Campbell and the British industries supporting him were about to find out.

It appeared that Craig's project had been scuttled right from the start. Then Bill Moore showed up with a sketch on a napkin and everything changed.

Bill was Craig's oldest friend. They had gone to elementary school together, built models together, fooled around in the backyard together pretending to be professional wrestlers, Craig acting the part of his idol Gorgeous George. Bill had gone on to win the Fisher Body Craftsman's Guild competition and a scholarship to the Art Center School with one of his car models and was now working as a graphic artist at Hughes Aircraft—where he got talking to an engineer in the cafeteria one day about the land speed car his friend Craig was going to build.

A four-wheel car? said the engineer, pondering Bill's description of the racer. *Too much frontal area. Too much drag. What your friend wants is three wheels.* He started sketching on a napkin. *Two wheels in the back, spread way out, and one in the front. That way it's nice and stable and there's a lot less drag.*

Craig gazed at the sketch and instantly saw the advantage. Here was the perfect racer configuration, the embodiment of stability and low drag: a dart. Combine it with the massive power of a jet and you had the perfect land speed equation. He had known it all along, going back to when he was a kid flying model airplanes. Why did a land speed vehicle have to have four wheels? Why not three, like an airplane? And if it had only three wheels, why did he need sanction from the FIA, which insisted that a vehicle needed at least four wheels to be considered a "car"?

The answer was that he didn't. Craig contacted the Geneva, Switzerland-based Fédération Internationale de Motocyclisme instead and got a much more favorable answer. The FIM, delighted by the thought of a motorcycle claiming the ultimate LSR, agreed to certify his planned racer as a motorcycle with sidecar and created a new category just for jets, with no stipulation about power being directed to the wheels. That was good enough for Craig. If he broke the record, the public wouldn't care if his racer was technically a car or a motorcycle or if it was thrust- or wheel-driven. He would be the fastest driver in the world and the FIA would be left scrambling to catch up with the times. "If you had the world's fastest elephant," he would say a few years later, "you wouldn't necessarily have the world's fastest animal. Somebody might come along with a cheetah and run the elephant's legs off."

He and Bill set to work developing the engineer's sketch on the napkin into a more detailed drawing, then gave it form with a three-foot-long model. What emerged was an entirely new type of racer—pointy nose housing a single front wheel; two outrigger rear wheels enclosed in swept-back fairings; a tailfin on the back for additional stability, like the feathers on a dart. The overall effect was something out of science fiction, like a wingless F-104 Starfighter on wheels.

Wheels? Craig already had that figured out. He was going to need custom-made wheels and tires capable of withstanding the tremendous centrifugal forces of land speed racing, forces that would tear stock tires apart. To get them, he would simply design his racer around 48-inch-diameter tires identical to the ones Firestone was custom-making for Nathan Ostich's *Flying Caduceus*, which according to newspaper reports had been tested at speeds over 500 mph. When the time was right, Craig would approach Firestone and ask them to knock off an extra set of Ostich's tires for him. It wouldn't cost them much, since they had already done all the work—the developing, the equipment setup, the testing. And in return they would get their name on Craig's racer. It therefore stood to reason that they would agree.

It was time to get serious. If Craig was going to do this, he had to do it full time. That meant quitting his job at the fire department, selling the house in Costa Mesa, and moving back to L.A.

Marge took the news badly. She wanted nothing to do with the jet car, she said. If Craig was dead set on moving back to L.A. to chase this pipe dream, then he should leave. Their marriage was over. But she and the kids were staying right here.

"I really want you and the kids with me," Craig pleaded. "This is the biggest opportunity of my life. It's the time you *should* be here. We're gonna make it big now, honey."

Marge didn't see it. So Craig packed his bags and moved out. If she didn't believe in him, if she wanted a husband whose only ambition was to earn a paycheck and stay home on weekends, then he would go it alone.

Craig's parents were unhappy about it too. "It was hard for people to understand why I'd quit my job to take on something like this," Craig recalled in the *Los Angeles Times* in 1965. "My parents thought I might turn into a bum. My dad [Norm] thought I was heading for a big disappointment that could ruin my life. . . . He thought what I was after would never materialize, and so did mom."

Craig moved into the spare bedroom of his dad Norm's new house on Sepulveda Boulevard following the breakup of his marriage. He would support himself and make child support payments by drawing unemployment insurance and working part-time for cash as a mechanic in the dirtiest workshop he had ever seen.

Strike that. It was the second-dirtiest workshop. The dirtiest was the abandoned space at Perkins Machine Company that Ed Perkins had said Craig could use to build his jet car. It had once been a car battery factory, the floor so deeply encrusted with decades of slopped tar that it would have to be chipped away with a pickax. It was going to need a major cleanup before Craig could move in.

The idea for the jet car, meanwhile, continued to evolve, thanks to an article Craig stumbled on in *Hot Rod* magazine. It was a feature on Chet Herbert's *Beast* dragster, designed by Task Corporation engineer Rod Schapel based on the results of wind tunnel testing. That,

Craig decided, was what his racer needed: scientific testing to perfect the design.

He cold-called Schapel and got an appointment. "Sure, I'll help you design a car," Rod said as he examined Craig's model. "But not this one." He liked the overall three-wheel concept but not the pointy nose and wheel fairings and swept-back tail—supersonic shapes you would put on a vehicle going Mach 2, not on a car going 400-plus. For a low-drag racer intended for subsonic speeds, rounded curves made more sense.

Working under Rod's guidance, Craig smoothed out the lines of the racer, then set to work building a full-sized wooden mock-up in his dad's garage, which first had to be enlarged to hold it. Norm helped him out. "We built it pretty fast," says Craig. "We got plywood panels from a lumberyard down the street and sawed the thing out and built a framework, and we positioned the engine where it would be in the car. It was really just a way to visualize the layout for all the components, where to put the air ducts, the fuel tank, where to put this, where to put that. Rod would come over and look at it when he was making the drawings. It helped him finalize the configuration." As a final touch, Craig painted "Firestone" on the fake front wheel, carefully copying the company's distinctive font.

With the jet car having taken on a rounder, more refined shape, a new model had to be built for wind tunnel testing. It would be fabricated with the assistance of another of Craig's high school friends, Art Russell, who by a remarkable coincidence had won the Fisher Body Craftsman's Guild contest the year after Bill Moore. Art fashioned a number of interchangeable parts to go with the model—four different nose shapes, two wheel fairings, a removable tail—so that various configurations could be tested. When it was ready, Rod secured some after-hours testing time with the smallest wind tunnel at the Naval Postgraduate School (NPS) test facility in Monterey. Over the course of several weekends, NPS employee Ron Burthoff and Craig's friend Stan Goldstein tested every possible configuration, painting a mixture of lampblack and alcohol onto the model to reveal the airflow.

The results were surprising. First, it was discovered that the tailfin wasn't needed, the model performing just as well with it removed.

Second, the wheel fairings turned out to be even more essential than Craig had imagined, drag increasing a whopping 30 percent when the wheels were left exposed. And third, a straight nose was found to be the best frontal configuration. A downward-sloping nose, which had been used on the wooden mock-up, caused too much downforce and in turn too much drag. To Craig, it all seemed like irrefutable science. He went where the test results led him. The design of his jet car assumed its final appearance.

It was around this time that Craig met Leota "Lee" Roberts, a beautiful young carhop who worked at Roberts Drive-In (no relation) down the street from Norm's house. "Lee was a biker chick," he says, "a really great gal, hardworking, had a lot of common sense." They were kindred spirits, for Lee was also coming out of a failed relationship and had two young kids of her own. She remembers having coffee with Craig at the drive-in, then going out for dinner. "Afterward, he took me over to where he was living with his father and showed me the wooden mock-up of the jet car and tried to explain what he was trying to do, and that he needed help." Craig and Lee were soon seeing a lot of each other, then started living together in Lee's nearby apartment when Norm got remarried—his third marriage—and Craig had to move out.

"Lee's place was on Sawtelle," says Craig, "just a block from my dad's house. She slept in the living room and her kids took the bedroom. I'd been there only a few days when we get woken up by this crashing on the front door, *BAM-BAM-BAM-BAM*. Lee jumps up and says, 'It's my ex!' She'd been with a biker gang guy named Stanley who had been violent with her. So she ran for the bathroom and climbed out the window and left me there with this guy breaking in the front door.

"So Stanley launches his way through the door and I'm standing there facing this huge guy maybe six-four and three hundred pounds. He looks at me and gets kind of puzzled and he says, 'Who are you?' And I said, 'I'm Craig.' And he calms down and says, 'Shit, I thought Lee was sleeping with one of my friends.'

"So that's how I met Lee's ex. We ended up drinking coffee together waiting for Lee to come back, sitting at the kitchen table. Actually, it was a picnic table made out of two-by-fours. That was Lee's kitchen table."

It was at a similarly modest piece of furniture, an old school desk in the hallway of Lee's apartment, that Craig came up with the name for his jet car. His inspiration was Charles Lindbergh, the first person to fly nonstop across the Atlantic in his monoplane the *Spirit of St. Louis* and the subject of a major Hollywood movie starring Jimmy Stewart just two years before.

"I was always impressed by Lindbergh's flight. So when I was trying to come up with a name for the car, I thought, what can I call it that would be similar to *Spirit of St. Louis*, but that represented what we were trying to do, which was to bring an international record to the United States?" *Spirit of the United States* was the obvious first choice for his car but it wasn't quite right. It sounded clunky. So Craig settled on . . . *Spirit of America.* "I remember sitting at that school desk that I had at Lee's, writing a letter about *Spirit of America* and mailing it to myself so it would be postmarked, hoping to copyright the name for the car project, to show intent. It survived for years and years, but it's gone now. I don't know where the heck it went."

———————

Craig's jet car dream was now coming together. He got a pickax and started preparing his workspace, chipping away at the tar on the floor of the building that Ed Perkins said he could use. It was going to be a big job, maybe two or three weeks. Craig also contacted Firestone and got an appointment to see George Eckel, manager of racing tire sales at the company's Akron, Ohio, headquarters. It would mean shelling out forty-one bucks for an air ticket, a major expense—the first plane ride Craig had ever taken in his life.

He took a night flight to Cleveland and from there went on to Akron by bus, running though his presentation again and again. The high school kid who had been afraid to give a book report in front of the class was about to blow a company executive away with the greatest sales pitch in the world. It was amazing what proper motivation could do. He arrived in Akron, shaved and changed his shirt in a gas station bathroom, then made his way to Firestone's imposing headquarters. He was all set.

The meeting was a disaster. "Eckel was just totally rude to me," says Craig, the memory still fresh after nearly six decades. "He was picking up the phone and calling people, and I'm standing there in front of him trying to do this presentation. It was like I didn't even exist. And so I just stopped talking. I just stood there. He finally looked up with this kind of curious look on his face, and I said, 'Mr. Eckel, I've never been treated so rudely in my whole life. I traveled all night to come here. I flew all the way from Los Angeles just to talk to you, and you won't even listen to me.' I don't know why I said that. I just did. I said it real calmly and I just looked at him. And he was embarrassed. He was this bigwig trying to blow me off and I really embarrassed him. He put the phone down and said, 'You're right. I apologize.' And I got his full attention."

It didn't help. After Craig got through his presentation, Eckel turned him down cold. "But all I really need is the tires," Craig pressed, "and you're already building them for Nathan Ostich. I'm not asking for money." Eckel wouldn't budge. Craig returned to the wind tunnel data. Didn't Eckel understand? The tests *proved* that Ostich's car couldn't break the record, that its four exposed wheels would create too much drag, that it wouldn't get much past 350 mph according to Rod Schapel's calculations.

"We appreciate your input, Craig," Eckel said, showing him the door. "But our engineers tell us that Ostich's car will break the record, so we're going with that."

Craig had struck out. He headed home without tires, the whole project suddenly in peril. In a way, however, Eckel's rejection only served to strengthen his resolve to make it all work, to get his jet car built and to drive it to the record. For now he had a self-important naysayer, and the whole company behind him, to prove wrong.

You blew it, Firestone. You really blew it.

Back in L.A., Craig played the only other tire card he had left. On March 23, 1960, his birthday, he wrote to Firestone rival Goodyear, Mickey Thompson's tire sponsor, outlining his project and asking for tires. Two weeks later he got a call. Goodyear engineer Walt DeVinney, he was informed, would drop by during an upcoming trip to the West Coast to look over Craig's project.

This was Craig's last chance. When it came to racing tire sponsorship, the two Akron-based giants, Firestone and Goodyear, were the whole ball game in the United States. Craig went into overdrive getting ready for DeVinney's visit, pulling his friends in to help. He and Art Russell painted and buffed the wind tunnel test model and made it look gorgeous. Bill Moore made sleek artwork showing the car streaking along. A whole set of blueprints was prepared. Craig was going to get a set of tires out of this Goodyear engineer or die trying.

DeVinney came. And this time Craig conquered. Goodyear agreed to make him custom tires, good to 500 mph, in whatever size he wanted. The design of Craig's jet car had by now advanced so far based on the assumption of 48-inch tires that it was too late to change. He therefore asked for 48-inchers, the Ostich-Firestone size.

The jet car was a go. Craig now had an engine, high-speed tires, a finished design, and more than eight grand in sponsorship money still to come from Ed Perkins. He happily went back to work in the Perkins Machine Company building, removing the tar buildup, painting the floor, scrubbing the soot off the walls, repairing the broken windows. He got the place looking so good that Ed felt even worse when he stopped by to break the news that he had to pull the plug on the whole thing. He had hit a rough patch financially, he said, and couldn't afford to give Craig any more money. In fact, he was going to have to rent out the building that Craig had just cleaned up to make ends meet. He had gotten a lease offer and he had no choice but to accept it. He said, "Craig, I feel terrible, after saying you could use the place and you went to all this work. I will give you the jet engine and all that steel tubing but that's going to have to be it."

It was a crushing blow. And it was followed immediately by another, when Goodyear called back to rescind its offer of tires. "We're sorry, kid," Walt DeVinney said over the phone, "but we can't do it right now. We're cutting way back on our racing division budget."

It was the summer of 1960 and Craig's jet car project had just fallen to pieces. "It all happened in what seemed like two weeks," he remembers. "I went from being on top of the world to being on the bottom." He vacated Ed's building, moved the jet engine and the chromoly (chromium-molybdenum steel) tubing for the chassis into Norm's garage, and sank into a depression. He drove out to Costa Mesa and pleaded with Marge to take him back, promising to give up the jet car and to make it all right. She refused. Craig was so upset after hugging his kids good-bye and leaving to drive back to L.A. that he started weeping uncontrollably and had to pull over.

It felt like he had screwed up his whole life.

5

SPIRIT IS BORN

IT TOOK A FEW WEEKS, but Craig snapped out of his depression. He decided to begin construction of the jet car on his own, without a sponsor and without tires, working on it during the day and taking on part-time jobs at night to bring in some money. He would build it in the garage at his dad's house, which was only a block from Lee's apartment, where he was living. Norm grudgingly agreed, but he was getting worried about his son. "Craig," he said, "you've put so much into this and I just don't see how you are ever going to come out the other side. I just don't want it to ruin your whole life." Craig pushed ahead anyway. He had sacrificed too much—his fire department job, his wife, his kids—to give up now. He was all in. To raise funds, he sold the only property he still possessed after the divorce from Marge, a small lot in Palm Desert, to Jim and Lucy Johnson, a couple he knew from the Clock Drive-In. They had come into a sizable inheritance and were glad to help Craig out.

Fabrication of *Spirit of America* began in the summer of 1960. The first thing Craig did was to run a piano wire down the length of Norm's garage and screw it up tight with a pair of turnbuckles. This was the simplest way he could think of to get a dead-straight centerline to work from as he welded together the chromoly tubing frame of his thirty-six-foot-long racer. Otherwise it would come out crooked. Even a quarter-inch bend in the frame would be a problem. At 400-plus mph, *Spirit* would not go straight.

Once the piano wire was up, Craig cut out bulkheads from the wood salvaged from the disassembled mock-up, drilled holes through the center, and mounted them on the wire. These would serve as templates for positioning the circular sections of tubing that would comprise the frame. With the wooden bulkheads propped up in place, Craig began welding. This had to be done with great care, for chromoly tends to shrink and contort when it's welded. The trick was to start in the middle of the racer and work outward in both directions. Craig tacked the two centermost sections together, measured and adjusted them until they were perfectly straight, then welded them securely, laying down a flawless bead. He moved outward, fore and aft, to the next two sections, tacked, measured, and adjusted, then welded, then he moved farther outward to the next two sections, gradually working his way toward the nose and the tail. In every weld he painstakingly made, he left a little something of the person who had taught him how to work with chromoly, so much more difficult to do than the garden-variety welding he had learned back in his mid-teens. Her name was Dot. She and her lesbian partner had lived next door back when Craig and Marge were in the house on Venice and they had occasionally babysat the kids. "Dot was a really great welder," says Craig. "All through the Second World War she welded motor mounts for the war effort. She was the one who taught me how to weld chromoly. That's where I got the skills."

As *Spirit of America* slowly started to take shape, volunteers began showing up to help. Among them was Gordon "Nye" Frank, a hot-rodding friend of Craig's since high school who had made a name for himself as cobuilder of the *Freight Train* dragster, which Craig had driven. Nye was a superb fabricator and first-rate mechanic, one of the best. He would be Craig's chief mechanic during *Spirit*'s construction and go on to become the most important member of Craig's two land speed car projects in the 1960s.

Nye also brought his eighteen-year-old sidekick Bob Davids into the project. Bob, the youngest member of the team, started out as a gofer, then took on a more important role as his skill working with fiberglass, which he learned making surfboards, came into play. "I've had seven great mentors in my life," says Bob, who would go on to achieve great business success, "guys who taught me how to be successful. Craig was the first. He had confidence and energy and a charisma about him. He'd walk into a place like he owned everything, like he was in charge. That was the first thing I learned from Craig: 'Act like you own it.' The second thing I learned from him was: 'Think big.' Before I met Craig, I had no idea what it meant to think big."

Another volunteer from the garage days was electrician Allan Buskirk—"Buzzy" to the guys. "I first heard about Craig's car when I was hanging around at Roberts Drive-In," Al remembers. "I just thought it was some guy who was building a car. Then I met Craig and we got talking, and I'm thinking, *This guy is serious. He's really going to make this happen.*" Al started dropping by after work to help make brackets or do whatever else needed doing. Later, when the project moved into high gear, he would do the electrical wiring. "One thing you learn working with Craig, when you build a bracket or anything that went on the car, first off, it had to be functional. Period. I mean, there was no compromise on that. And second, it better look good. If it didn't look good you were taking it off and making another one."

And so Norm's garage became a beehive of activity and noise—welding and grinding and hammering, loud voices, work spilling into the driveway. It became too much for Norm's new wife Laura. Norm finally told Craig the jet car had to go.

"Where am I supposed to take it?" implored Craig. "Where am I supposed to go? There's nothing I can do."

Norm was firm. "Well, you've got to get it out of here. Or it's going to cost me my wife too."

Craig had to get creative to come up with a solution. If he couldn't move his jet car, why not find a new place for his dad? He went to Jim and Lucy Johnson, who had as yet paid him only half the amount for the Palm Desert lot he had sold them, and talked them into returning the land to him in exchange for his beloved '34 Ford coupe, the only other thing of value he still possessed. Jim, who had always admired the coupe, jumped at the offer. Craig then signed the lot over to his dad, who used it to buy a new house closer to Goldwyn Studios, where he was now working. The house on Sepulveda, number 2808, and the garage out back housing the jet car thus became Craig's. He moved in with Lee and her kids Dawana and Jimmy and his two dachshunds. And the *Spirit of America* project kept moving forward, the whole house becoming a production facility for the car.

The neighbors, understandably, weren't happy about it. "Mr. Tuchen owned the apartment building next door, a fourplex," says Craig. "He was a little Jewish man, spoke with a real strong accent. He would come over and he'd say, 'What's this? What's this? What are you doing?' And I'd say, 'It's my hobby, Mr. Tuchen. I'm building this jet car.' And he'd say, 'Craig, this is not a hobby. This is a business! You can't have it here!'"

As the chassis was being fabricated in the garage, inside the house the air ducts were being formed. There would be two of them running down either side of the chassis and joining together behind the cockpit to feed air into the engine. Getting these ducts right was in fact a major concern, just as important as the overall shape of the car, because the pressure of the air passing through them would be so extreme that they could easily explode or implode if not designed right.

Once again it was through his friends that Craig got the help he needed. Out at the Van Nuys air base, group commander Glenn "Snake" Reeves, a test pilot on Lockheed's F-104 supersonic jet fighter, overheard Mike Freebairn talking about Craig's jet car and offered to put him in touch with Lockheed engineer Walt Sheehan, who was a car buff and might be willing to help. Walt was vastly knowledgeable about aerodynamics, jet engines, and testing experimental vehicles. And air ducts? He had been in charge of designing the air ducts on the F-104. Nobody in the whole world knew more about air ducts than Walt Sheehan.

Mike passed Walt's name and number on to Craig. The contact was gold. "I just cold-called him," says Craig, "told him who I was and what I was doing. Walt didn't seem especially interested over the phone but he agreed to meet me after work at a restaurant close to Lockheed. We talked about the program and he got interested, said he'd help us on the air inlet ducts. You know, I can't tell you how I was able to pull all these people in. I guess I managed to grovel enough to get them to help me. And I guess I just had the gift of the gab. Anyway, Walt designed the ducts and John Peters's uncle, Shorty [Frank Fellows], a plaster pattern maker, helped me build the tooling. It turned out to be a huge job."

Building the tooling, using lumber and steel rods and aluminum plates, was just the first step. A plaster core mold then had to be made in the cavity of the tooling, left to dry, then removed and finished with lacquer and polished. "It had to be flawless," says Craig. "It was shiny glossy when I got it all done." These two plaster cores, ten feet long and "ungodly heavy," served as the forms over which the actual air ducts were made using fiberglass. This was where young Bob Davids with his surfboard-making skills started to shine. The kid was a virtuoso. When the fiberglass cured, the plaster cores inside had to be chipped away piece by piece and the interior of the ducts polished. Bob did some of this work—he was six foot four and as thin as a rake—but most of the job fell to Lee. She was the only one small enough to comfortably squeeze inside the ducts to do the endless hours of chipping. "Those things were so hard to get out," says Craig. "Lee was in there in the living room taking out little half-inch chunks of plaster from those ten-foot-long ducts. It was amazing. But she got it all out of there and got it all polished. She must have spent, I don't know, six weeks in those air ducts getting the plaster out of them. She worked on them every day when she was off work. God, I don't know how she did it. It was a Herculean task." The entire process of building the air ducts, from start to finish, would end up taking six months.

Seven hundred miles to the northeast, out on the Bonneville Salt Flats, the 1960 land speed season was beginning. Competition this year was going to be intense, with five major players vying for the land speed record.

First up, on August 1, was Athol Graham in *City of Salt Lake*. Out of money and perhaps feeling pressure from expectant spectators and reporters, he set out to break the record on his very first run, ignoring reports that the course was too windy. Somewhere over 300 mph, his rear wheels started spinning and the rear end of his racer swung around, enough for the wind to catch it and send it into a barrel roll down the salt. It tumbled for half a mile, leaving behind a trail of metal and smears of red paint before coming to rest as an unrecognizable mass of smoking wreckage. By then Athol was beyond saving. He was loaded into a plane and rushed to Salt Lake City, where he was pronounced dead.

Nathan Ostich, in his recently unveiled *Flying Caduceus* jet car, was the next to try. His week on the salt did not go well. During an engine test a massive explosion sent the crew scrambling backward. The J-47 jet, blasting air out the back faster than it was being sucked in at the front, had created a vacuum and imploded one of the air ducts. The duct was replaced but the same thing happened the next day. Ostich would return to Bonneville in September to try again with reinforced air ducts, only to be foiled by steering problems. He finally gave up and hauled his racer back to L.A., having got only halfway to his stated goal of 500 mph.

Mickey Thompson's first Bonneville week was a different kind of disaster, the course so washboard rough that it almost shook him to pieces. "The pounding I went through was terrible," he would write in his autobiography a few years later. "When Judy [Mickey's wife] and Fritz pulled me out of the car I was vomiting and in a great deal of pain." Mickey tried again in September, after seeing the course graded. He did 406 mph on his first run and seemed all set to grab the record. *Challenger* was turned around and prepped and got away within the hour for the required return run. Then, in a cloud of black smoke, it ground to a halt. One of its four engines had stayed in neutral and been destroyed when Mickey shifted into second. There was still plenty for the team to celebrate, for 406 mph was the fastest anyone had ever driven, four miles an hour faster than John Cobb's best pass. But the fact remained that there was no such thing as a one-way land speed record. Winning the LSR required two runs. Cobb's official record of 394 mph still stood.

In early September the sole British competitor in the game, Donald Campbell, arrived on the salt flats with his turbojet *Bluebird*, the pride of British industry, built at a cost of $3 million. Of all the drivers at Bonneville that year, Campbell seemed most likely to break the record. But he didn't. He lost control at 300 mph and crashed, sending *Bluebird* airborne for 825 feet, bouncing four times and sliding for a quarter mile. Campbell was unconscious when he was pulled from the wreckage but soon revived. When he arrived glassy-eyed at the hospital in the nearby town of Tooele, he was able to walk inside with only a little assistance and even managed to greet the staff with a cheery "Good morning!"

There was one more entry in the land speed contest that year, one the *Deseret News* called "the darkest of dark horses." He was Art Arfons of Akron, Ohio, a World War II US Navy veteran and feed mill owner who had turned to professional drag racing in the mid-1950s, teaming up with his half brother Walt to build a series of Allison engine–powered machines they christened *Green Monster*. The two brothers were estranged now, working side by side in neighboring garages on competing cars and never speaking to each other. Art's latest machine, *Green Monster* number 15, a.k.a. *Anteater* on account of its drooping nose, was his first attempt at an LSR racer. The Allison streamliner would prove to be a disappointment when Art ran it on the salt, the clutch repeatedly burning out when he got it up into the mid-200s. The taciturn Akronite was forced to give up and go home. But he wasn't done. He was just getting started.

For his next car, he would use a jet.

The results of the 1960 land speed season reassured Craig that he was on the right track. The wheel-driven cars had all failed due to either mechanical complexity or wheel spin, as he had foreseen, and the sole thrust vehicle, Ostich's *Flying Caduceus*, had demonstrated the wisdom of seeking help from professional engineers. With *Spirit of America*, Craig was confident, there would be no imploding air ducts—not with those babies Walt Sheehan had designed.

The flurry of competition at Bonneville nevertheless turned up the pressure on Craig. Here he was still laboring on a racer that wasn't even half-built while other guys were already deep in the game, vying for Cobb's record. He knew he needed to get a sponsor to kick his project into high gear or he would be left behind. A part of him, however, dreaded courting all that rejection again. It was easier to stay in the garage and continue plugging away with his friends. So that's what he did, on into 1961.

It was Rod Schapel's nagging that finally prompted him to take action. "Craig," he would say, "if you don't stop working on the car and go get a sponsor, this thing is never going to get done. We need money! You've got to get your ass out there and sell this thing."

"I needed somebody to tell me that," admits Craig, "to scold me on it." With pushing from Rod, he started working on a new and improved sales pitch, one that would grab the listener right at the start and hold him all the way through. Bill Moore once again stepped up to help, this time with a slick series of twenty-five-by-thirty-inch flip charts that Craig would repeatedly practice on to get his delivery just right. There were charts on the car's professionally engineered configuration, proven through wind tunnel testing; on "Builder Driver Craig Breedlove" with his ten years of experience and a top speed of 234 mph to his credit; on a precise cost estimate of $30,230 to get the car finished and to run it on the Bonneville Salt Flats ("Seat: $50; Controls: $60; Windshield: $30; Canopy Glass: $80 . . ."). The *Spirit of America* model also got a velvet-lined mahogany carrying case and a fresh coat of paint, two complementary shades of blue that Bill Moore suggested.

Letters requesting meetings were mailed to potential sponsors, together with brochures that Craig and his team made by hand. Some elicited rejection letters. Most were ignored. Out in the garage, meanwhile, the jet car continued to take shape . . . and evolve. Rod Schapel, unable to find a way to fit a steering assembly into the narrow confines of the nose, had come up with the novel idea of locking the front wheel in position and controlling the racer by other means. Starting out, Craig would steer with his feet by applying differential brakes to the rear wheels—brake the left wheel to turn left, brake the right wheel to turn right. When he got up over 150 mph he would use the steering wheel to control a fin or air rudder on the underside of the nose, as the wind pressure on it by then was sufficient to make the vehicle turn. "God, it seemed like a really far-out kind of concept," says Craig. "But I really looked up to Rod and his expertise, so I just sort of acquiesced. I said,

'Well, I don't know, Rod. I've obviously never driven anything like that. I'll just accept your word that it's going to work.'"

There was little land speed activity at Bonneville in 1961. The salt was in such poor shape that Mickey Thompson and Nathan Ostich stayed home, hoping for better conditions in 1962. The postponement gave Craig time to catch up, *Spirit of America* being roughly two-thirds finished by the end of the year. A sponsor, however, continued to elude him. Finally, out of desperation, he approached Shell Oil again. He had already contacted Shell three times in the past two years and been turned down each time. Yet the company seemed like a good prospect. They sold gasoline, the most essential automotive product; they were interested in racing, as demonstrated by the race cars they were sponsoring on the European circuit; and they currently had no motorsport involvement in the United States. What if Craig were to try an in-person approach, just walk into Shell's local office and pitch the manager there?

Craig stopped by the Shell gas station where he had worked part-time back in high school and asked the owner, his old boss Andy Anderson, where the Shell office was. Andy pointed to the building directly behind the station. It housed the Shell district office for the whole of Southern California. The name of the boss was Bill Lawler. *He's a tough ex-marine major*, said Andy, *and is on his way up Shell's corporate ladder. He'd be a good guy to try.*

Craig gathered up his flip charts and the car model in its case and marched over, reminding himself that he had come first in the interview portion of the fire department exam. He could do this. He could win Lawler over.

He presented one of his freshly printed business cards to the receptionist outside the Shell manager's office. She turned and called through the half-open door behind her desk: "There's a Mr. Breedlove to see you."

A deep voice inside: "Send him in."

This was going well. Craig had half expected Lawler wouldn't see him. He entered the office and was met with a welcoming smile.

The smile turned to a scowl. "You're not Vic Breedlove," said Lawler. As Craig would learn later, one of the Shell station owners in Lawler's district shared his last name.

"No sir, Mr. Lawler, I'm *Craig* Breedlove and I'm here to talk to you about a project that will not only benefit myself but Shell Oil as well, and I'm sure it will interest you because I am going to bring the world's land speed record back to the United States after thirty-four years, and after many people have tried and failed, and I have the car that can do it."

Lawler eyed him sourly. He leaned back and crossed his arms. "You've got ten minutes."

Craig launched into his spiel. Seeing Lawler's skepticism give way to interest, he kept on going long past ten minutes, impressing the executive with the professionalism of his project and the scope and depth of his knowledge. As the presentation wound down, Lawler's eyes began darting to the mahogany case still sitting unopened on the floor.

"All right," he finally said, "what's in the box?"

Craig shifted the case in front of Lawler's desk, just out of sight, and removed the lid. "Mr. Lawler," he said, rising with the model in his hands, "this is the *Spirit of America*."

Lawler's eyes lit up as he beheld the beautiful model, its two-tone blue paint job polished to a high shine. He seized it and bolted from the office, his voice booming down the hall, "Look at this! Look at this!"

Craig had just sold Bill Lawler. But he didn't have Shell yet. There were still two more hurdles to clear. The first was Lawler's boss, Shell's West Coast division manager, Al Hines. In a subsequent meeting, Craig repeated his presentation for Hines and hooked him just like he had Lawler. That left just one more executive to win over, Purdom "Purd" Thomas, director of marketing at Shell's head office in New York. Thomas was going to be a very tough sell, for he was the one who had turned down Craig's previous approaches to Shell.

Al Hines tried first on his next trip to New York. Thomas responded with a flat "No." The land speed record was too risky, he said, not the sort of thing he wanted to get Shell involved in. Lawler didn't tell Craig about the rejection. Instead he waited for Thomas's next trip to L.A., then he and Hines took him out for a night on the town, plied him with martinis, and tried again. "Please just listen to this kid and see what he has to say," pleaded Lawler. "If you still turn it down then, we'll drop the whole thing." Finally Thomas relented.

"Boy, I hope you've got your selling hat on today," said Lawler as he drove Craig to the meeting with Thomas the next morning. "Because this guy's tough. And he's going to have a hangover."

Purd Thomas sat through Craig's presentation with a neutral expression. Craig got to the end and opened the mahogany box and held up the *Spirit of America* model. Still no reaction. "Mr. Thomas," he said, "Texaco comes out with its toy tank truck every year at Christmas. Wouldn't it be great for Shell if you came out with some of these *Spirit of America* models at the same time? People would flock to Shell stations to buy them and most of them would fill up at the same time."

He handed the model to Thomas. "How would you like to have this model, with the Shell logo on it, on the mantel of millions of American homes at Christmas, just like the Texaco tank truck?"

That did it. The stony Shell executive's resistance crumbled. "All right," he said, "I'm going to do this goddamn thing. But if it doesn't work out"—he turned to Bill Lawler and Al Hines—"I'm coming after you guys. It's going to cost you."

Craig had just landed a major sponsorship deal, the full thirty grand he needed to bring his land speed project to fruition. The news was met with incredulity as it spread and the occasional comment made that Craig had just gotten lucky. Behind the luck, however, lay dozens of rejections and a whole lot of persistence. The experience of landing Shell, of all the trying and failing that had gone before it and all the work it had taken, would have a profound impact on Craig's approach to life going forward. "The only time you really lose is when you quit," remains one of his favorite maxims today. And, usually delivered with a chuckle: "I've generally found that the harder you work, the luckier you get."

With the clout of Shell behind him, Craig reached out again to Goodyear with a renewed request for tires. "You really have Shell?" Goodyear engineer Walt DeVinney exclaimed when Craig phoned him up. "You mean Shell Oil in New York?" Within days Craig was on a plane to Akron, at Goodyear's expense, for a meeting with company president Russell DeYoung and the top brass. This time it was an easy sell. With Shell a $30-million-a-year customer of Goodyear's, there was no way the tire company was going to refuse him. Craig was nevertheless extremely anxious when he was asked to step outside after giving his presentation so that the matter could be discussed. He tried to concentrate while DeVinney gave him a tour of the factory, but it wasn't easy. Finally DeVinney was called to the phone. He listened, then turned to Craig. "You got it, Craig. They said yes."

The jet car project was a go. It was February 1962 and Shell wanted it operational in August. That gave Craig barely six months to complete *Spirit of America* and get it ready for the Bonneville Salt Flats.

Craig was back in L.A., getting *Spirit* ready for the move out of the garage, when he looked up to see racing greats J. C. Agajanian and Parnelli Jones strolling up his driveway. *Holy cow*, he thought, *what are these guys doing here?*

They had been sent by Firestone. They were there to talk Craig into signing with Goodyear's archrival. Craig said he was already verbally committed to Goodyear and was just waiting to sign a contract. "Well," they said, "if you haven't signed yet, believe me, Firestone is prepared to make it worth your while to run on their tires." That meant money, which Goodyear hadn't offered Craig, in addition to tires.

Craig declined, saying he had already given his word to Goodyear. As Agajanian and Jones turned and walked away, he remembered that morning two years before in George Eckel's office, when the Firestone executive had ignored him and been so openly rude. It felt like vindication.

Firestone, I knew you blew it.

6

BLACK LINE ZIGZAG

CRAIG WAS FACED WITH A BIT OF A PROBLEM. *Spirit of America*, roughly two-thirds complete, was trapped in the garage, its outrigger rear wheels too wide to fit down the driveway. He managed to clear an extra foot of space by taking a sledgehammer to the concrete steps at the side door of the house, but it wasn't enough. Mr. Tuchen's hedge on the other side of the driveway had to go too. And there wasn't much chance of Mr. Tuchen giving permission to cut it down. Craig remembers Stan Goldstein turning to him and asking, "What are we going to do?"

"Well," said Craig, "what we're going to do is you're going to go down to Sam's U-Rent and get a chain saw, and we're going to fire that baby up and take the hedge down in one fell swoop before Mr. Tuchen can get outside."

So that's what they did.

"It took Mr. Tuchen a while to figure out what this new roar was coming from next door, but God, when he did he came flying down the stairs, screaming about his hedge, just as we were getting the last of it cut down. I said, 'Mr. Tuchen, Mr. Tuchen, the car is going!' That settled him down. 'The car is going?' 'Yeah, yeah, the car is going. We'll plant you a new hedge.' And he said, 'That's good boys. Good boys.' Poor Mr. Tuchen. He put up with a lot. But the car was gone."

After being manhandled down the driveway, *Spirit* was hauled to L.A. International Airport for its jet engine to be tested, then was taken to Quincy "Quin" Epperly's cinder-block shop in a scruffy neighborhood in Gardena, where fabrication would be completed. Quin was one of the most experienced race car builders on the West Coast, in the business since 1938, but even he was taken aback by *Spirit*'s sheer size. "It's the biggest thing I've ever seen," he marveled as he took it all in. Quin and his full-time employee George Boskoff would play a key role in the racer's fabrication. A scrappy Irishman named Don Henry who hung around the shop—Boskoff describes him as "kind of a USAC roustabout"—would also help out.

The plan was to unveil the car in late July 1962 and run it at Bonneville starting at the beginning of August. That meant Craig had scarcely five months to get everything done. He quickly made a production schedule and started hiring additional workers, mostly young guys already on board with the project: Nye Frank as chief mechanic, Allan Buskirk for electrical work, Bob Davids for fiberglass, Stan Goldstein for getting parts and supplies and running the office, "tin bender" Wayne Ewing to work with Quin and Boskoff in shaping *Spirit*'s aluminum skin. A total of fourteen guys would work on the car, six of them just on the aluminum body, an indication of how time consuming "tin bending" was. Craig was in charge but in most things he deferred to Epperly. "Craig would never question Quincy," says Bob Davids. "Everybody in the shop thought Quincy was like God. For critical welds, on the suspension and things, Craig insisted on him doing it. The master would come over. He was like an artist. I remember Craig saying, 'My life is riding on every weld, and the weld I trust is Quincy's.'"

Bill Lawler called Craig into his office just as work was getting under way. It was about Lee, whom Bill had met on a visit to Craig's house the previous day. "Look," he said, using the tact he had learned in the Marine Corps. "About that babe you're shacked up with, here's the deal. Either marry her or move her out of your house. I want you back in here with a resolution on Monday morning." Shell, Lawler went on to explain, was a conservative company and did not want someone representing it in the public eye living in sin.

There was no way Craig was going to kick Lee out of the house, not after all the help she had given him, letting him move in with her when he needed a place to stay and putting in all those hours of work on the car. But he wasn't going to lose his Shell sponsorship either. And so, even though he wasn't eager to get married again, he popped the question that weekend. Lee said yes.

"So we drove straight through to Yuma and got married on Sunday evening," says Craig, "then we drove all night long to get back home. I dropped Lee off at the house on Monday morning and went right in to Bill Lawler's office and put my marriage license on his desk. He was really surprised. 'Well, OK,' he says. 'I really thought you'd go the other way and move her out. But OK, fine. Congratulations!'"

Back at Epperly's shop work had kicked into high gear on the car. As the weeks ticked down and the inevitable complications and hold-ups occurred, it became clear that the team wasn't going to make the July deadline. They started working eighteen and twenty hours a day, seven days a week, bringing food into the shop to save time. "We didn't stop," Craig wrote in his autobiography in 1971, "and some of the guys would work until they dropped. Then they would sleep on the floor. It was a complete, all-out crash program." And then another problem: the $30,000 sponsorship from Shell was being burned through far more quickly than Craig had imagined, everything costing more than he had budgeted for because it had to be done at top speed. He had to go to Lawler and ask for more money. Lawler smiled and, to Craig's enormous relief, explained that Shell had discounted his original estimate right from the start. The *Spirit of America* project had been budgeted for the seemingly impossible sum of $100,000.

It was now the middle of July. Crunch time. The unveiling was pushed back a week, then another, and the time-consuming job of skinning *Spirit*'s rear wheel fairings in aluminum hadn't even been started. It was at this point that nineteen-year-old Bob Davids, the youngest member of the crew, came to the rescue, convincing Epperly to let him do the fairings in fiberglass instead. Bob ended up making the nose cone and the steering fin out of fiberglass too, plus thirty-two disposable covers for the parachute compartment. "It's duck soup, man," Bob brashly said, selling Quin on how quick and easy fiberglassing would be. Just like a surfboard. And it was . . . until he started on the underside of the fairings.

Bob was still slaving away on the right fairing one day when the rest of the crew went out to lunch. Don Henry, an old-timer with little regard for fiberglass on race cars, stayed behind to watch. "So it's a hot day in July," Bob remembers, "and I'm soaking this forty-ounce cloth in resin and trying to laminate the underside of the fairing. The cloth is heavy, I'd never used it before, and I'd put too much catalyst in the resin, so it's not sticking. I got resin all over my hands and running down my arms and it's going down my neck and it's burning me, and the cloth is sagging, it's not sticking, and Don Henry is sitting there watching me and puffing on his cigar, and I'm going, 'Holy shit, I'm stuck. How do I save this?' So I'm struggling and struggling, the cloth is falling off and I'm trying to press it back on just as it's starting to get tacky. And finally Don gets up to leave and he says, 'You know, kid, money can't buy the experience you're getting right here.'"

"It's a car," began the Spotlite Newsreel, "believe it or not! In Los Angeles, Craig Breedlove unveils the *Spirit of America*, his jet-powered, three-wheeled streamliner designed to go 500 miles an hour . . . or more! Breedlove will attempt to better the late John Cobb's 15-year-old mark of 394 miles an hour and bring home to America the world land speed record, in British hands since 1929. . . . All America is with you, Craig. Good luck!"

Spirit of America was unveiled at the beginning of August at the Wilshire Country Club near Hollywood in central L.A. The exhausted crew came in jeans and T-shirts and immediately made for the food tent. Craig, in a new suit with a name tag and ribbon on his pocket, was obliged to circulate among the invited guests and reporters, smiling and answering questions and posing for photos. Then it was back to Quincy Epperly's, for the racer still wasn't quite finished. Finally, in the third week of August, a cavalcade of cars and trucks headed out from Gardena bound for the Bonneville Salt Flats, *Spirit of America* on its trailer leading the way with a big warning sign, WIDE LOAD, stuck on the back.

Mickey Thompson by this time had retired from land speed competition. He had come up short during his week on the salt in July and would not run *Challenger* for the record again. Nathan Ostich's Bonneville week in early August began in promising fashion, with *Flying Caduceus* quickly reaching speeds over 300 mph and looking all set to break Cobb's record. Then disaster struck. It started as a sickening shimmy just as Ostich was entering the mile at 331 mph. The bearings in the left front wheel were seizing up. He cut the engine just as the wheel tore off the racer, sending it spinning out of control. Fortunately *Caduceus* didn't go into a roll. It ground to a halt at the end of a long trail of scraped-off red paint and Ostich struggled out of the cockpit, shaken but unhurt. "Well, I accomplished one thing," he quipped to a reporter from the *Deseret News*. "I likely set a three-wheeled record of some sort for Craig Breedlove to shoot at."

Speed Week followed and three new jet cars entered the picture. The first was a J-46-powered racer called *Valkyrie*, built by Bill Fredericks and with a young up-and-comer named Gary Gabelich as the driver. *Valkyrie*, with just under 4,000 pounds of thrust and tires that wouldn't have stood up to very high speeds, was unable to satisfy the insurance requirements of the meet organizer, the United States Auto Club, and thus was not allowed to compete. It would spend the rest of its long life running on drag strips.

The second jet car was Art Arfons's *Green Monster* number 16, nicknamed *Cyclops* on account of the single headlight in its nose. Art had built the open-cockpit dragster mainly for touring the drag strips, where it drew big crowds and earned him good money. But he also wanted to take a crack at the land speed record. And he did. Sitting entirely exposed in front of the J-47 jet intake, the wind blast nearly tearing his face off, Art hit a top speed during Speed Week of 342 mph—the fastest anyone had ever gone in an open-cockpit machine. He returned home to Akron determined to build a bigger and better jet car specifically for the LSR.

And then there was the *Infinity* jet car, built by a team up in Oakland, California, headed by Romeo Palamides and driven by Kansas native Glenn Leasher. It was scheduled to arrive at Bonneville on

September 7, after the two weeks Shell had booked for Craig on the salt. By then, Craig was confident, the LSR would be his.

The *Spirit of America* convoy arrived in Wendover, Utah, on August 22, in the middle of Speed Week. It pulled into the parking lot of the Western Motel and Craig got out and stretched. Down at the far end of the straggling town, mostly a collection of gas stations along the highway, he could see the ninety-foot-high statue of cowboy "Wendover Will" waving his mechanical arm in front of the Stateline Casino. WHERE THE WEST BEGINS read the sign on the pedestal under Will's feet. And, in blinking neon: THIS IS THE PLACE . . . THIS IS THE PLACE . . . THIS IS THE PLACE.

Craig was shocked to learn that Shell had booked nearly the whole motel for his two Bonneville weeks, including a spacious double, sheer luxury, for him and Lee. It was yet another reminder that he was now in the big leagues, beyond even Mickey Thompson. There was also a film crew on hand to make a movie of his record attempt, and a professional photographer to take photos, and a chartered B-25 for aerial shots. So this was why Shell had tripled the budget for the project.

Spirit was first taken to Wendover Air Force Base for a complete strip down and to test the engine. The massive facility, largely abandoned after the end of World War II, had been where the 509th Composite Group had trained to drop the atomic bomb on Japan. Its empty hangars, away from blowing salt and rubbernecking spectators, made excellent workshops. The racer was then hauled onto the salt following Speed Week for the start of test runs. Its arrival made quite an impression. "Breedlove's jet is by far the most impressive yet seen on the flats," gushed the *Deseret News*, "not only in size but in workmanship and design." Unloaded from its trailer, the three-ton *Spirit* stood 36 feet long, 11 feet 4 inches wide between the rear fairings, and 6 feet high at the cockpit. Craig would need a stepladder to climb in.

From this point on Rod Schapel was in charge. He had put himself forward as operations manager and Craig and Bill Lawler, Shell's top man on the scene, had agreed. Schapel's plan was for Craig to use 100 percent power on his very first run to quickly get up over 150 mph, where the nose fin would come into play, then to throttle back to 70 percent and test out the steering. Craig didn't like the idea, starting out like this with the J-47 going full blast. It seemed an awful lot like jumping into the deep end of the pool before learning to swim, for the fact was that he had not yet driven even a yard with jet thrust. Rod seemed absolutely certain this was the way to go, however. He could in fact be quite intimidating. So Craig went along.

Spirit was positioned on Bonneville's "international course," where official land speed runs were made. It was eleven miles long—five miles for building up speed, the measured mile, and five miles to slow down. The international course was in reasonably good shape in 1962, freshly graded by the Utah Highway Department to remove the ridges that formed on the otherwise smooth surface, then a black line of used crankcase oil was sprayed on. The line was essential to give Craig something to follow. Without it, the course was virtually indistinguishable in the featureless, blindingly bright sea of whiteness. Without it, it would be impossible to go straight.

Craig got strapped in and donned his air mask. In the event of an accident, with fire-suppressing carbon dioxide released into the cockpit, he would need it to breathe. A start cart got the jet engine going, then was wheeled away. Craig advanced the hand throttle to 100 percent— "full military power" as it was called in the Air Force—pressing down with both feet on the brakes. He had run through these steps dozens of times before but only in stationary practice. Now he was actually going to go.

He released the brakes.

Spirit leaped forward, the acceleration more intense than anything Craig had ever felt on the drag strip. "I had the sort of feeling in the pit of my stomach that you get in a car when you go over a big dip in the road at high speed. The only difference was that this feeling just stayed there, like I was going over the biggest dip in the world."

The sensation lasted for just a few seconds, then was replaced by alarm as *Spirit* began veering off course to the right. Craig pressed down on the left brake to ease back to center only to overshoot and veer off course to the left. He went to the right brake, more gently this time, only to overshoot in the other direction, zigging to the right, then zagging to the left, back and forth and back and forth as the needle on the speedometer swept past 150.

Craig was going fast enough now for the nose fin air rudder to work. He began using the steering wheel but got no response. He turned the wheel all the way over, his speed passing 200. Nothing. He turned the wheel back the other way. Nothing. He frantically returned to the differential brakes but only got more wild zigzagging. Speed 220 now, 230, 240. *Spirit of America* was leaving the graded course, careening across the desert. Craig had no control.

He killed the engine and hit both brakes and came to a stop, utterly distraught, almost in tears with frustration. His beautiful racer, the focus of his life for the past four years, was a disaster. He couldn't even steer the damn thing!

Rod Schapel came roaring up in one of the crew's rental cars. "What's wrong? Why did you shut it off?"

Craig pulled himself together. "The brakes didn't work, the fin didn't work, nothing."

"They had to work!"

"Well, I'm telling you right now they didn't. I was out there still trying to steer it with the brakes at 240. The fin didn't work."

Craig returned to Wendover and retreated to his motel room, so upset that he couldn't eat dinner. The next morning, after a sleepless night of reflection, he climbed back into *Spirit* to try again. This time he insisted on starting out slow, idling down the course at 100 mph, the throttle at 70 percent. He managed to get some control this time with the rear brakes but not nearly enough. The racer still had a tendency to wander about as if it had a mind of its own. Rod Schapel, increasingly irritated, refused to believe it. His design *had* to work, he insisted. Craig must not be using the rear-brake steering and air rudder correctly. He was probably trying to steer with both of them at the same time.

"Well, there's one way to settle this," said Craig. "Let's take the air rudder off."

The air rudder was removed and still *Spirit* continued to wander, Craig running with the canopy off in the hopes of picking up some clue as to what was happening. Finally, with the crew completely stumped, the racer was torn apart and all the wheel bearings were checked. It was only then that the problem was discovered. The front wheel pivot bearings were sliding about in their housing, allowing the wheel to shift just enough to send the racer drifting off course.

The problem was fixed, *Spirit* was put back together, and testing resumed. Craig, his optimism mostly restored, took another run and this time found that he was able to control the car with the rear brakes. It wasn't easy but he could do it. When he got up over 150 mph, however, the air rudder wouldn't come into play. Rod Schapel insisted that it would work, that Craig just needed to go faster to get enough wind resistance. So Craig did. He took *Spirit* all the way up to 279 mph but still got no response. He was turning the steering wheel from lock to lock and getting nothing at all. The air rudder steering system was useless.

The crew was becoming demoralized as they ground through their second week on the salt. Craig was frustrated and fed up, all faith lost in Schapel's far-out steering system. He told Bill Lawler that it would probably be best just to pack it in and go home to regroup, maybe find some way to make the front wheel steer like he had originally planned so that they could ditch the rear brakes and the useless air rudder. Schapel, meanwhile, was becoming defensive to the point of belligerence, proclaiming that there was nothing wrong with the car and claiming that Craig was to blame. Finally, inevitably, a blowup occurred.

"It is impossible for the fin not to steer the car," said Schapel, confronting Craig. "You are just afraid to go any faster and you are using the fin for your excuse."

The accusation of cowardice was the last straw. Schapel actually seemed to think that Craig was steering off course on purpose. "This car doesn't need an ignition key," Craig shot back. "Park your fat ass in the seat and try driving it yourself!"

Schapel, too big to fit into the custom-made cockpit, suggested that Mike Freebairn, present as a spectator, take *Spirit* for a test run. "I was sitting in on a team meeting when Schapel came out with that," Mike remembers. "He said that, because of my experience flying jets, I should drive the car and see if the canard fin would work." Bill Lawler came to Craig's defense. "Lawler took my side in most things," says Craig. "He saw what was happening, that Rod was trying to buffalo me and buffalo everybody, and he wasn't going to have it. Lawler was tough, boy. Schapel didn't like that at all."

The second and final week on the salt ended on that acrimonious note. *Spirit* was loaded back onto its trailer and the crew started packing up to return home without the record. It was only then, late in the afternoon of the last day, that the steering problem was finally solved. Nye Frank could hardly believe it when he discovered the cause. Neither could Craig. The steering linkage on the nose fin had never been properly set when they arrived two weeks before. It had been left cinched up tight, locked in place for transportation, and in all the strain and confusion no one had thought to check it. That was why Craig had no steering. The fin had been moving scarcely half an inch when he was cranking away at the wheel.

Spirit was quickly unloaded from its trailer and Craig got a run in just as the sun was setting behind the mauve hills. "I made a pass at about 325 and I was steering it with that damn fin. The air was dead calm and I could steer the thing right, steer the thing left. In fact I almost went too far under power because I was having such a good time driving with the fin after this horrible ordeal we'd been through. But we were out of time. Shell was pulling the plug."

The *Infinity* jet car crew had the next week on the salt. Craig and some of the *Spirit* team ran into them during a junket out to Wells, Nevada, the team cramming into a big station wagon with HARD-ON EXPRESS traced in the salt film on the doors. The two crews spent the evening together drinking and bonding, neglecting the ladies who were the main reason for going to Wells. "When are you guys going to stop talking race cars and have some fun?" one of them asked. *Infinity* driver Glenn Leasher was a real hit with Craig and the guys. They all immediately liked him.

Craig stopped by the *Infinity* camp to look the competition over before heading home. Glenn's jet car was essentially a J-47 encased in an unpainted aluminum tube with a cockpit capsule precariously perched in the intake—not as sophisticated as *Spirit* and no doubt costing much less. He wished Glenn good luck and left, fearing that this bargain-basement racer just might snag the record and make him look even more like a failure.

He was on the highway with Nye Frank a couple days later, nearing home, when the news came on the radio that *Infinity* had crashed, a catastrophic end-over-end roll that obliterated the racer and literally tore Glenn to pieces. He had been twenty-six, a year older than Craig.

Failure was a natural part of developing a new vehicle. That's what Walt Sheehan, with his lifetime of experience at Lockheed, told Craig back in L.A. "Craig," he said, "there's never been an airplane in the history of the aircraft industry that went through flight testing without things going wrong and having to be changed, sometimes a lot. That's why we do testing. That's the whole point."

Craig knew that Walt was right. But this wasn't Lockheed. He was being backed by Shell and it looked like the company might pull out altogether. As Bill Lawler now explained, there were executives at the New York head office who had been opposed to sponsoring Craig from the start, arguing that involvement in land speed racing was too risky, that Craig might get himself killed and blacken Shell's name. They had been outvoted earlier in the year. Now, after the Bonneville debacle and the death of Glenn Leasher, they had fresh ammunition. They were going to try to shoot *Spirit of America* down.

Craig thus feared the worst when Lawler was summoned to New York to face company CEO Monty Spaght and the top brass. For the next several days he was in a state close to panic. If Shell dropped its sponsorship, what would he do?

7

BRINGING IT BACK

THE GODS OF LAND SPEED smiled down on Craig Breedlove. Bill Lawler returned to L.A. from New York with the good news that Shell had agreed to extend its *Spirit of America* sponsorship into 1963, giving Craig one more chance, one *last* chance, to get the record. First, though, the company insisted on having the car assessed by outside experts. If it had fundamental problems, as its underperformance at Bonneville suggested, Shell wanted them fixed.

Craig was all for making changes. He had already told Lawler that he wanted to make the front wheel steer and install a stabilizing fin on the tail as he had originally planned. He nevertheless felt tremendous anxiety going to the first meeting with the high-powered engineering consultants that Shell brought in, for his future was no longer in his control. It was in the hands of outsiders.

The steering issue was the first thing addressed. Rod Schapel's rear-brake and air-rudder system had been made to work at the very end of *Spirit*'s two weeks on the salt, but was such a complex arrangement really necessary? Wasn't there some way to make the front wheel turn? No there wasn't, Schapel insisted. A steering assembly wouldn't fit in the nose. Not enough space. End of story.

Silence around the conference table as the matter was pondered. Then Bob Heacock, an engineer Shell had brought in from Hughes Helicopters, spoke up.

"Well, why don't you use a focusing link?"

Everybody started looking around—Craig, Schapel, the other engineers. Finally someone spoke up: "What's a focusing link?"

"So Heacock gets out a piece of paper and draws a focusing link," says Craig, laughing as he tells the story. "And it was the simplest way to make the front wheel steer, after we'd gone through this whole thing and all Rod's bluster about it being impossible. We were five minutes into the first meeting and this front wheel steering thing came up, and right away we had the solution. We just had the right guy in there. Rod didn't want to hear it, but that's what we did."

Craig's idea of installing a tailfin was subsequently addressed. Schapel was adamant that a tailfin wasn't needed, that the wind tunnel tests proved that it added no stability to the racer for all the extra weight. It only ramped up the drag. An engineer from Aerospace Corporation named Bernie Pershing disagreed. Craig was right, he said. *Spirit of America* needed a tailfin. No, Schapel said, it didn't. Yes, Bernie gently insisted, it did. The car was fundamentally unstable without a tailfin and the problem would only get worse the faster it went—so much so that a crash was likely if it approached record speed.

"Rod Schapel was a really good intuitive aerodynamicist," says Craig, "but he didn't have a degree. And here was Bernie Pershing with a PhD in aerodynamics. Rod would say something and Bernie, he was a small guy, a real sweetheart, very diplomatic, he would very quietly explain how he was wrong, using all this irrefutable logic, and Rod would just have to shut up. But after the meeting he would say, 'I still think a tailfin's not necessary.' By then I'd just about had my fill of Rod Schapel."

That's how *Spirit* got a steerable front wheel and a tailfin. The experience of having his design changed and then being pushed aside left Schapel bitter and contemplating legal action. A lawsuit would follow, but that still lay a few years ahead. As for Craig, he emerged from it all more mature and with greater confidence in himself. He would continue to seek out the best advice he could find but never again would he subordinate himself to someone else in the design and operation of his racers. In all important things, he would ultimately rely on his own judgment going forward.

Craig would never again rely on wind tunnel tests either. A wind tunnel, he was coming to see, did not accurately reproduce a land speed racing environment and thus did not generate reliable results. "With an actual car racing down a track, the air and the ground are going the same speed [i.e., they're stationary] and the car is going a different speed. In a wind tunnel, the ground and car are going one speed [i.e., they're stationary] and the air is going another speed. So this can cause you to make bad design decisions. You can end up building a whole car based on data that isn't any good." Looking back on *Spirit*'s wind tunnel–influenced configuration today, Craig even regrets discarding the drooping nose he had originally designed and used on the mock-up. "We should have left it the way it was. But the wind tunnel told us we had a problem with the nose pushing down too heavy. And actually that wasn't the case."

It took five long months for the committee of experts to complete its review and approve the changes Craig wanted. Craig, obliged to attend meetings as his racer sat in storage, felt so much strain that he lost his appetite and had pains in his chest. It was not until spring 1963 that the committee submitted its final report and Shell allocated funds to rebuild *Spirit* for a return to the salt.

Released from enforced inactivity at last, Craig threw himself into working on the car with ferocious determination and drive. Rod Schapel was out. From now on Craig would make his own decisions. It was he, after all, who was putting his life on the line. It would therefore be on his terms. As a grim reminder of the stakes involved, he obtained a copy of the film that had been shot of Glenn Leasher's crash and showed it to the reassembled crew. Most of the guys had gotten to know Glenn the previous September. They had talked to him, looked him in the eye, shaken his hand. And now he was dead. "The film probably did more to reunite the crew than any other thing," Craig would say. "We became a tightly knit group again."

Once again the work had to be done at top speed, for the Bonneville season was now less than six months away. The racer was stripped down to the bare chassis and a new control system was hand-built around Bob Heacock's focusing link. The steering yoke could now be turned right there in Quin Epperly's shop and Craig could *see* the front wheel turning. And when he tested it on the tarmac at L.A. International Airport, it worked like a charm. By then the new tailfin, six feet high and covered in fiberglass, had been installed, restoring *Spirit* to something closer to Craig's original vision. And there, prominent on the tail, was the American flag.

Craig's belief in *Spirit of America* was now stronger than ever. "I was somebody with a vengeance and a purpose," he says of his return to Bonneville in 1963. "I was completely confident we could get the record because now I knew I could control the car."

It was time to bring the land speed record back to the United States.

———————

America's involvement in the LSR went back to 1902, when William K. Vanderbilt II, heir to the Vanderbilt fortune, drove a French-built car on a road outside Paris to a record speed of 76 mph. The record had the additional significance of initiating a shift in the sport to the internal combustion engine. Previous marks, going back to Frenchman Gaston de Chasseloup-Laubat's 39 mph in 1898, had been set in electric or steam-powered cars. Vanderbilt's record would be bettered by Henry Ford in January 1904 in a bid to attract publicity to the budding industrialist's Ford Motor Company. Steering with a bicycle-style iron bar, his face spattered with oil from the uncovered engine, Ford pushed his racer *999*, a.k.a. *Arrow*, to 91 mph on the frozen surface of Michigan's Lake St. Clair. Vanderbilt responded less than a month later, this time driving a German-built Mercedes, with a run of 92 mph at Daytona Beach.

Fred Marriott was the next American to enter the picture, shooting the LSR up to 127 mph in the steam-powered *Stanley Rocket* in 1906. He subsequently crashed the *Rocket* trying to better his record. The twisted wreckage was buried in the Daytona sand. Marriott survived but never competed again. His record stood for nearly four years before falling to a Frenchman. Then the English took over, beginning their almost undisputed hold on the ultimate speed mark.

The LSR had been in British hands for fourteen years when Ray Keech of Philadelphia came along in a three-engine, 36-cylinder, 81-liter behemoth called the *Triplex Special*. On April 22, 1928, Keech hit 207 mph at Daytona to edge past Malcolm Campbell's record by less than one mile an hour. His mark stood for a year, then Henry Segrave blew it away with a two-way average of 231 mph to reclaim the LSR for Britain. *Triplex* builder and owner J. M. White asked Keech to take his monster racer out again to snatch the record back but Keech declined. It was too dangerous, he said.

It was instead *Triplex* mechanic Lee Bible who would take the wheel on March 13, 1929. The Daytona garage owner had no experience with high-speed racing but he wasn't going to pass up what he called the "golden opportunity of a life time" when White asked him to drive. With twenty thousand spectators lining the dunes, Bible roared off down the beach and entered the mile at 202 mph. Then he lost control. The *Triplex Special* made a lurch and a bound and went into a barrel roll up toward the dunes, cutting a movie cameraman in half and flinging the pieces about. Back down on the beach Bible lay inert on the sand, head smashed, neck and all four limbs broken. He had been thrown a great distance. Eyewitnesses said he tried to sit up, then gasped and fell back, dead. His wife, who saw it all, went into hysterics. J. M. White broke down and had to be helped back to his hotel, vowing he was through with racing.

Ray Keech, the last American to hold the record, went on to compete in the Indianapolis 500 later that year. He was killed in another race shortly after that, on June 15, 1929.

A new land speed jet car opened the 1963 Bonneville season. It had been built by Walt Arfons, Art Arfons's estranged older half brother. Walt had been building jet dragsters going back to the late 1950s but was only now getting into the LSR game with a purpose-built racer, named *Wingfoot Express* after the logo of his primary sponsor, Goodyear. In backing both him and Craig, the tire company was hedging its LSR bet. Like every record contender before it, *Wingfoot* was beset by problems on its first trip to the salt. Walt and driver Tom Green were eventually forced to go home when salt got sucked into the jet's hot compressor and baked on to the blades.

Spirit of America had the salt for the next nineteen days. It was hauled onto the international course on July 28—right past the shattered remains of the *Infinity* jet car. It had been dumped alongside the road coming in off the highway. "It bothered us seeing that wreckage," crew member Al Buskirk remembers. "Finally, about the second day, Craig goes to Bill Lawler and says, 'Get that wreckage out of there. If I have to drive past it one more time, I'm not running.' We didn't blame him a bit."

Spirit, the new tailfin its most prominent feature, was two feet longer than the previous year, thirty-eight feet altogether. The chute compartment, shifted farther back to accommodate the tailfin, now projected out over the jet exhaust like a beak. The air rudder, reduced in size, was still in place under the nose. It would turn in tandem with the front wheel to steer the racer. And a new feature for 1963: "Craig Breedlove" freshly painted under the cockpit.

There was no longer any question of who was in charge. As Bill Lawler made clear in a letter to the crew, "Craig Breedlove will have over-all authority in the Project." Shell engineers Roy Van Sickle and Frank Bollo would oversee testing and provide guidance on the salt; Quin Epperly would serve as crew foreman; Nye Frank would have charge of steering and wheel bearings; Dick Compton and Bob Johnson the J-47 jet engine; Al Buskirk electrical; Jack Carter and Bob Davids the chutes. Craig's old friend Stan Goldstein, a new crew addition, would be the inspector, checking that all required procedures were completed before every run. Walt Sheehan once again would be responsible for data acquisition from the strain gauges installed on the car, all of them feeding into an onboard recorder from an F-104 jet fighter. Rod Schapel would assist him. Bernie Pershing would also be on hand to help interpret the data. If the nose started to lift up excessively or press down too hard, Walt and Rod and Bernie would know it. It would all be revealed in the wavering lines recorded on the roll of photographic paper in the data recorder that they would develop back in Wendover in their motel room sink.

This onboard data recorder, which was largely kept secret, was in fact *Spirit of America*'s ace in the hole heading into the 1963 Bonneville season. "Our car was the first in motorsports history to have data acquisition put into it," says Craig. "We were just light-years ahead of everybody else from a technological standpoint. Nobody had even thought about this stuff." The reason it was so important was that it allowed Craig and his crew to monitor the car's aerodynamic performance as it went faster so that adjustments to lift could be made and problems headed off right there on the salt. This was a revolutionary approach to speed, at a time when all racing, aerodynamically speaking, was done blind. Whether at Bonneville or the Indianapolis 500 or the Paris Grand Prix, the first hint a driver usually had that his car was lifting was when he became airborne, the first inkling of excessive downforce when one of his tires blew out. Going forward, Craig's unique ability to acquire aerodynamic data and respond immediately to it would give him a tremendous advantage in the LSR game.

Test runs began on July 29. There were the inevitable glitches. The disposable chute compartment lids tended to buckle and pop off at higher speeds, releasing the chute prematurely. They were reinforced to better withstand the wind blast but the problem was not fully solved. The cockpit breathing system also failed, making it necessary for Craig to run with the canopy off for the first two days, until replacement parts were flown in. Overall, however, *Spirit* performed very well and so did the crew; competence, efficiency, and morale were all much better than the previous year. In a dozen practice runs over three days Craig steadily advanced the throttle and built up his speed to within striking distance of the record—John Cobb's record, the ultimate record. He had already left the motorcycle record far behind. He ran up to 349 mph with the canopy off, surpassing Art Arfons's open-cockpit record, the wind violently buffeting his head. Breathing system fixed and canopy in place, he pushed on further to 365. The racer was then given a thorough overhaul in preparation for the LSR bid. Testing had gone so well that D-day was moved forward three days, to Monday, August 5, 1963.

Craig arrived on the salt at five thirty that morning, as the dawn sky was turning from mauve to cobalt blue. He ducked into the trailer-workshop at base camp and changed into his fire suit: baggy blue pants cinched at the ankles and matching zip-up jacket with Shell and Good-year logos over the heart. On his feet: white athletic socks and navy blue sneakers, the kind he had worn in high school gym class. He hadn't had any breakfast, just a cup of coffee and some orange juice. It was better to have an empty stomach in case he crashed and doctors had to operate on his innards. Besides, the butterflies he was feeling left no room for food.

The sun appeared over the mountains. It was going to be a good day—cloudless sky, no wind, temperature heading to the low nineties. *Spirit* was towed north from base camp to the two-mile marker, past the worst of the roughness that the Highway Department's grading over the weekend just couldn't fix. This left Craig with nine miles of course on which to set the record. He walked around his racer, methodically checking things over, then pitched in to rub polish on its gleaming body. It would help reduce drag and increase speed as *Spirit* cleaved through the air—not much, but every bit helped. He tried to be affable with the reporters on the scene but it wasn't easy, particularly with the guy who kept pressing, *What are you feeling? Are you afraid? Are you nervous?* "Of course I'm nervous," Craig finally snapped, unable to maintain his forced smile.

The United States Auto Club would once again be timing Craig's runs. This would be done by means of a light beam shining across the course into a photoelectric cell, one set at the entrance to the measured mile and a second set at the end. Electrical wiring would convey the signals to head timer Joe Petrali and his team in the "USAC shack" at the center of the mile, set well back from the course. When *Spirit* entered the mile it would break the light beam shining across the course and start the electronic clock in the shack. Passing out of the mile, it would break the second beam and stop the clock, giving Joe an elapsed time in the mile accurate to one-thousandth of a second. From this he would be able to precisely calculate Craig's speed. His speed over a kilometer distance, more meaningful to continental Europeans, would also be measured. All of this would be observed by two representatives from the Fédération Internationale de Motocyclisme, who would certify the results and officially sanction a record. To satisfy the FIM, which classified *Spirit* as a "cyclecar," Craig had thirty kilos of ballast aboard to nominally approximate the weight of a passenger in a sidecar. It was actually a tank of water under the seat, part of a water injection system to give the jet engine more power. It had not yet been needed.

Six thirty. *Spirit* was ready. Craig just needed the verdict on the wind. The half dozen observers stationed along the course reported dead calm, with just a slight breeze in the mile, well within the margin of safety. "She's all clear," said the USAC official manning the field telephone at the two-mile marker.

Craig turned to the crew. "Let's go."

Norm Breedlove and Lee gave him a hug and headed up the course to watch from the timing shack, Norm looking anxious, Lee remarkably calm. Craig stooped to feel the salt. It had rained in the night and was still a bit damp. He rose and looked up the eighty-foot-wide course. Even starting at the two-mile marker, the first section of course down here was still pretty rough. It would impede his acceleration on his run going north. Coming back, as he was slowing down, it would give him a shaking.

He stuffed cotton into his ears and donned his helmet. It was a new one painted in *Spirit of America* colors with stars on the sides and "Breedlove" across the front. He mounted the stepladder positioned alongside *Spirit*, pausing at the top for Nye Frank to brush the salt off his sneakers, then squeezed into the cockpit. The U-shaped steering yoke was turned upside down to give him a little extra space as he wriggled in past the roll bar. He settled into the custom-made seat, a padded cavity at the top cradling his head, the whole thing nesting him in chromoly tubing like a full-body crash helmet.

The steering yoke was rotated 180 degrees into position, the ends of the "U" now pointing forward, a button on either end within easy reach of his thumbs, like the gun buttons on a WWII fighter. These were the parachute releases, main chute on the right side, backup on the left. The instrument panel held five indicators: speed in knots, tachometer, exhaust temp, fuel pressure, air bottle pressure, chute release light. A hand throttle for the jet engine was by his right hand. Five toggle switches for starting the engine and arming the chutes were by his left. At his feet were two pedals. Only one of them now controlled the rear brakes. The other was an accelerator. After setting the hand control to the power level he wanted, Craig had simply to slam the accelerator to the floor and hold it down to maintain precise throttle. It was the only way to use the foot pedal, stepping on it hard and holding it to the floor. Anything more gentle than that and his foot might get knocked off the pedal when the ride got rough and threw him around.

Nye helped Craig with his harness and snapped his air mask to his helmet, then set the canopy in position over the cockpit. Craig turned the inside latches, locking it down. He was now sealed off from the world.

He made his first run with the throttle at 90 percent RPM. The chutes once again released prematurely but otherwise it went well. He coasted to a stop at the north end of the course, close to where the advance crew was waiting to get the turnaround started. The clock was ticking. Less than an hour left. They set to work removing *Spirit*'s deployed chute, cleaning the windshield, and wiping salt buildup off the body. The B-25 that had been circling overhead, filming, came in for a landing alongside the course. Reporters who had hitched a ride aboard tumbled out and came running forward.

The rest of the crew came roaring up in rental cars and team trucks. They got the dolly under *Spirit*'s nose wheel and muscled it around, pointing south, for the return run. New chutes and explosive charges were installed. Battery power was checked, and tire pressure, and the temperature in the wheel bearings. The clock was ticking.

The verdict arrived from Joe Petrali. Craig had done 388.47 mph through the mile. To beat Cobb's 394 mph record he would have to do at least 412 on the next run.

"We'll have to give it more throttle," he said. "We'll pick it up going back."

The turnaround procedures continued. Install new air bottle for Craig's breathing system; replace photographic strip in the onboard data recorder; top up the oil in the J-47; refill the fuel tank with Shell aviation fuel. *Spirit* had burned most of the forty-five-gallon tank on the run. Craig, nervously pacing the whole while, passed the word to the B-25 pilot to stay out of his field of vision. He didn't want any distractions.

It took the crew forty minutes to get the car ready. The wind by this time had picked up a bit. *Spirit* was positioned forty feet over from the black line to give it drifting room and the engine was started. Craig was heading south in a blast of salt at 7:13, throttle at 95 percent RPM, roughly three-quarters of the engine's full power.

The wind was stronger than expected. It quickly nudged *Spirit* back to the line and then past it, Craig making big turns with the yoke to get back to center, for from lock to lock the steering moved the nose wheel a mere 2 degrees. The wheel itself initially did most of the turning. Then, as Craig got up over 200, the air rudder increasingly took over.

Tremendous noise. The jet engine's compressor was screaming; the shock strut on the front wheel was banging; the tires sounded as if someone were beating on them like a drum. The roar of the exhaust could no longer be heard. It was being left far behind.

Severe shaking. It came on at around 300 mph, got worse, then subsided as Craig streaked past 350, the racer now going so fast it was barely skimming the surface. The sensation was intense, sharpening Craig's focus. It was like driving on ice.

Smoke. It was starting to creep into the cockpit. It had alarmed Craig the first time it happened—he thought his racer was burning. Now he knew it was salt pulverized to dust by the nose wheel and working its way in. This was where his tinted goggles came in handy, protecting his eyes from the irritation more effectively than the full-face bubble mask he had worn the previous year.

Spirit reentered the measured mile, breaking the photoelectric beam. In the USAC shack the HP 5532A digital recorder marked the precise time. One second . . . two seconds . . . three seconds. . . . The digital recorder clicked again as the racer broke the second beam at the kilometer marker, then a third time as it exited the mile. Joe Petrali jotted the numbers down on a yellow pad and started his manual calculations. Craig's elapsed time in the mile: 8.404 seconds.

Out of sight down the course, Craig took his foot off the accelerator and hit the knob at the center of the steering yoke, killing the engine. The roar of the exhaust stopped. He coasted for a bit, the screaming of the still-turning compressor slowly dropping in pitch.

He punched the chute button with his thumb. *Bang!* The explosive charge blew off the rear lid and the eight-foot-wide canopy deployed, throwing him forward against his harness. Then he hit the rough section at the south end of the course and the ride turned violent, giving Craig a tremendous shaking. It was only thanks to the cup-shaped headrest that his helmeted head didn't smash through the canopy glass. He gutted it out, waiting for his speed to drop off. When it got below 135 knots— 150 mph—he eased down on the brakes.

Spirit coasted to a stop. The entire nine-mile run had taken less than two minutes. The compressor continued to spool down, a diminishing whine. Craig sat there for a moment, numbness receding. Had he done it? Yeah, he was pretty sure that he had.

He undid the latches and lifted up the canopy for one of the Shell people to take. He undid his harness, wriggled out of the cockpit, and jumped down to the ground, turning back to wipe his footprint off the air duct. Expectant faces all around now. *What do you think you did?* someone asked. Craig had previously said he could get a pretty good sense of his speed from how fast the mile markers whipped past. He replied, "It felt like about 425."

All eyes shifted to USAC official Ben Torres, in contact with the timing shack by field telephone. "What's that?" he was saying, straining to hear over the excited voices and static. "I can't hear you. . . . Four? . . . Four what? . . . Four-two-eight?" A collective cheer rose from the crowd, drowning him out.

Craig had done 428.37 mph on the return trip, giving him a two-way average of 407.45 mph. He had just broken the world land speed record. After thirty-four years, he had brought it back to the United States. "We did it, huh?" he said, seizing Lee in a bear hug when she arrived from midcourse.

The scrum of photographers and journalists closed in. *How does it feel, Craig?* they wanted to know. *What's it like to go more than 400 miles an hour?*

"It feels great!" Craig exulted. "It's great! Just great!"

The idea of making a third run within the hour to increase the record was quickly abandoned. The car had endured a hard pounding and needed a thorough inspection before it ran again. Craig also wanted to see the readouts from the onboard data recorder, for the earlier test runs had revealed that *Spirit* had a tendency to get light in the nose. It was another instance of the wind tunnel tests having led them astray. Before going any faster, Craig wanted to make sure his racer wasn't about to fly. They would take a couple days to regroup, he decided, then try again.

Shell head office had other plans. The company wanted Craig back east to make the most of the publicity jackpot they had just scored. So did Goodyear. Press conferences, interviews with magazines and newspapers, public appearances, TV guest spots—it was all being arranged.

L.A. hot-rodder, fireman, and mechanic Craig Breedlove had just become famous. He was about to enter a whole new world.

8

AMERICAN HERO

THE DELUGE STARTED WITH A FLOOD of telegrams to the Western Motel. "Congratulations on your record run," cabled Nathan Ostich. "Since I didn't do it first I am glad you as an American driver did." "Hearty congratulations. Magnificent achievement," read the one from Donald Campbell. And from Roger and Gene Rourke, Craig's old lakester partners: "Super." The messages kept pouring in and the *Spirit* crew started getting a bit crazy, chugging beer and roaring and singing and some of the more agile ones climbing up on the roof. Then everybody piled into cars and headed off to Salt Lake City for a lavish dinner laid on by Shell.

It was the next day that Craig's life really started to change, when he and Lee were hustled onto a plane to New York, where the city was waking up to the *New York Times* headline: BREEDLOVE SETS WORLD LAND SPEED RECORD OF 407.45 MPH. They arrived in the afternoon and were driven to the Americana Hotel, through the concrete canyons of Manhattan, everything totally foreign. Apart from Bonneville and his two hurried trips to Akron, Craig had never done any traveling before. There was a crowd of reporters waiting at the hotel to interview him. There would be a whole lot more of them the next morning, when Craig was ushered into an auditorium downstairs.

"I was just so overwhelmed. The place was packed with international press, a sea of people, cameras and flashbulbs going off. I mean, I'm kind of a shy person. I was the guy in high school who dreaded giving a book report in front of the class. I'd gotten pretty good talking to people one-on-one and giving presentations to small groups, but nothing like this. Within twenty-four hours of setting the record, here I was having to conduct this huge press conference in front of three hundred people."

Craig rose to the challenge. When he was talking about *Spirit of America* the confidence and the eloquence just somehow came. "He's a remarkable salesman," an unnamed Shell executive was quoted in the *New York Times* as saying, "modest but with a commanding personality when he talked about his car." The same paper included a write-up on Craig's mother Portia. "I must admit I didn't encourage him," she said. "It seemed to be too big a thing to be shooting for. He's taught me a lesson."

The whirlwind New York visit included appearances on *The Tonight Show* with Jack Parr and *The Today Show* the next morning. Craig, nervous under the hot lights, was watched by four million people. Guest spots on *The Mike Douglas Show* and the game show *I've Got a Secret* would follow. Somewhere in between he was hustled into a meeting with smiling Shell and Goodyear executives to be presented with an offer he couldn't refuse. They would jointly pay him $2,000 a month for three years to serve as a "racing consultant," plus $200 a day and all expenses to go on a publicity tour. That was big money in 1963, a CEO's salary. "It was incredible. . . . For the first time in my life I would know what it feels like to have money. . . . The record had been important to me and I was proud of what I had done, but the money was like the biggest present in the world." Lee cried when Craig told her the good news. To help Craig handle his newfound wealth, Shell fixed him up with a business manager, Don Gardner.

Ads were now appearing in all the major newspapers. Shell headlined theirs FASTEST MAN ON WHEELS . . . USING SHELL FUEL! Goodyear's lavish full-page spreads trumpeted, NEW LAND SPEED RECORD! 407 MPH ON GOODYEAR TIRES! With the name "Breedlove" suddenly a household word, Craig set out on a thirty-eight-city nationwide tour organized by Goodyear's PR department. "Advance teams would go out and work in an area lining appearances up before I got there. I would literally get off the plane and they would hand me a schedule that went from early in the morning until nearly midnight, attending functions and meetings and whatever you can imagine, all the radio shows in the area, visits to television stations, sports interviews."

Lee by this time had returned to L.A., leaving Craig alone with his Goodyear handler Bill Neely. He became more polished dealing with the press and speaking in public, but the pace was brutal and telling the same story again and again was a grind. It was ironic, really. He had achieved exactly what he wanted. He had won the LSR and made himself a somebody—and here he was yearning to escape the attention. It had all happened so fast. The crew had been there celebrating with him one minute . . . and then they were gone. He hadn't even had a chance to properly thank them. Somehow it didn't feel right.

———————

Back out at Bonneville, Nathan Ostich had taken over the salt. His *Flying Caduceus*, like *Spirit of America*, had acquired a tailfin since the previous year, his team having independently arrived at the conclusion that the jet car was unstable without it. Things started out well, Ostich quickly building his speed up to 350 mph, the fastest he had yet gone. But then the *Caduceus* ran into a wall, topping out at 359 mph even with its J-47 going full blast. Ostich kept trying but it didn't do any good. The problem, which Craig had predicted to Firestone's George Eckel back in 1960, was that *Caduceus*'s four exposed wheels produced too much drag. And there was no way to fix it. Putting fairings on the wheels would make the racer, already three and a half tons, too heavy.

After three seasons on the salt, Ostich had struck out. If there was a silver lining to it all, it was that "Doc," well liked by all, would live to old age.

———————

Craig visited thirty-eight cities on his cross-country publicity tour, his schedule packed from morning to night, the whole thing a whirl of airplanes and hotels and people. It was such a marketing bonanza for Shell and Goodyear, with over ten thousand write-ups in the press and massive TV and radio coverage, that they decided to squeeze in junkets to England and Australia as well. The weeks, then months of unrelenting stress were almost more than Craig could handle. By the time it was over he had lost nearly twenty pounds off his already lean frame.

One stop Craig didn't make was at the White House. The ringing close of John F. Kennedy's inaugural address had been a particular inspiration for him back in January 1961: "And so, my fellow Americans, ask not what your country can do for you; ask what you can do for your country." Those words, coming at a time when Craig was struggling without a sponsor to get *Spirit of America* built, had helped him keep going. They had been an affirmation that he was doing the right thing, that winning the land speed record for America was what he had been born to do. It was thus a thrill when he was invited to meet President Kennedy in the Oval Office—and a crushing disappointment when Kennedy was assassinated before the meeting could take place.

Craig was anxious about how he would be received when he arrived in London, for the Brits had been doing the most carping about his record, hammering away on the point that it wasn't recognized by the FIA because *Spirit* wasn't technically a car and because it was powered by pure jet thrust. "You really haven't broken Cobb's record, you know," a reporter from a London paper had told him over the phone just hours after he set his 407 mph mark. "Breedlove's was made in a jet car and couldn't be considered a record," groused Sir Alfred Owen, one of the industrialists involved in building Donald Campbell's *Bluebird*. "It is just like putting an aircraft engine in a car." Craig responded modestly in public, conceding that yes, John Cobb's mark still stood for a wheel-driven car. Privately, however, the denigration left him feeling angry and hurt. "Who the hell are the FIA?" he would say in an unguarded moment. "If they don't like the car they can do the other thing—we got the record."

As it turned out, Donald Campbell himself became Craig's biggest defender in England. Campbell had endured tremendous frustration in his own LSR bid, crashing at Bonneville in 1960, then being flooded out on his second attempt in early 1963 on Australia's Lake Eyre desert lakebed. If anyone had reason to express resentment about *Spirit of America*, it was Campbell. When he hosted a reception for Craig at his home in Surrey, the British press thus went hoping for some choice sniping, perhaps even a UK-USA confrontation. Craig was oblivious to these undercurrents. It was only on the drive down to Surrey, sharing a car with a group of British reporters, that he learned that "fireworks" were expected. Campbell, however, didn't deliver. Far from being critical, he called Craig's achievement "brilliant" and his record the new mark he would aim for on his return to Lake Eyre. But Craig did it with a *jet*, the newsmen prodded. His vehicle wasn't *wheel driven*. "I only wish I had been smart enough to think of it first," Campbell responded. "Instead, we buckled under to FIA's intractable ruling and have ended up on the short end of their thinking."

Campbell's generosity in the face of disappointment and his grace in handling the press made a deep impression on Craig. The forty-two-year-old racer—who coincidentally shared Craig's birthday—became his new role model and a close friend. As for the FIA, it found itself slipping into irrelevance in the eyes of the public, where *speed* was what mattered, not the niceties of how it was attained. Within months it would create a "Special Vehicles" category to accommodate pure jet thrust.

Returning to London, Craig stumbled into the belated realization that being famous brought with it temptation. It happened when he was taken to a nightclub, his first such experience in four months of nonstop publicity work. "I couldn't believe my eyes. The place was crowded with mostly drunk and partying guys, and there must have been a hundred of the most beautiful nude women dressed only in high heels and catering to these guys." For Craig, starved of female companionship, overworked and worn out, it was too much. He did not return to his hotel alone. He felt a twinge of guilt the next morning, but more than anything there was a sense of relief at having escaped the unrelenting pressure, at least for one night.

It was in fact another turning point in his life. In justifying marital infidelity as a matter of survival, a way of coping, Craig had opened the door to other women. When he arrived in Australia on the next leg of his tour, he requested a female traveling companion, someone to help him relax after the packed days of public appearances. His Goodyear handlers, used to the womanizing ways of race car drivers, quietly fixed him up with a beauty from Sydney's Playboy Club. At the end of the junket Craig had fallen for her and didn't want to leave. He stayed in Sydney for an extra week, phoning Lee to say he was exhausted and needed the rest. "Ninety percent of a young guy getting into trouble is having the opportunity," is how Craig sees it today. "No opportunity, no trouble."

Opportunity of the female kind would beckon again the following May, when Craig attended the Indianapolis 500. She was named Linda Vaughn, a buxom blond bombshell employed by Pure Oil to pose in skimpy outfits with the cars. Craig once more delayed his return home to spend a few extra days with Linda, and this time Lee found out. When Craig finally got back to L.A., it was with the determination to end his marriage. He sat down with Lee, apologized for everything, and tried to explain what his life had become—the pressure, the temptation, the loneliness of being on tour. It would be best for both of them, he said, if they just got a divorce. He would give her the $50,000 house they were building in the affluent L.A. suburb of Palos Verdes—five bedrooms, three baths, swimming pool in the backyard, stunning view of the ocean—and make her a fair settlement too.

To his surprise, Lee refused. Craig could do what he wanted when he was away, she said, just so long as she didn't hear about it. She only expected him to behave himself when he was at home. So that was that. The marriage continued . . . for now.

They were singing about Craig when he got back to the States from Australia, a new hit song by the Beach Boys called "Spirit of America": "*Half airplane, half auto, now famous worldwide / The Spirit of America the name on the side / The man who would drive her, Craig Breedlove by name / A daring young man played a dangerous game . . .*" "I thought it was the neatest thing," says Craig. "I was really excited the first time I heard it. Don Gardner [Craig's new business manager] was talking about suing the Beach Boys for writing a song about me, for using my name. I thought that was crazy. I'm going, 'I don't want to sue them. I want to *meet* them and tell them how much I like their song.'"

And then an even bigger surprise: Hollywood came calling. Producers Stan Jolley and William Veragas approached Craig through his dad Norm with the idea of making a feature film about his life, to be titled *Spirit of America*. After getting Craig on board, they began developing the project out of a Goldwyn Studios office and writing a script and talking Shell and Goodyear into footing most of the budget. The plan was to wait until after the 1964 Bonneville season, when Craig was hoping to improve his record and maybe even break 500 mph, then to go into production with this as the spectacular third act for the picture. Who would star? Steve McQueen, whom Craig had known for several years through Norm, was at the top of the list. Steve was interested—he loved cars and racing—but he had to decline, his schedule being booked solid for the next couple years. "Why don't you just do it yourself?" he told Craig when they met. "It's real easy. You'll just be playing yourself." The producers gave the suggestion serious consideration, which terrified Craig. A small part of him, however, was drawn to the idea of starring in a movie. It was the part that had enjoyed pretending to be flamboyant wrestler Gorgeous George back when he was a kid, the part that he had inherited from his mother Portia, who never got beyond the chorus line in her own movie career. Heck, if Steve McQueen said he could do it, then he was willing to give it a shot.

Could life get any better for Craig? Yes, it could. Shell Oil went for his idea of selling *Spirit of America* toy racers through its thirty-eight thousand gas stations across the country and tens of thousands more Shell and Goodyear outlets worldwide. Texaco had enjoyed great success with its tanker truck toy campaign, advertising the thing to kids on TV and selling many millions through its stations. If a mundane toy truck, well advertised, sold like that, imagine what a sleek *Spirit of America* model would do. Kids would go crazy. Shell signed a contract with Wen Mac to begin manufacture of the toys and started putting together a marketing campaign for the 1964 Christmas shopping season. The royalties alone would make Craig a millionaire.

Craig Breedlove, American hero, was riding high. He was famous, living in a beautiful house, money rolling in and lots more to come. And best of all, he was back doing what he loved, fabricating a racer, this time with full backing from Shell and Goodyear right from the start, a slingshot dragster called *Spirit II*. The quickie project, begun in early 1964, was conceptualized by Craig and Bill Moore and built with the help of Quin Epperly and Nye Frank. The finished machine was revolutionary, unlike anything ever seen on the drag strip, a fully streamlined dragster with an enclosed cockpit and the front wheels encased in drag-reducing fairings, otherwise known as wheel pants. Craig ran it for the first time at the *Hot Rod* magazine meet in Riverside, California, in June, aiming to be the first to crack the 200 mph barrier from a standing start on the strip.

It didn't happen. The wheel pants acted like air rudders at high speed and made steering tricky. *Spirit II*'s tires, the very first batch of drag slicks produced by Goodyear, also proved to be lousy alongside the M&H Racemasters everyone else was using. "I guess they didn't have the compound down yet," said George Klass, "[because] it was like driving on grease." The biggest problem, however, was that *Spirit II* didn't have enough power, a 354-cubic-inch engine having been installed in the rush to get it finished, at a time when most top competitors were running 392s. "Connie Kalitta offered to let me use his engine," says Craig, "but we didn't have enough time to do it for the *Hot Rod* meet. Man, if we had put Kalitta's engine in that thing—he had some killer engines. He was probably the best engine guy that NHRA ever saw, an absolute maestro."

Although it never achieved its potential, *Spirit II* still played an important role in drag history, introducing streamlining to dragster design and marking Goodyear's entry into the drag tire market. It was an ignominious entry. But great things lay ahead. In just a few years, with Craig himself playing a key role, Goodyear would greatly improve its slicks and come to dominate the drag scene. *Spirit II* by then had been largely forgotten. Craig had to shelve it after the *Hot Rod* meet to get ready for the 1964 Bonneville season and never got back to working on it again. It sat neglected in his garage, slowly becoming obsolete.

Then an entrepreneur named Jay Ohrberg approached Craig with an offer to take it on tour and split the money.

"So I gave Jay the car—and he stole it! I tried to chase him down but he just dissolved. I guess he didn't want me to find him because he swiped the car. It ended up with George Barris, then Don Garlits bought it. It's in Garlits's museum right now. I guess it's better sitting there than in my garage, where nobody would see it."

July 1964. It was time to get *Spirit of America* ready for the return to the salt. Donald Campbell was now effectively out of the unlimited LSR picture. On July 17 he gutted out a two-way average of 403 mph on Australia's Lake Eyre, enough to break Cobb's wheel-driven record but short of Craig's mark. To Craig, reading about Campbell's tremendous effort, his weeks of frustration, and heartache, it was clear that *Bluebird* couldn't go much faster. It was the finest wheel-driven racer ever built . . . and it had topped out. From now on, competing for the land speed record at the ultimate level would be all about thrust. With Nathan Ostich retired, that left Craig with only two serious rivals: Walt Arfons with his *Wingfoot Express* and Art Arfons with his latest *Green Monster*.

Craig had visited both men earlier in the summer during a trip to Goodyear headquarters in Akron. He had driven out to Pickle Road, the dirt lane outside town where Walt and Art had their garages side by side, and had a pleasant visit with each. He already knew quite a bit about Walt's *Wingfoot*. It had made an unsuccessful bid for the record in 1963 and would likely do better this year, the bugs hopefully ironed out. As for *Green Monster*, Craig had heard little more than rumors. Alarming rumors. Now, walking over to Art's neighboring garage, skirting the junked cars and old engines littering the yard, he saw they were true.

Art had somehow gotten his hands on a J-79, the jet engine that powered Lockheed's cutting-edge F-104 fighter. A civilian wasn't supposed to have a J-79. It was too new, still considered classified by the military. But there it was, installed in *Monster*. Art had put the word out for a 79 to junk dealers all across the country and finally located one in a bin of scrap in Miami. It had been "fodded"—foreign object damaged—by dirt and pebbles being sucked in, and so the Air Force had junked it, thinking it beyond repair. But it wasn't. Not for Art and his fabrication partner Ed Snyder. They got it working fine, testing it out behind the shop where the grass was blasted away down to the dirt.

Craig walked slowly around *Monster*, taking it in. It looked something like his very first idea for a jet car, a simple tubular shape, sidesaddle cockpit on one side, a second cockpit on the other side for balance. The front intake of the engine comprised the nose of the car, a big gaping hole that at first glance seemed like an aerodynamic disaster—way too much frontal area, way too much drag. In studying up on jet aircraft, however, Art had learned that the intake didn't count toward frontal drag because it wasn't pushing its way through the air in flight—it was sucking it through. So why not just leave the damn intake wide open and save yourself the trouble of building air ducts? It wasn't science, just down-to-earth logic. So that's what he did. The whole car, Art proudly explained, had cost just $10,000 to build. That included the five grand he had spent on the engine.

Craig peered into the intake. He was looking at serious competition. What *Monster* lacked in aerodynamics it made up for in power—monstrous power, three times what *Spirit* had, around 17,000 pounds of thrust in full afterburner. It was so much juice that if you placed *Monster* on end it could literally blast off into the sky.

"It really looks strong," said Craig.

Art smiled. "It is."

The race for the LSR was about to get hairy.

9

SPEED WAR

SPIRIT OF AMERICA WAS HURTLING DOWN THE SALT, Craig's thundering heartbeat louder than the screaming wind and the engine. He was out of control. Then he was crashing. The black line dropped away and the view through the canopy became nothing but sky, then a jumble of blue and white as *Spirit* started tumbling end over end. When the world settled Craig was hanging upside down, the smell of leaking aviation fuel permeating the cockpit. He struggled to free himself. The fuel smell got stronger. Then the crackle of flames . . .

Craig awoke with a start in his room at Wendover's Western Motel. It was October 12, 1964, his first day on the salt. Lee wasn't with him. He had asked her to stay home, not so much due to the tension in their marriage as his need to focus, to regain his edge, to find the intensity he had lost after more than a year of distraction. He was feeling more anxiety this year, for so much was riding on him not just winning back the record but on pushing it all the way to 500 mph. The producers at Goldwyn needed a 500 record to make the perfect ending for the Craig Breedlove movie. Shell Oil was counting on it too for the huge *Spirit of America* toy sale planned for the lead-up to Christmas, a marketing blitz that would make Craig a millionaire from the royalties alone. And then there was the bigger publicity picture, the reality that breaking the land speed record, as Tom Green and Art Arfons had just done, wasn't in itself worth very much. Craig had to break it *and hold it* at the end of the season to give sponsors Shell and Goodyear a full year of marketing value. So that meant that he had to set it very high. He had to deliver a fabulous new record—and privately he wasn't at all sure he was mentally prepared.

Craig frankly was scared. The fear had started to creep in earlier in the summer, when he witnessed the fiery crash that had killed Dave MacDonald and Eddie Sachs at the Indianapolis 500. "It was a period of time when a lot of drivers were killed," Craig remembers, "guys I knew, that were friends. Fireball Roberts had just had that bad crash and been burned, and then my friend Bobby Marshman was killed. And at Indy there was just a whole series of things that happened throughout. In fact, I left early. Once Parnelli Jones caught on fire in the pits, I just had to walk out. I couldn't watch it anymore." It had helped spending time with Linda Vaughn in Las Vegas before coming on to the salt flats. Linda seemed to know just what to say to psych Craig up and make him feel better. But then he got to Wendover and there in the paper was that terrible photo of George Koehne's crash at the Riverside racetrack, where Craig himself had recently run *Spirit II*. It showed Koehne seated in his car, seemingly calm as the flames engulfed him, eerily like that Buddhist monk who had recently set himself ablaze in Saigon to protest the Vietnam War. It was the race car driver's worst nightmare, being burned alive. It was the nightmare that was jolting Craig awake in a sweat almost nightly.

The 1964 Bonneville season, condensed into the single month of October, was the most intense period of competition in LSR history. It was kicked off by Walt Arfons and driver Tom Green with their Goodyear-sponsored *Wingfoot Express*, returning to the salt for a second try after the previous year's disappointment. Once again they ran into a wall of frustration, *Wingfoot* barely touching 300 mph. Walt tried cutting away some of the paneling behind the cockpit—and part of the Goodyear logo along with it—to give the jet engine more air. It didn't help. He replaced the engine with a spare. Still no good. Finally, on the afternoon of the very last day, Tom punched the afterburner, unleashing *Wingfoot*'s full power, and squeaked past Craig's year-old mark to set a new record of 413 mph.

The record lasted only three days. Walt and Tom were on the long drive home, bound for a celebratory bash laid on by Goodyear, when the news came over the car radio that Art Arfons in his Firestone-sponsored *Green Monster* had snatched the LSR away with a new mark of 434 mph. Art had been right there in Wendover, waiting his turn while *Wingfoot* was running. He had arrived in the middle of his half brother's week, parked his old bus at the Western Motel, and defiantly hoisted a big red Firestone flag. "He parked his bus right here, on this side of the swimming pool," Walt would privately grouse. "And it was all Goodyear here. It was my week here. He come in on Wednesday, on *Wednesday*, of my week." When Art got up the next morning, the Firestone flag was lying on the ground, the flagpole bent over. It was the opening shot in the land speed battle that was about to explode between the two tire giants—what Humpy Wheeler, sales manager of Firestone's racing tire division, would call "all-out blood-stinkin' war."

"Absolutely fantastic," Craig said when he heard the news of Art's record. "I think they did a tremendous job." He had good reason to be impressed, for what Art had done was amazing, showing up on the salt with a backyard-built car that had never been driven and breaking the LSR in only two days. It hadn't been easy, however. Art had found *Green Monster* almost impossible to handle on the first day of testing, the ride so rough he could hardly stand it, half his view from the sidesaddle cockpit blocked by the side of the car. It was such a bad experience that he almost packed it in before deciding to give it one more try the next morning. That's when he discovered that the ride smoothed out in the high 300s, that once *Monster* got going fast enough "the damn thing held like a dream." It took Art just one more run to set his 434 mph record, using scarcely half the power of his J-79.

He tried for 500 mph two days later. It didn't go well. *Monster* blew a tire in the mile, a 250 psi explosion that wrecked the right rear end, but luckily didn't roll. Art escaped the fastest blowout in history unscathed. Firestone pushed the story that the blowout had been caused by a stray bolt kicked up off the salt but that wasn't true. The reality was that the tire had been overloaded by the rightward torque of Art's salvaged engine, the result of the repairs he had done to get it running, filing down dinged compressor blades and removing others altogether, the ones too bent to fix. In static tests behind his workshop, his rebuilt J-79 had produced so much torque that the left side of the chassis had lifted up off the ground.

That was it for Art's week on the salt. Craig was up next.

———————

Craig announced when he arrived on the salt on October 10 that his goal was 500 mph. He was confident he had the car to do it. On the 428 mph return run of his record the previous year, the 95 percent RPM throttle setting had utilized scarcely three-quarters of *Spirit of America*'s potential thrust. Going those last few clicks to 100 percent therefore meant a whole lot more power. And that was only the start. *Spirit* now had a new engine, a rebuilt J-47 that burned hotter to produce an extra 500 pounds of thrust. That alone would likely get Craig to 500. And if it didn't, he would use water injection—spraying water into the inlet ducts to vaporize in the engine, thereby making the air heavier to substantially boost thrust. The system was in fact already in place, in the form of a forty-gallon water tank under the seat. Craig, in satisfying the FIM's ruling that his racer carry ballast to qualify as a "cyclecar," had been thinking ahead. And if water injection wasn't enough, there was still the possibility of fitting an afterburner onto the tailpipe like on Art's *Monster*. Craig didn't think he would need it, however—not with *Spirit*'s low-drag design. "From an aerodynamic standpoint, *Spirit of America* was superior to *Green Monster*. Art was relying just on the sheer power of the J-79, while I was relying on the refinement of the aerodynamics."

Craig not only had an aerodynamically superior racer, he had the ability to know what those aerodynamics were doing thanks to *Spirit*'s onboard strain gauges and data recorder. These had played a crucial role in his 1963 record and would do so again, allowing *Spirit*'s lift to be monitored and problems identified and corrected. These corrections were done by changing the shape of *Spirit*'s rear axle, the strut connecting the outrigger wheels to the body. The metal tabs attached to the rear of this axle were curved like the airfoil on a wing. When the strain gauges revealed that *Spirit*'s nose was starting to lift, these tabs were removed from each side of the axle and bent ever so slightly to give the "wing" more lift, thereby easing up the back of the racer and shifting some of the load to the nose. It was all very precisely done according to Walt Sheehan's and Bernie Pershing's calculations, the tweaks to the axle so subtle as to seem inconsequential. At 400-plus mph, however, it took very little additional "flap" to change *Spirit*'s lift. For Craig, it all added up to a tremendous advantage over Art Arfons, who had no way of knowing what his *Green Monster* was doing. And what was it doing? Judging from Art's rear tire blowout, it was likely experiencing too much downforce and overloading the rear wheels. That made a lot more sense than Firestone's story about a stray bolt.

After helping get *Spirit* unloaded at base camp, Craig mounted his Triumph motorcycle and headed off down the salt. It was a practice he had started back in 1962, after Lee turned him on to bikes. He would ride up and down the course to locate the bad patches and map the best route—steer to the left at the mile 3 marker, over to the right at mile 6, that sort of thing. There was more usable course this year, eleven miles as opposed to nine in 1963, but the multiple runs by *Wingfoot* and *Monster* had left it rutted in places. *Spirit* handled especially poorly in ruts, its single front wheel apt to tram along in a depression like a bicycle wheel stuck in a streetcar track.

Spirit sailed through the first day of testing. The air rudder under the nose, increasingly effective at higher speeds, had been further reduced in size and checked out fine. So did the chutes, so problematic the previous year. Confidence building, Craig did a 300 mph pass first thing the next morning, October 11, then hit 452 coming back, in record territory already.

He almost lost it on the return trip when *Spirit* hit a bump and pitched sideways, thrown up onto its left rear wheel. Craig released the chute, stabilizing his racer, and coasted to a stop. *OK*, he thought, *that's where my big problem is.* There was a slight hump in the course heading south out of the mile, a foot-high elevation several football fields long—imperceptible at highway speeds but the world's biggest speed bump at 400-plus. You couldn't see it with the naked eye in daylight. It was only after dark, riding the course on his bike, that Craig could make it out in the low-angle beam of his headlight. He rounded up Roland Portwood of the Utah Highway Department and showed him where the course needed more grading. Roland set to work. He continued on through the night.

Craig went for the record the next morning. The day began with *Spirit's* J-47 failing to light. The car had to be lifted up by the nose to drain out the fuel and the crew tried again. Craig finally set out at nine forty-five, a late start but thankfully still no wind. The first run was good: *Spirit* clocked at 438 mph with the throttle at just 90 percent RPM. Craig's new J-47 engine was really kicking out power. A quick turnaround, Craig nervously pacing, then he was heading back south, throttle advanced five ticks to 95. He could tell just by the feel of the ride, by the way the mile markers flashed by, that he was going much faster. He streaked through the mile, bracing for the rough portion of the course that still lay ahead. Had Roland Portwood's work overnight helped?

It hadn't. Hitting the rough stuff a moment after releasing the chutes was like going over the railway tracks all over again in Stan Burnhaley's coupe. It threw Craig violently around in the cockpit, his helmeted head smashing so hard into the canopy that it shattered the glass. He hung on, an iron grip on the steering, heart pounding, wind screaming in, and fought *Spirit* to a stop. It was the second time in two days that he had come within a hair's breadth of crashing.

The wait was longer this time for the verdict, as Joe Petrali drove down from the USAC shack to personally hand Craig his speed. Onlookers and crew marveled at *Spirit's* shattered canopy and the gash on Craig's helmet. The course would have to be walked again to pick up the pieces of glass. "I hardly felt it," Craig was saying. "I heard it more than anything when the glass exploded."

Here at last was Petrali. As his car pulled up the call went out, "Make an aisle for Joe!" Then, seeing Joe's scarred lip twisted into a grin, murmurs of, "It's a hot paper, it's a hot paper."

Joe handed Craig the slip, folded in two. Penciled on it was Craig's return speed, a blazing 498.13 mph, and his two-way average of 468.719 mph. He had just reclaimed the land speed record. Art Arfons and Firestone had held it for scarcely a week.

"We're going to stay," Craig announced after the cheering subsided. "We haven't got 500 yet."

The next day was spent overhauling *Spirit*. It had taken a serious pounding, with bolts from nose to tail that needed tightening and parts that needed replacing. It was also given a thorough cleaning, for salt had worked its way into every nook and cranny. "It powders up in a very fine dust off the tires," Craig said, "and this dust floats through the entire car. It gets into all the wheel bearings, all the steering mechanism—every place you think is sealed off and completely protected against the salt, it corrodes, it rusts." Quin Epperly and Art Russell repaired the canopy, fitting in a piece of aluminum where the glass had been.

The wheel bearings as usual received particular attention. They always did in land speed racing, because if they failed the wheels would tear off the car. *Spirit*'s bearings were all taken apart, carefully cleaned and regreased. The seemingly mundane grease that was used had in fact played a significant role in Craig's two records. At the extreme speeds of land speed racing, the wheels rotate so fast that regular automobile grease would liquefy and the bearings would seize up. That's what happened to Nathan Ostich in 1962, resulting in the loss of his left front wheel—a Firestone wheel. To avoid this, *Spirit*'s bearings were packed with a new type of heat-resistance grease, Darina AX, specially formulated by Shell. It effectively had no melting point.

Out on the course, Craig showed Roland Portwood the section that needed leveling, the invisible speed bump. Roland this time used the blade on his truck to shave down the hump before using his grader. Hopefully that would do the trick. After seeing the job started, Craig returned to working on *Spirit* and kept at it on into the evening. He was tired out when he finally got back to his motel room. That was good.

Fatigue was his Bonneville sleep aid. It took the edge off the nervousness he always felt going after the record and helped him drift off.

Not tonight. Craig lay awake into the wee hours of the morning, visions of disaster floating through his brain. Dave MacDonald and Eddie Sachs at Indy, burning to death . . . George Koehne in Riverside, trapped in his racer, flames all around . . .

You're going to get killed.

He had already escaped two near crashes in the 400s. The chances were good, considering the condition of the course, that it would happen a third time tomorrow, at 500-plus. Would he be so lucky again?

You're going to get killed.

The sense of foreboding was so deep, so dark, that Craig finally got up and wrote notes to his three kids, Chris, Norman, and Dawn, telling them how much he loved them. Tears were running down his cheeks by the time he was done.

10

ROLL THE AMBULANCE

OCTOBER 15, 1964. There was frost on the car when Craig left his room and headed out to the motel parking lot before dawn. It got cold at night out here in the high desert, four thousand feet above sea level, halfway into the fall. No breakfast again, just a sip of water. He got into the car with his dad Norm and Nye Frank, all of them bundled in winter coats, for the drive east on Highway 50 and out onto the salt flats to base camp. It was still dark when they arrived and parked alongside the red-and-white awning sheltering the racer. Most of the crew was already present, together with a handful of spectators and reporters, the Bonneville greenhorns shivering in thin sweaters and light jackets.

"How's everything, Craig?"

"Sleep OK?"

"How do you feel?"

How did he feel? He was tired from having lain awake for most of the night. He was anxious. He was irritable. He had a knot in his stomach as big as his fist.

"Fine," he said, brushing aside the questions. "I'm fine."

He started checking and rechecking his racer, pausing to wipe off a spot here and there. "Craig was very particular about how the car looked," says Bob Davids. "No scratches, no dings, none of that stuff." Final prep done, the crew reinstalled the aluminum side panels over the engine and on the outrigger wheel fairings, sealing in *Spirit*'s brand-new set of tires. They were Goodyear's latest and best, tested at over 600 mph under brutally heavy loads, everything that could be piled on the test rig. They consisted almost entirely of tightly wound nylon plies, twenty-four layers of the stuff to hold them together under massive centrifugal forces. The outer covering of black rubber was paper thin, so thin that the nylon plies showed through. Nitrogen gas rather than air was used to inflate them. Air contained moisture that heated up and expanded when a tire was spinning, something you didn't want to happen when that tire was already inflated to 250 psi, six times more pressure than regular passenger tires. *Spirit's* tires in fact scared the crew a little, like bombs that might go off if mishandled. They were so rock hard that if you flicked them with your finger they would ring like a bell.

Norm came over for a final word with Craig. He was visibly anxious—all the more so knowing the strain his son was feeling. He gave Craig an emotional hug, then headed up the course to join the spectators gathering outside the USAC shack at the mile. Inside the shack, head timer Joe Petrali was already hunched over his equipment, making sure it was working and ready to go. Fellow USAC official Ted Gillette was manning the field telephone, in touch with observers along the course, checking the wind. Ted's regular job was driving the ambulance that was parked outside. He had been called to hundreds of accidents on Utah's highways over the years and was a regular fixture at Bonneville land speed attempts. It was Ted who took Donald Campbell to the hospital after his 1960 crash. It was Ted who picked up the pieces of Glenn Leasher in 1962.

Seven thirty. The sun was just coming up, the morning air almost dead calm. *Spirit of America* was towed out to the black line behind the Ford F-350 the crew called the "farm truck." The plan, dictated once again by the relatively poor condition of the south end of the course, was for Craig to make his first run south to north. That way the worst of the pounding would be saved until after he exited the mile on the return trip and hopefully had the record. Both runs would be made without water injection, which had yet to be used. Craig figured he could get to 500 mph without it. Throttle setting for the first run: 97.5 percent RPM.

Craig removed his warm winter jacket. He was down now to his one-piece fire suit, a trimmer, snappier outfit than the one he had worn the previous year. The gym shoes were gone too, replaced by boxing boots, black leather with crisscrossing white laces. He had stumbled on them in a sporting goods store and thought they looked more professional. Being in the spotlight had made him more aware of his image.

He mounted the stepladder and climbed into the cockpit. The seat was cold. Nye helped him with his harness and air mask. Just behind them, jet fuel was being pumped from the Shell truck into the tank. To the right, the start cart was being wheeled alongside and its umbilical plugged into the chassis. At the back, Bob Davids and Al Buskirk were putting on asbestos jackets, getting ready for engine start-up, fire extinguishers in hand. Quin Epperly in the meantime was slowly circling the racer, checking that the body panels removed during the overhaul were all firmly in place and secured.

Craig mechanically checked the cockpit switches, making sure he hadn't brushed against any of them squeezing into the seat. He looked at his hands. They were steady. Deep down inside, however, he had a sick feeling. It was worse than mere butterflies, worse even than fear. It was dread. He had never experienced anything quite like it before. It felt like he was on the edge of a yawning abyss with a voice whispering up at him from the blackness: *You're going to be killed, Craig. You're going to be killed.*

The start cart, operated by Bob Johnson and Dick Compton, roared to life, blasting air through the J-47 to get the compressor turning inside. Craig advanced the throttle. He watched the RPM gauge, waiting for the needle to reach 10 percent, then turned on the fuel switch and hit the ignition. A whoosh as the fuel ignited and the jet whined to life. Craig switched the ignition to idle and watched the RPMs continue to build, the compressor spinning faster and faster, 20 percent, 30 percent, 40, 50. When it hit 70 he switched off the ignition. *Spirit*'s engine was now running on its own, the thousands of blades inside the compressor churning the air into a hurricane blast, 500 degrees centigrade and climbing at the tailpipe. The umbilical was disconnected and the start cart wheeled away.

"The engine's started," the mile 0 observer radioed to the timing shack. "Give us a clearance."

A static-crackling response: "Stand by." A pause while observers along the course checked in. Then: "OK, roll him when you're ready."

Nye hoisted the canopy into position. Craig guided the pins into the holes and turned the latches, locking the canopy down. His view through the blue-tinted Plexiglas was partly blocked on the right, the pane where his head had smashed though having been hastily replaced with a piece of aluminum. It didn't matter. He only needed to see straight ahead.

Nye backed away and gave a thumbs-up.

RPMs 80 percent.

Craig gazed out at the nose of his racer, sleeker and more stream-lined this year for greater stability at the higher speeds he was going. A small red piece of metal rose from the nose like a gun sight. This was a pitot tube for measuring air speed. It was connected to the speedometer, which would indicate the reading in knots.

RPMs 90 percent.

Beyond the pitot tube, the black line pointed the way forward, from mile 0 all the way to mile 11 and the rocky outcrop known as Floating Mountain beyond. Craig would be driving straight at it. From down here at the south end it looked like a shimmering smudge hovering on the horizon.

Nye flashed the final hand signal: two fingers. It was a reminder to activate the onboard data recorder and the camera attached to the right wheel fairing. Craig flicked the switches to "ON."

RPMs 97.5 percent.

A vision of flames, burning up, trapped in the cockpit.

You're going to be killed, Craig.

He released the brake and slammed the accelerator to the floor.

Norm Breedlove was standing outside the USAC shack at the mile, star-ing up the course, anxiety etched on his face. "I don't care if he doesn't get the record," *Salt Lake Tribune* sportswriter Marion Dunn heard him saying. "I just don't want anything to happen. I love that boy."

A call from the open door of the timing shack: "He's rolling!"

Norm had never been a religious man. But right now he needed it. He lowered his head and whispered a prayer.

———————

Spirit took off in a blast of salt, 2 Gs of acceleration pressing Craig back into his seat. The speedometer needle swept past 100, 200, 250, 275. The rough salt was giving the racer a pounding, the shock struts on the nose wheel clanging. Craig hung on as he was thrown about in the cockpit, *Spirit*'s single front wheel causing it to lurch from side to side.

The mile 3 marker. Craig eased the yoke over, nudging *Spirit* to the left side of the course, following the path of least roughness that he had mapped out. Speed passing 350 now. This was where the hump was. Craig didn't feel much. Roland Portwood had shaved most of it down.

The mile 4 marker. Get over to the right side. The ride was now smoothing. Speed passing 400, 450. Measured mile coming up. Steer back to center. Speed 470, 480, 490.

Whoosh. The fluorescent green-on-black marker streaked past on the right. Craig was into the mile at 500 mph and climbing, hurtling down the salt at nine hundred feet—nearly three football fields—per second, faster than a bullet from a Saturday night special. He was traveling so fast that he could pass over a knee-deep trench three feet wide and not feel a thing. *Spirit* would be over it and a hundred yards down the track before its suspension could respond. It was an utterly strange, almost indescribable sensation. It was no longer like driving. It wasn't even like flying. It was more like Craig was skating, skimming along on an icy surface, the wheels barely in contact with the ground, the racer scarcely under control.

Whoosh. The second marker whipped past, fluorescent red checks on black. He was out of the mile. Foot off the accelerator. Kill the engine. Coast for two miles, letting the speed fall off. Floating Mountain was no longer a shimmer in the distance. It was getting close.

Craig hit the chute release button on the end of the steering yoke handle. *Bang!* The lid blew off the chute compartment and sailed up into the air. A slight shudder as the drogue deployed, hauling out the chute on its eighty-foot line, then a massive tug as the canopy opened, throwing Craig forward against his harness. The deceleration so upset his inner ear that the world seemed to tip over, like he was driving straight down a cliff. Then it passed, the horizon righted, and he was slowing, slowing.

Parked vehicles ahead, the farm truck and a few others. Craig applied the brakes and rolled to a stop. He had traversed the entire eleven-mile course in just under two minutes.

The advance crew was already getting the dolly under the nose wheel as Craig exited the cockpit. The clock was ticking, fifty-five minutes remaining to get *Spirit* away on its return run. While the racer was still being muscled around, Jack Carter, wearing an asbestos jacket to work in the lingering heat of the tailpipe, yanked the pins securing the chute lines to the chassis and bundled up the canopy and cast it aside. The farm truck was pulled up alongside, a drum of aviation fuel in the back. A hose was run to *Spirit*'s tank, nearly emptied by the run, and thirty-five gallons of fuel were hand-pumped in. The bottle of compressed air in the cockpit was topped up, replenishing Craig's breathing system. The rear wheel fairings were removed to check the tires for damage. They looked OK. Pressure was good. Craig stayed out of the way, pacing back and forth as all this went on. He was too keyed up to stay still. Off to the side, the USAC observer was radioing messages down the course: *The car is stopped. . . . The canopy is off. . . . Craig is out of the car. . . . The car is being turned around. . . .*

The rest of the crew arrived from the south end of the course. Bob Davids grabbed the used chute off the salt and stowed it and helped Jack Carter load a new one into the chute compartment, packed tight in its bag. The film was removed from Walt Sheehan's data recorder and the right fairing camera. Fresh film was loaded. Other guys were wiping the racer down, removing salt buildup. The start cart was wheeled alongside to restart the engine. That would take crossed fingers all around. If the J-47 flooded it would take an hour to drain it and try again. The run would be shot.

"OK, the mile . . ." It was the course observer at mile 11. Word was coming in over the field telephone of Craig's speed. "Five-one-three—"

The crew broke out in a cheer. Craig had just become the first person ever to drive 500 mph. His exact speed: 513.33 mph.

"Beautiful! All right! You got it, Craig!"

Craig shied away from the congratulatory backslaps and outstretched hands. "Don't touch me," he said, needing to stay focused. "We have to do this two ways." He did the same thing when Bill Flemming from ABC's *Wide World of Sports* came over and asked for a comment. "I'm sorry, Bill, but I can't talk right now. I have another run to make before it's official."

Outside the USAC shack five miles to the south, Ted Gillette was on the field telephone, Jim Economides nearby, tape recorder in hand. "Two seconds and he'll be ready to go," Ted was saying. Then: "He's on his way. Hey! Hey!"

The warning cry was taken up in the background. "He's on his way! Get off the track!"

Norm Breedlove raised his binoculars and peered up the course, silently praying, scarcely able to breathe. "He's standing on it," Ted Gillette was saying, repeating the messages from the north end of the course. "They said he's really standing on it now. He's really moving."

The turnaround had taken scarcely thirty minutes. The crew had become that efficient. Craig was on his way on his return run before nine o'clock. He took off in full military power—100 percent RPMs. The hand-painted letters at the maximum setting on *Spirit*'s hand throttle said it all: BANZAI!

Hard acceleration. Craig passed the mile 10 marker, then the Nine. Rough patch ahead. He steered to the left side of the course, where it was smoother, then back to center. Bumpy section at the Seven. He eased to the right. He was doing 400. The mile 6 marker. Steer back to—

Snap!

Craig heard it over the wind and the engine. The racer gave a shudder and started veering off course. He turned the yoke to correct. Nothing. He kept turning, turning. *Spirit* finally responded, sluggishly moving back toward the black line. By then the yoke was upside down.

In a flash of intuition Craig thought of the ⁵⁄₁₆-inch bolts. Bob Heacock's focusing link had been a godsend, making it possible to steer the nose wheel. But with his aircraft design background Bob had designed the thing light, with tiny ⁵⁄₁₆-inch bolts supporting the wheel steering bearings, little bits of steel that had made Craig uneasy. He should have insisted on ½-inch bolts. You could lift the whole car with a ½-inch bolt, bounce it up and down, and it wouldn't shear off. *You should have insisted on ½-inch!*

All this raced through Craig's mind in the space of two seconds. He knew what the nose wheel was doing. He could feel it through the steering. It was leaning over, the bearings sagging with the bolt sheared off on one side, the car's forward weight thrown onto the opposite bolt, scarcely three times the thickness of a coat hanger. It was a bad situation. He would have to abort.

He hesitated. He was still going straight, the checkerboard marking the entrance to the mile now in view up ahead. Could he make it? Could he hang on and finish the run?

He kept his foot down. *Spirit* streaked into the mile.

––––––––––––

Ted Gillette, on the field telephone at the timing shack, was repeating the messages from the north end observers: "He's by the eight. . . . Nice and straight. . . . He's really rolling. . . . He's into the mile. . . ."

"I see his smoke trail," somebody said.

Norm Breedlove was looking up the course through his binoculars. At first he could only see the rooster tail of salt. Then *Spirit of America* emerged through the shimmer and streaked past at phenomenal speed. In less than seven seconds it had traversed the mile and disappeared from view in the south.

"Wait a minute." Ted Gillette pressed his headphones to his ears, straining to hear. Then: "Something fell off the car. Something fell off the back of the car."

———————————

They were the longest seven seconds of Craig's life, the seven ticks in the mile, willing *Spirit* to go straight. It didn't. It started veering toward the side of the course and this time he couldn't muscle it back. If he ran over the timing lights—

He took his foot off the pedal. The loss of acceleration caused the racer to straighten out and return to center. The kilometer marker streaked by. Craig slammed his foot back down and hung on.

A red blur on the left. Craig exited the mile at 550 mph. He killed the engine. On his earlier runs he had coasted for a mile or two to lose some speed before releasing the chutes. Not now. He stabbed the button on the right end of the yoke with his thumb. He heard the bang of the cartridge blowing the lid off the rear compartment and releasing the primary chute. He felt a slight tug, then nothing.

His primary had failed. It had ripped off, the line breaking under the strain. He forced himself to wait before trying the backup. *Let it slow down*, he said to himself. *Let it slow down.* The mile 4 marker whipped past. The speedometer needle dipped below 500 mph.

He punched the left-side button on the yoke. He heard the bang of the cartridge but this time there was no tug at all. He punched the button again and again. Nothing.

His backup had failed. He had no chutes. That left only the brakes. They were intended for use at 150 mph and below, not at 450.

The mile 3 marker flashed by. Craig was running out of course.

———————————

Back at the north end, Nye Frank, Al Buskirk, and Stan Goldstein had piled into the Ford F-350 and were now driving down the salt. "We were going down the course chasing after Craig," Al remembers, "going about

85 flat out in the farm truck. Suddenly Roy Van Sickle from Shell goes racing past us in one of the rental cars. We would always beat Roy down to the other end. He didn't like to drive very fast. But not this time. Nye says, 'Hey Buzzy, look.' So I look over and I see Roy shouting into his radio—that car had a radio in it—and he's just flying past us. 'What the hell . . . ?' Right then we knew something was wrong."

Jack Carter and Bob Davids were farther ahead in the blue pickup, Craig's friends Bill Moore and Art Russell hitching a ride in the back. They had their eyes peeled coming out of the mile for *Spirit*'s ejected chute compartment cover and empty chute bag. These had to be picked up so no debris would be left on the course. "All of a sudden there on the salt we find the whole chute," says Art Russell, "and then just a little bit later the second chute, and we said, 'Oh-oh, he's really in trouble.'"

Roy Van Sickle streaked by at high speed, followed by the farm truck. Bob heaped the chute into the pickup and jumped back in beside Jack. "We're going down the salt flats as fast as we could go, probably 100 mph," says Art, "and it seemed like we could have gotten out and walked faster. We thought we were never going to get to the end of the course."

———————

Four hundred on the speedometer. *Spirit*, with its superb aerodynamics and minimal drag, didn't want to stop.

Craig gave the brake pedal the gentlest touch he could manage in the shuddering cockpit. If he just feathered the pedal, maybe he could—

The brakes turned to ashes. The pedal went right to the floor.

The mile 2 marker whipped past. Craig kept pumping the brakes, the pedal thudding uselessly against the floor. There was nothing else he could do.

The mile 1 marker. He could see base camp up ahead now, cars and trucks parked off to the side at the end of the course. And people. They were standing too close.

———————

"He's coming, he's moving right along!"

Ted Gillette at the USAC shack was repeating messages from the observer at the south end.

"He's really pouring it on! Here he comes! He's getting close to the finish line. He's approaching it right now. He's past the finishing line. Oh—!"

A shriek inundated Ted's headphones as *Spirit* streaked past the south end observer and hurtled off the end of the course. It was heading for the flooded south end of the salt down by the highway.

"He's in the water! He's in the water! Better roll the ambulance down here! Roll the ambulance!"

That last message was for Ted himself. He was the ambulance driver. "I'll roll down there," he answered. "OK, I'll roll!"

11

"I ALMOST DROWNED IN THAT THING!"

CRAIG ROARED PAST MILE 0 at nearly 400 mph. All of Bonneville's space, two hundred square miles, equal to the state of Delaware, was now behind him. A fleeting glimpse of horrified faces as the black line disappeared. His chutes were gone and his brakes were burned up and his steering was almost useless. *Spirit of America* was careening off course and out of control.

A line of telephone poles was coming up fast. Beyond that: the salt's flooded south end, a shimmer of water, then Highway 40 and the train tracks. He cranked the yoke over, trying to make a giant U-turn to the right. If he could get turned around and heading back north, he could ride it out and burn off his speed.

Craig leaned to one side as he steered, willing the racer to turn. It responded a little but not nearly enough. He was coming up on the telephone poles. He was approaching them at an angle, not much clearance between. If he could just get over a little bit more—

He shot between the poles, somehow clearing them on each side. A second line of poles lay ahead. *Spirit* was coming at them at too sharp an angle to slip between this time. No doubt about it, he was going to hit.

Craig squeezed the yoke hard and dropped his head, bracing for impact, the rending metal, the tumbling wreckage, the fire. Time slowed down. He was aware of the wind shrieking past the canopy, the banging of the wheel struts, the crunch of rough, shingled salt under the tires. He remembered a jumble of innocuous things: drilling the holes to mount the instruments in the cockpit, forming the metal supports for the windshield, the custom upholstered seats in his old '34 coupe. *What put me in this damn thing?* he would distinctly remember asking himself. *Why am I here in the first place?*

Thock! Spirit's right outrigger sheared off the telephone pole like a machete through a cornstalk. Craig hardly felt it. The racer gave a shudder and kept on going, its speed down to 300 mph, still way too fast. He wasn't going to make the U-turn. Not even close. He was now getting into the flooded section of salt down by the highway, *Spirit's* speed dropping more rapidly as it plowed through the slushy brine, throwing up spray. The embankment was coming up fast, a six-foot-high wall blocking the way. It was the diggings from an eighteen-foot-deep drainage ditch, currently submerged beneath shin-deep floodwater, used to convey brine to the evaporation ponds south of the highway. To Craig the area beyond the embankment up to the train tracks looked like a lake.

Spirit hit the embankment at 200 mph. It struck at an angle and started to roll over as it shot up into the air. Then, by pure luck, the right outrigger wheel clipped the edge of the bank and tipped the car back to level.

"So now I'm airborne, flying through the air, and I could see I was going into the water. And I'm thinking, *I've got to get the canopy off before I hit.* Because if I don't and the frame bends, the canopy pins will be stuck in the frame and I won't get out. So I twist the knobs and push up with the heel of my hand and the canopy's gone. The air just took it. So now the cockpit's wide open. The next thing I thought was, *Boy, this thing is going to hit hard.* So I let go the steering wheel, put both hands on my stomach and leaned forward against the harness to get ready for the impact."

Spirit slammed into the shallow floodwater, throwing Craig forward as he hung on to his guts. It skipped like a stone and came down again, raising a second geyser of water, rolled a ways, and dropped into the submerged drainage ditch.

The racer, its outriggers straddling the ditch, started sinking nose first, water pouring into the cockpit.

"Come on, let's go. He's in trouble!"

Back at mile 0, Roland Portwood jumped into his Utah Highway Department truck to chase after Craig, *Deseret News* reporter Hi McDonald beside him. They set off across the shingly salt, following *Spirit*'s triple tracks to the flooded area down by the highway. Up ahead, they saw the racer hit the embankment, fly up into the air, and disappear just as a train was passing on the tracks farther on. "Our first thought," Hi would write, "was, 'Oh, Lord, he's crashed into that train across the highway.'"

"Hang on," said Roland, "we're going right through."

The four-wheel-drive truck charged into the water, wipers going as it made for the embankment. Farther back, other chase vehicles skidded to a stop at the edge of the flooding and guys started running the last quarter mile.

The water was to Craig's waist and rising, *Spirit* sinking fast. He frantically reached down and fumbled with his harness buckle. The water was to his chest.

He got his harness undone. He heaved himself up out of the seat to escape. Something pulled him back down. The water was over his shoulders now, touching his chin.

He heaved up again. Again he couldn't get out. He tried a third time. Something was holding him down.

The water rose to his mouth. It would soon be over his head. Craig wasn't going to be burned alive. He was going to drown.

The water continued to rise. It was covering his nose. It was covering his nose and he was still able to breathe. That didn't make sense. The water was lapping at his goggles now, his vision murky. He was starting to panic.

"I'm pulling, trying to get out, but I couldn't get out. I'm thinking, *What the fuck is going on?* And then I thought, *Oh shit, my air mask is still plugged in.* So I reached down and popped the air mask fitting and then I was loose. I got around the roll bar across the top of the cockpit and got out."

He was free, standing on *Spirit*'s rapidly sinking front end. Then it was gone in a hiss of hot engine and steam and he was floundering in salty brine over his head, weighed down by his fire suit, his helmet, his boots. He flailed about, struggling to keep his head above the surface that was alive with air bubbles. The embankment was scarcely twenty feet away but the way he was floundering it might have been half a mile. And then he was out of the ditch, solid ground under his body. He dragged himself out of the water and crawled on his hands and knees up onto the bank and collapsed.

———————

Roland Portwood skidded to a stop at the embankment. "He's OK!" he shouted into his radio. "He's out of the car!"

He and Hi McDonald leaped out of the truck and ran forward just as Craig was struggling to his feet and pulling off his helmet. Craig's knees started to buckle. The overload of adrenaline was leaving his body. "Hold me," he said. Roland grabbed him in a bear hug and kept him upright. "Just let me kiss the ground," Craig breathed, hanging on.

The strength returned to Craig's legs and with it came a flood of relief. It was so overpowering, this realization that he had survived, that he was *alive*, that everything suddenly seemed wonderful, delightful. "I almost drowned in that thing," he marveled, gazing at *Spirit of America*'s tailfin sticking up out of the water. He grinned, then started laughing, for he was in the desert, for God's sake. He was in the *desert*. "I almost *drowned* in that thing!"

By now a dozen guys were frantically splashing their way forward through the ankle-deep brine, Goodyear PR man Bill Neely in the lead. "I'm all right, baby!" Craig called out. "What's the speed?" Nobody knew. They ran up to Craig and crowded around, touching him, slapping him on the back, Jim Economides among them with his tape recorder, capturing every word.

"Jesus Christ . . . holy mackerel . . . suppose you get a water speed record on that too?"

Craig, laughing: "I think so!"

The farm truck reached the edge of the standing water, where Ted Gillette in the ambulance had gotten bogged down. Nye, Buzzy, and Stan bolted out and ran forward, followed by Jack Carter and the rest of the guys in the pickup. "I was running through seven inches of salt slush for like what seemed half a mile," Bill Moore would remember. "I thought Craig was dead. I really thought so."

Up on the embankment, Craig was laughing and having the time of his life. "What a ride!" he said. "For my next trick—I'll set myself afire. Did I break it? Did I break the record?"

"We didn't wait to see."

"If Petrali missed the time on that, boy, he's out of business. I'm not doing it again!"

Jim Economides held out his microphone. "Craig, that was a tremendous run. You must have broken the record by a big margin."

"I obviously did!" Craig turned to Roland Portwood. "Hey, you did a pretty good job on that course, old buddy."

"I tell you, that was the last we expected to see of Craig Breedlove."

Craig turned to see Nye Frank and the others from the farm truck scrambling up the bank, looking frantically from Craig to the *Spirit's* upended tail. "Did you see that telephone pole, Nye? I damn near drowned. Look at the racer!"

Nye was looking. He could hardly believe it. "I almost had a heart attack," he said.

"I'll tell you one thing," Stan Goldstein said, "you're spectacular, man."

"What's my time? Nobody waited to get it! How fast did I go? How fast did I go!"

"Nobody heard, Craig."

Norm Breedlove arrived, ashen faced, and pushed through the crowd. "Oh God," he moaned, seizing his son, holding him close. "Oh God . . . oh God, Craig."

"It's OK, Pop. We did it."

Norm clung to him. "I couldn't afford to lose you," he said.

"I damn near drowned in that thing," Craig said, emotion momentarily catching in his voice. "I couldn't get out." Then the merriment returned. "If you can't win, be spectacular!"

"I thought I had it when I hit the pole," he continued. "I saw that pole coming and I said, 'Oh . . .' and I gritted my teeth and that pole just sheared off like nothing. *Boom*, and no pole. And I thought, *Oh boy, another chance.* I looked up, and I hit the water, and the water started slowing me down and I see this big old bank coming up and I thought, *Oh no . . .*" He was laughing again with sheer joy.

"I hit the bank and I went right over the top there and I'm flying through the air about thirty feet and I said, 'Now I'm gonna drown!' I get the canopy off and I'm trying to get my belt off and I couldn't get my mask off and the water was filling up like that, and I thought, *What a way to go. I'm gonna drown!*"

It was hilarious. Everybody was laughing. "Next run, scuba gear, baby!" somebody said.

Bill Moore straggled up the bank in his ruined shoes. "Hey, Bill!" Craig said. "For my next trick, I'll set myself afire!" Bill tried to smile, then his face crumbled. He threw his arms around Craig and burst into tears. "Everything's OK," Craig said as they hugged.

He turned to the others. "How fast was I going, damn it? Did we break the record, goddarn."

The call went out to every new arrival: "What was the time? What was the time?"

The verdict was that Craig had done 539.89 on his return run, giving him a two-way average of 526.277 mph. It was almost 60 miles an hour faster than Art Arfons's mark—the biggest jump in LSR history.

A crane was brought in the next day to fish *Spirit of America* out of the water. The racer was hoisted by the tail and held up until the water drained out, then set down and loaded onto its trailer. The outrigger camera had broken away in the crash but after prolonged poking about in the water it was recovered. The spectacular footage it had captured would be used in a film coproduced by Shell and Goodyear called *The Wildest Ride*.

Craig tried to be upbeat when he spoke with reporters, claiming that the car was in remarkably good shape, that it could be quickly repaired for an early return to competition. It was gamesmanship pure and simple, intended to discourage Art Arfons from trying to break Craig's new record before the Bonneville season ran out. He felt fairly confident that Art couldn't do it, not this year, not with winter closing in and with *Green Monster* having a torque overload problem, which Craig knew about. But why take the chance?

"I was basically putting out the word that we were going to clean up the car and be right back. But then Roy Van Sickle, Shell's new project manager, he told the press that there's no way I'm going to run. I guess he assumed that I was in shock or just crazy. I knew that it was going to take to the next season to get the car running, but the strategy was to not let the opposition know that. Anyway, Roy told the press that there was no way we'd be ready to run again this year. I was upset with him because of that."

Sure enough, a couple days later, Art Arfons announced that he was going to return to the salt flats. "I can't quit," he said. "[Craig]'s given me a tough mark to shoot at. We're going to come out and try, anyway." As Art would tell Craig some years later, "The only way I ever convinced Firestone to let me come back was to tell them that your car was destroyed and Goodyear couldn't defend its record."

Spirit of America was hauled back to Quin Epperly's shop in Gardena and stripped completely apart to wash out the salt. The most obvious damage was the mangled right outrigger and dented body panels. Closer inspection revealed that the engine mounts were bent as well and needed replacing. The engine was of course shot from the salt water immersion but that didn't matter. Craig had a spare J-47 on hand, an even newer model, ready to install. With this new engine and water injection he was confident that his racer could go even faster. His goal for 1965: 600 mph.

After seeing work begun on *Spirit*, Craig hit the publicity trail to make the most of his record while it was still all over the news. There were press interviews and public appearances and TV talk shows, a special on ABC's *Wide World of Sports*, a guest spot on *What's My Line?* A week passed without any news from Art Arfons. It was now so late in the season, flooding imminent at Bonneville if it wasn't flooded already, that Craig began to relax. His 526 mph record was looking increasingly secure for the year.

And then it wasn't. On October 27, in the middle of a press conference in Detroit, Craig was informed that Art had just reclaimed the record with a two-way average of 536 mph. The torque from *Green Monster*'s J-79 had once again overloaded its right rear tire and caused a blowout as Art was coming out of the mile on his return trip. Miraculously, the racer didn't tumble to pieces. Art, the man with nerves of steel, released his chutes and fought *Monster* to a stop, cutting a miles-long furrow in the salt on bare rims. Craig's mark, which had nearly cost him his life, had stood for only two weeks.

The news hit him like a slap in the face. It wasn't just that he had lost the record. It was everything that was tied up with it: the year's worth of publicity, the Craig Breedlove movie, the Christmas sales blitz for the *Spirit* model—all of it was suddenly at risk.

He faltered in front of the room full of reporters.

He shook his head and smiled.

He said, "Boy, isn't that something."

12

SONIC I

THE FALLOUT FROM LOSING THE RECORD turned out to be worse than Craig had imagined. It started with the shelving of the *Spirit of America* feature film. Shell pulled its promise of funding and the project fell apart. Shell also canceled its Christmas advertising campaign for the *Spirit of America* model and reduced production to the three million units already made, turning over part of that to Goodyear to sell through its stores. The models would quickly sell out when they hit the market, record or no record, but for some reason Shell refused to order more, stunning both Craig and toy manufacturer Wen Mac. It was a huge financial blow, for Craig had relinquished his royalties on the initial order to push the deal through, counting on follow-up orders for his big payout. Now, with no follow-up orders, he would not make a cent.

Another disappointment that occurred at this time was the scuttling of Craig's plan to become a professional race car driver like his idol Parnelli Jones. Lindsey Hopkins had broached the idea. The plan was for Craig to train with Hopkins's driver Bobby Marshman and to have his first race in Sacramento, driving a Champ Car. Then, when he was ready, he would drive one of Hopkins's backup cars at Indy, where his charisma and movie-star looks were sure to be a hit. It all fell to pieces when Marshman suffered a horrific crash while testing a new car for Hopkins. He staggered from the flaming wreck with burns on 90 percent of his body and died a few days later, on December 4,

1964. Hopkins, shaken by the death, pulled the plug on Craig's planned racing debut after that.

And then came the phone call. It was from Shell. The company had received an inquiry from the Museum of Science and Industry in Chicago about putting *Spirit* on permanent display and they were eager to comply. Goodyear liked the idea too. "But we're getting the car ready," Craig said, taken aback. "I want to go back to Bonneville and go 600. Can't we put it in the museum *after* we run?"

No, Shell wanted to do it now. It was a great honor and a great opportunity and the company wanted to seize it. "Look, if you'd be willing to do this," Craig was assured, "we'll consider sponsoring you for a new car. Maybe one with a J-79 engine or something like that."

Spirit was everything to Craig. He didn't want to give it up. But he didn't want to alienate Shell or Goodyear either. He therefore agreed. The repair work being done at Epperly's was scaled back to a cosmetic restoration, preparing the racer for its new life as a museum exhibit, and Craig threw himself into designing a new car. Being sponsored for a bigger, better racer was "a pretty good incentive," he says, to let his three-wheeler go. "But it was really going to be a tremendous crash program. We only had eight or nine months until the next season started to build a whole new car from scratch and I didn't even have a line drawn on a piece of paper."

Craig was suddenly looking beyond 600 mph to the speed of sound, Mach 1. It varied with temperature, rising the hotter it got. For Chuck Yeager, the first person to break the sound barrier in an aircraft, Mach 1 in the frigid air at forty-five thousand feet had stood at 660 mph. For Craig, driving on the ground on a cool Bonneville morning, it would be around 750 mph.

It was this new speed-of-sound target that gave Craig the name for his racer. He would call it *Spirit of America–Sonic I*.

The two things Craig knew he wanted for *Sonic I* right from the start were a J-79 jet engine and four wheels. The switch to four wheels was to qualify the racer with the FIA as a "car" and to avoid the tendency a single nose wheel had of following ruts. With these basic parameters set, he started sketching. He found inspiration in a photo of a German land speed racer from the late 1930s called the Mercedes T80, the "Rekordwagen," a masterpiece of Nazi-era engineering that was overtaken by the war and never ran for the LSR on the Autobahn as planned. What attracted Craig's interest was the way the T80 was pinched in at the waist and had wings projecting out from the sides. The wings were obviously to generate downforce to keep the racer on the ground. The pinched-in waist was a more subtle concept Craig recognized as embodying the "transonic area rule" used in the design of such advanced military aircraft as Convair's F-102 and F-106 and Northrop's F-5. By squeezing in the fuselage at the wings and expanding it fore and aft, drag in the transonic zone could be substantially reduced. Amazingly, the Germans had apparently figured out this concept nearly three decades before. Craig now decided to use it for his new car.

The design that emerged in Craig's feverish sketches had a cockpit in the pointy nose, a single air duct above the cockpit, a tailfin, four enclosed wheels, and a body pinched in at the waist. Its overall shape would often be likened to a Coke bottle. He ended up not using central wings as on the Mercedes T80, fearing that they might be too effective at high speed, like the air rudder on the three-wheeler had been. "We didn't want to go ahead and put those big wings on," he says, "and then learn we didn't need them, that the car was pushing down too hard." He opted instead for small horizontal fins fore and aft, just in front of the wheels. With Walt Sheehan's strain gauges and onboard data recorder he would know exactly what the car was doing when he ran at Bonneville, whether it was lifting up or pressing down, and would be able to make adjustments by angling the fins. And if for some reason that wasn't enough, there would still be the option later on of installing larger T80-style wings at the waist.

Things on the home front, meanwhile, were not good. Craig's marriage was on the rocks. It took a turn for the worse when Linda Vaughn called Craig at home—she wanted to tell him that Bobby Marshman had just died—and Lee answered the phone. After the blowup that followed,

Craig vowed to break things off with Linda and remain faithful. And he did. His obsession with the new car, however, became a new source of alienation. The more it came to fill his life, the less time he had for Lee and the kids.

And then another blow: Craig made the shocking realization that he was practically broke. He and Lee had been spending their newfound wealth too freely, starting with the house in Palos Verdes. And now, with the record gone and with it a year's worth of promotional earnings, they found themselves living close to the edge. Things were so tight that Lee got a job as a waitress at a local Red Onion restaurant and started doing some modeling work on the side.

Fortunately Craig still had Shell's assurance of sponsorship for the new car. He had Art Russell quickly build him a model, something sleek and glossy that he could show the top brass. When he took it to Shell with his preliminary *Sonic I* proposal, however, he was shocked to learn that they weren't interested. "Shell has reevaluated the land speed program," public relations vice president Gordon Biggar told him, "and in view of the danger involved we've decided that it's something we no longer want to participate in."

It now became clear what had occurred behind the scenes at the company's New York head office, the corporate power shift that had already resulted in funding being pulled from the Breedlove movie and the cancellation of the car model campaign. In the wake of Craig's crash, the executives who had been against sponsoring *Spirit* from the start, led by Gordon Biggar, had won the upper hand over Bill Lawler and the pro-LSR faction, pressing the view that Shell's reputation would have been damaged if Craig had been killed and that it had been a mistake to get involved in something so risky in the first place. From now on the company's main sports sponsorship would shift to a TV show Biggar himself created, a safe and sedate Sunday afternoon program called *Shell's Wonderful World of Golf.*

The world had been Craig's oyster just a few months before, opportunities boundless . . . and now everything was falling to pieces. He didn't even have his racer anymore, having already signed the papers committing it to the Chicago museum. He was down to just one asset:

his relationship with Goodyear. If he could get Goodyear to commit to being his secondary sponsor for the new car, covering half the cost as it had done with the three-wheeler, he could use that to attract a new primary sponsor to replace Shell and foot the rest.

That was Craig's hope when he flew to Akron in early 1965 to meet with Goodyear's public relations director Bob Lane. "I've just come from Shell," he said, laying it on the line, "and they've declined to sponsor me for the new car. So I was wondering if Goodyear would be willing to do the tires and sponsor 50 percent, like before. It'll take a while, but with Goodyear on board I could get another petroleum company to back me."

Lane contemplated the *Sonic I* model that Craig had brought with him. He thumbed through Craig's sketches. A long pause. "Craig," he finally said, tossing the pictures back on his desk, "I don't see us taking 50 percent of this thing."

Craig's heart dropped into his shoes. He had just struck out.

"No, we don't want half," Lane continued, seemingly enjoying the moment. Then he looked up and smiled. "We want the whole thing."

"So that's how Goodyear got involved," says Craig. The company would sponsor him for $100,000 to build the car, to be followed by an additional $34,000 to run it for the record. He returned to Shell after that and this time his old mentor Bill Lawler took him under his wing.

"Bill told me, 'Stop talking to Gordon Biggar. He hasn't liked your project from Day One. The person you need to talk to is Ed McGee.' So Bill took me to see national sales manager Ed McGee. I told Ed, 'Goodyear's sponsoring me for a hundred percent and they've given me permission to get sub-sponsors. So now I've got an offer for you, a chance to bet on a horse after it's won the race. If Shell will give me the fuel and lubricants, I'll put you on the car as a sub-sponsor. And if I go 600 miles an hour I want you to pay me $50,000. If I don't, you pay me nothing, so there's no risk.' McGee chewed on that for a while, then he said, 'Here's what we'll do. We'll let your contract with Shell run for another two years. That's $24,000 a year, 48 grand total, that you won't get if you go to another petroleum company. You can have that, and if you go 600 we'll give you an extra 35 grand.' I said, 'Sold.'

"So I picked Shell back up. Gordon Biggar was probably grumbling, but anyway . . ."

———————

Craig returned to L.A. with a $30,000 check from Goodyear to get the car started. The task ahead seemed almost impossible: to turn a handful of drawings into a transonic racer and use it to break the land speed record, all in the space of six months. It was going to take a crash program like never before.

The first step was to find space to work in, the original *Spirit* taking up all of Quin Epperly's shop, where it was still being restored. Craig and Stan Goldstein, hired as project business manager, rented a building on Compton Boulevard just off Central Avenue, on the edge of a rough, predominantly black neighborhood known as Watts. "It was kind of small," says Craig, "but it was cheap. It was also less than three miles away from Quincy's, so we could draw on his expertise and job out work to his shop."

Craig next bought a pair of used drafting tables and set to work finalizing the car's design and preparing blueprints. He didn't have a J-79 yet or even an idea of where to get one, so he had to proceed relying solely on engine specs and drawings provided by Walt Sheehan and hope that a 79 would eventually turn up. The final design that emerged was no-frills, straightforward, and almost entirely Craig's, far more the product of his brain than his original *Spirit*, which had incorporated ideas from Walt Sheehan, Rod Schapel, and other engineers. A model was built by Art Russell but it was not wind tunnel tested. There was simply no time. Even if there had been, Craig had no desire to go down that road again. He had come to the conclusion that wind tunnel testing was effectively useless.

Fabrication began in April 1965. "We worked seven days a week," says Craig, "huge long days. It was tough." Nye Frank once again served as chief mechanic and Bob Davids returned with his fiberglass and paint skills. Stan Goldstein managed the shop, ordering materials and keeping the books. Gordon Barber and Leon Lake, both of whom had worked on the original *Spirit*, returned to do the electrical systems. New team members included Jim Jefferies and Paul Nicolini to build the chassis; George Klass for logistics; Wayne Ewing, Bob Sorrell, and Tom Hanna to form the aluminum body; and drag racer Connie Swingle and "Lump-Lump" (the nickname Bill Fordham got saddled with, along with "Garbage Mouth") to help out where needed.

"Connie Swingle was crazy," remembers Bob Davids. "I asked him once if he was ever scared running Garlits's *Swamp Rat* dragster and he said, 'No, man. When I go, I want to go a ball of flames into the crowd.' He was a friend of Craig's and Stan's and didn't have a job at the time, so Craig hired him. Craig said, 'OK, Connie, what can you do?' and Connie said, 'Nothin'.' So Craig says to me, 'OK, Bobby, you take him. Connie'll be your grunt in the fiberglass shop.'" When Craig was subsequently looking over samples of canopy glass for the cockpit, one of which the manufacturer claimed was bulletproof, Connie grabbed it and took it outside to test it with the rifle he carried in the back window of his pickup. *BANG!* Connie came back in. *Hey Craig, that's total bullshit. That glass isn't bulletproof at all.*

The build was already well underway when Craig hired Quin Epperly fabricator George Boskoff to help with a particularly difficult part of the body: the transition in the aluminum skin from the car's rear rectangular shape to the oval shape of the nose. "I came into the shop and looked at it," says George, "and said I could do it. But then I woke up in the middle of the night thinking, *What in the hell did I get myself into?* I'd been involved with at least three Indy drivers who got killed, Dave McDonald and some other guys, and I'm thinking Craig's going to get killed too and it'll be something I did. I got up and I paced and paced, and drank coffee, and it wasn't until sunrise that I could calm myself down. Then I loaded up my tools and went in to the shop and figured out how to make those panels."

It was a colorful bunch of guys working on the car. It added to the ribbing that constantly took place—good natured for the most part but sometimes it went overboard. "What happens in a shop," says Bob

Davids, "is that guys can be sharks. Blue collar shops are like that. It's sort of a rite of passage, a sign of masculinity, everybody cutting at each other, trying to get a reaction. If somebody says something that provokes a reaction from you, then the other guys swarm in and pick on you. So you had to be a tough bastard to work in that shop. If you didn't have elephant skin, you couldn't work there."

"Yeah, some people didn't get along perfectly," says George Klass, "but everybody worked well enough together so it never got in the way. For that I really credit Craig and his easygoing personality. He was the easiest guy in the world to work with. He never had tantrums or yelled at anybody, none of that shit. He was the same with everybody, didn't treat anybody better than anybody else. I mean, I've been on other drag crews before, and I don't think I've ever seen any group of people working together so well." Even Wayne Ewing and Stan Goldstein became unlikely friends—unlikely because Wayne was "the most anti-Semitic son of a bitch," Stan remembers, "with Nazi flags and uniforms hanging all over his shop." Stan was Jewish.

Two final members of the team were a pair of chained-up dogs the crew rescued from a workshop on the other side of the alley. "The people across the way mistreated them and covered them with paint," says Craig. "I mean, it was pure animal cruelty. So we just took them. We told those jerks they were never going to get those dogs back and they'd better not do that to any more. We cleaned the dogs up and named them Stars and Stripes, took them to the vet, the whole thing, but Stars didn't survive. He got really sick from the paint and died. Stripes survived and we took him to Bonneville with us."

Work was well advanced, the initial thirty grand mostly spent, when the contract finally arrived from Goodyear. Craig scanned through the five pages of legalese, got to the last page, and froze. "On the very last page there was this clause, 'Upon completion of the car, it shall become the sole and separate property of Goodyear.' So I had got myself into a deal where I was designing the car, and building the car, and getting no pay to build it, and working seven days a week, sometimes twenty hours a day, as was everybody else, and now I find out I'm building a new car for free for Goodyear."

He phoned up Bob Lane and told him that *Sonic I* was his car and the deal was off. He would go to the bank and take out a loan and pay back all the money Goodyear had fronted. Lane asked why it was so important for him to actually own the racer. "Because that's how I'll earn money," Craig said, "by taking the car to auto shows, using it for ads and TV commercials. I get paid for those things."

"OK, so how long would the car be a hot item? How long would you do the shows?"

Craig thought for a moment. "Maybe two years."

"OK, so what if we let you use the car for two years after you set the record, you earn all the money you can, then we'll take it to show around at Goodyear stores and then maybe donate it to a museum, like the last car."

Craig relented. He was too deeply committed now to the project to stand up to Goodyear and risk throwing it all away. "Look," Craig said, squeezing all he could from the lousy deal, "I know that you and Shell paid the Santini Brothers more to truck the last car around on just one tour than I got for breaking the record three times. If Goodyear is going to be paying commercial rates anyway to take this new car around, why not pay me to do it? Let me do the trucking."

Lane agreed. A new contract was drawn up. Craig reluctantly signed it and got back to work.

Back at the shop, the rush to get *Sonic I* finished was taking a toll on the team. "Guys would get just wiped out," says George Klass. "Everybody was working their asses off and getting maybe five hours of sleep at night. We had cots in the shop so people could lie down for a few minutes."

"We worked seven days a week," says Craig. "We had huge long days. We had guys just freaking out from the stress."

The most dramatic incident involved Bob Sorrell. "Bob was an amazing craftsman," says Stan Goldstein. "But he had a reputation for being wobbly. He lived in a kind of industrial building in Harbor City and had a lot of cats. I used to have to go pick him up and you'd walk in the place and the smell from these cats would just overwhelm you." On this particular day Bob was working on the car when Paul

Nicolini said something innocuous that set him off. "Bob was emotional to begin with," says George Boskoff, who was there, "but suddenly he went *extremely* emotional. He started yelling and screaming and punched his fist through the door to the kitchen off the shop, and he took a whole box of clecos [sheet metal fasteners] and threw them all over. Paul pats him on the back and says, 'Bob, take your pills, take your pills.' He probably had tranquilizers in his toolbox. I took him home and he never returned after that."

Shortly after Bob Sorrell had his breakdown, a much bigger societal breakdown shook L.A., three days of race rage known as the Watts riots. California highway patrolman Gale Reed Gilbert, a regular visitor to the *Sonic I* shop, played a key role. It began with a routine traffic stop for drunk driving, "about a mile away from Breedlove's place," says Gilbert. The black driver was cooperative at first, then started fighting when his mother came out, which in turn set her off. Gilbert, responding to the call for backup, helped restore order, forming a cordon with other highway patrolmen and LAPD officers to keep back the crowd.

"There was a woman in the crowd," says Gilbert, "with a barber smock on and curlers in her hair. She'd come from a beauty shop down the street. She leaned out and spit on the highway patrolman on his motorcycle ahead of me. The sergeant said, 'Get her! Get her, Gilbert!' It would have been probably best to have ignored it. But I jumped off my motorcycle and grabbed the woman by the arm. She pulled back into the crowd, the crowd was trying to pull her away and I'm hanging on. The other policemen broke the crowd up and I led her to a patrol car and we all left. Well, the crowd just got bigger after that, and the word started going around, 'Did you see how that highway patrolman kicked that poor pregnant girl to the ground and knelt on her?' It didn't happen! Anyway, later that night they were overturning cars, setting them on fire. Crimey, I'd never seen anything like it."

George Klass takes up the story. "We were working inside all the time so we didn't realize at first that something was happening, not until somebody came in and said, 'Hey, there's a lot of smoke. Looks like a riot.' It didn't really affect us at first. We just kept working. But then it got closer, and some cop came in and said, 'You guys better not go out.' And then we see army trucks out front, and they're unloading National Guard soldiers. But we *still* didn't realize how bad it was.

"Then Craig and Stan came to me and said we needed some parts from this industrial hardware store we were buying a lot of things from. They said, 'Would you mind going and picking this stuff up? It's not too far away, but with all the shit going on . . .' And they actually gave me a shotgun. As if I'm going to go shoot somebody, right?

"So I head off in the truck. This was probably the second day of the riots. I get out there and people start throwing rocks and yelling and I'm thinking, *Holy shit, I'm driving a red, white, and blue pickup truck with 'Spirit of America' on the side in pretty big letters.* So now I'm having to weave in and out, and some streets are blocked, and I'm trying to go to this place and get back in one piece. It scared the shit out of me, I got to tell you. I get back and, I mean, I was shaking. I said, 'They got problems out there!'

"It lasted four or five days. We worked on the car straight through and took turns keeping guard up on the roof with the shotgun, because they were setting fires to buildings right on our street. It was a very tough time. And then when it's all over, these highway patrol cops, they'd been to the shop several times before, they stop by again and say, 'Yeah, we're the guys that started the whole deal.'"

Sonic I was now rounding into finished form. It was 34½ feet long and 59 inches high, somewhat shorter and lower to the ground than the original *Spirit*. With a J-79 engine installed, nearly half the car's weight, it would tip the scales at 8,000 pounds, a little more than the three-wheeler with its lighter J-47. The 100-gallon gas tank was more than double the size, for a 79 in afterburner would gulp a whole lot of fuel. The heavy-duty aircraft brakes were also much more substantial, as Craig was determined to never again find himself in a situation where he was unable to stop. To save time and money, he used the 48-inch tires from his original *Spirit* on the back; 36-inchers were up front, where there was less room due to the air duct. Goodyear, constantly striving to make improvements, would claim that it tested both to 850 mph.

As for the heart of the car, its J-79 jet engine, one still hadn't turned up. September rolled around, Craig's booked time on the salt flats was just a few weeks away, and the yawning cavity in *Sonic I*'s chassis had yet to be filled.

Finally, with the car almost ready for painting, Craig got a call on the shop phone with a lead. One of the many surplus dealers he had contacted in his search for an engine had heard of a J-79 in Charlotte, North Carolina, and suggested he give the place a call. Craig did, and sure enough it was true. He bought the engine on the spot for $7,500 and immediately went to Walt Sheehan with the good news.

"Walt," he said, all excited, "I just bought a J-79. I found it at Charlotte Aircraft."

"You're kidding. Which engine is it?"

Craig checked his scribbled notes. "It's a YJ-3."

"Craig, that's an early experimental engine. You don't even want to touch it."

"But I've already wired them the money and they're shipping it. It's on its way. I got an afterburner too from that guy in Tulsa."

"Oh shit . . ."

The problem was that the YJ-3 was one of the very first models of the J-79—no more than a handful were ever made—and was quickly superseded by a redesigned version. That meant that it probably wouldn't work very well and that whatever afterburner Craig had acquired almost certainly wouldn't fit.

"But we'll *make* it fit," Craig insisted.

Walt shook his head. "Craig, it's not that easy . . ."

The J-79 and afterburner arrived at the shop on almost the same day. "We opened the can to look at the engine," says Craig, "and we were just blown away. I mean the thing was gleaming, with no dust, all the blades brand new. We couldn't believe it." Walt Sheehan retrieved the paperwork that went with it, stowed inside the can in a little tube. It made him smile, for he knew this very engine. It had made the first flight in an F-104 back in 1955, the fighter taking little more than a hop off the runway. "Look," he said, showing Craig the papers, "I signed the log to send it back to General Electric because the seals in the turbine seized up." The engine had been rebuilt but never again used, the YJ experimental model deemed not airworthy. It had sat in its can for a decade before being scrapped.

And then came an even bigger surprise when they opened the wooden crate containing the afterburner and Walt bent down to examine the ID plate. "I don't believe this . . ." He turned to Craig. "You are absolutely the luckiest son of a bitch on this entire planet. This burner was made for this engine." It was a thousand-to-one chance, pure dumb luck. "In the matter of two days," says Craig, "we had the whole thing."

The next hurdle was to get the engine and afterburner running after sitting in storage for a decade. It took some high-level corporate string-pulling by Goodyear president Vic Holt, but General Electric agreed to do the work and even assigned a technician to join the *Sonic I* crew on the salt. Just five days later Craig got a call from GE's engine facility in Ontario, California, informing him that his J-79 was operational and inviting him in to watch it being tested.

"It was the first time I had seen a J-79 run at close range," Craig would recall in his autobiography a few years later. "When I had watched Art's practice run [in 1964], I had been two or three miles away. I hadn't even seen his second run; so when the technicians fired the engine up for the first time, I couldn't believe it. The J-79 made the J-47 sound like a peashooter. . . . It was the most impressive display of raw power that I had ever witnessed. Then they lit the afterburner. When a J-79 afterburner lights, there is a series of shock waves, and a reddish blue flame shoots out the back because the velocity of the thrust is well over supersonic speed. It sounds just like the end of the earth."

The rebuilt J-79 was installed in *Sonic I*. It was placed on the shop floor and the car was rolled overtop for the engine to be hoisted up and bolted in place. Bob Davids, the skinniest guy in the shop, wriggled underneath the chassis to insert the underside bolt.

"As soon as we line this thing up," Nye Frank told him, "slam that bolt into the hole. And do it quick because this fucking thing's heavy."

The massive engine, weighing nearly two tons, was slowly lifted and maneuvered into position, everyone being careful not to ding the fresh paint on the chassis. "OK, Bobby, try it!"

The holes weren't lined up. Bob couldn't get the bolt in. "It won't fit!" he said, frantically stabbing. "It won't fit!"

The guys on the chain hoist were straining now as the engine was jiggled. "Goddamn it, hurry! It's heavy!"

Bobby kept poking. "It's not lined up. Lift it up a little . . . I can't find the hole! I can't find the hole!"

That's when George Boskoff quipped, "Put some hair around it!"

"I almost couldn't stop laughing," says Bob Davids, retelling the story. "Everybody cracked up. You can see that we worked a lot of hours."

They got the J-79 bolted into place. Special sliding mounts like on a kitchen drawer were used to secure it to the chassis, because an operating J-79 needs room to expand. Craig's jet engine would grow a half inch in length as it heated up.

––––––––––

There were just days to go to the press unveiling, *Sonic I* freshly painted and logos applied, when Bill Neely of Goodyear's PR department phoned Craig at the shop. Bob Lane, he said, wasn't happy with how the car looked in the photos he'd just received. The Goodyear logo wasn't prominent enough. He wanted it not just on the racer's side, but up on the tail.

"That's a terrible idea," Craig said. "You don't put a commercial emblem over the American flag on a car called *Spirit of America*. Besides, I have a contract signed by Lane specifying where and what size every logo on the car is supposed to be. And there is absolutely no reference to any Goodyear logo on the tail."

Neely backed down and Craig went back to work thinking the matter was settled.

Howard Babcock, Neely's superior, phoned up next. "Hey, what's this I hear about you not wanting to put the Goodyear emblem on the tail?"

Craig went through it all again. "Look, Howard, the car is named *Spirit of America*. The promotional theme behind the whole thing is patriotism. So putting the Goodyear logo above the American flag on the tail—people are going to pick up on that and it's not going to be good PR for Goodyear."

"OK, I get your point," said Babcock. "Let me talk to Lane. I'm sure he hasn't thought this through."

Craig once again assumed the matter was settled. But it wasn't. Babcock showed up at the shop in person two days later to make sure the Goodyear logo went on the tail. "I know this is ridiculous," he said, "but Lane has flipped out. Frankly, I think it boils down to him getting his way. He wanted you to make a concession to him."

"Why does Lane want this?" Craig said, exhausted from overwork and about to snap.

"Well, in the photos of the car from the back, the Goodyear emblem is way up at the front and you can't see it. We need something in the foreground when it's photographed from the back."

It was the first thing Craig had heard that made any sense. "OK, fine. I'll add a second Goodyear logo to the back of the car and shift all the other sponsor logos forward."

"Fantastic," said Babcock. "Thanks, Craig. I know this will settle Lane down."

It didn't.

13

BACK INTO BATTLE

"The little shit lied to me," Art Arfons snarled to *Sports Illustrated* writer Jack Olsen. He had just learned that Craig had a new land speed racer built and ready to go. "M-Z Promotions. Ha! He told me he wasn't going to have a car this year and was going to take it easy for a year or two, and here he had this damn thing happening." M-Z Promotions was a Seattle-based PR firm that Craig had used to reserve the salt flats incognito.

"Yeah, but isn't that part of the game?" said Olsen, recording the conversation.

"Yeah, you got to admit that, Art," said Firestone's Humpy Wheeler. "You'd probably have done the same thing."

Spirit of America–Sonic I had its press unveiling on September 29, 1965, in the garden at L.A.'s Ambassador Hotel. The event was a tremendous success. "This car wins the [land speed] beauty contest," enthused *Deseret News* sports editor Hack Miller, and "Breedlove takes first honors as being racing's handsomest driver. He looks like someone who should shade for Robert Goulet. Dapper young man, but as friendly as old Rover."

When it was all over, Howard Babcock took Craig aside for a word. "Craig, you've got to put the Goodyear logo on the tail."

Craig's smile faded. "Howard, we already sorted this out. We put a second logo there on the back. Just like Lane wanted."

"Well, I'm sorry, but you either have to put the Goodyear emblem on the tail . . . or else."

"'Or else'? What does that mean, 'Or else'?"

"Or else you can't run. Lane's pulling the plug."

For Craig, it was the last straw. "Here I'd been working on this frigging thing for twenty-nine hours a day, eight days a week for six months, and I'm ground down to nothing. I've got nothing left. I'm physically ill over the thing. So we're driving back to the shop and I say, 'OK, that's it. I'm not doing it. My contract says that Goodyear will own the car "upon completion," right? Well, as the designer and builder, I'm telling you officially right now that the car's not complete. We have more work to do before it's complete and ready to run, so that means it's still mine. So you want to drop out? Fine. Drop out. Send me a letter.' Well, they went crazy. They didn't know what to do. My dad was upset too. He was saying, 'Calm down, Craig. This can be worked out.'"

The *Sonic I* project was suddenly in peril. Craig was angry and had his back up, and Bob Lane, furious at his own legalese being used against him, was ready to dump the whole thing. With Norm Breedlove mediating with Howard Babcock, however, a compromise was worked out and the crisis averted. Craig agreed to remove the diamond around the Goodyear logo and increase the size of the letters, making the "Goodyear" name more visible in publicity photos, and Lane dropped his demand that the logo go on the tail.

———————————

The battle for the ultimate land speed record was already underway on the Bonneville Salt Flats. Walt Arfons had kicked it off in the third week of September with a brand-new Goodyear-sponsored racer, dubbed *Wingfoot Express* like his jet car the previous year. This time he had built a rocket car, the first ever used in land speed competition. Walt had previously tried adding three JATO (Jet-Assisted Take-Off) solid-fuel rockets to his *Wingfoot* jet car but had been unable to run it, USAC withholding its sanction because the external rockets couldn't be controlled by the driver and weren't an integral part of the engine. Convinced that rockets were the way forward, Walt had gone back to the drawing board and built a whole new racer from scratch, one powered solely by JATOs—fifteen of them in a huge cluster sticking out the back, a cumulative total of 15,000 pounds of thrust. They weren't throttleable like a jet but they could be lit up and shut down from the cockpit and so passed USAC muster. A big drawback: JATOs burned for only fifteen seconds. They also cost a bundle. That meant that driver Bobby Tatroe didn't have the luxury of test runs. He had to strap in and go.

The *Wingfoot* rocket car underperformed in its first week on the salt. Its tremendous acceleration didn't last long enough to get it up to record speed and maintain it through the mile. Extending the burn time by firing the rockets in two stages helped, but not enough. The only solution was to add more rockets. Walt and Bobby hauled *Wingfoot* to a hangar at Wendover Air Force Base and began installing ten more JATOs, bringing the total to twenty-five.

Art Arfons had the next week on the salt. He had booked it months before but now didn't really need it. His 536 mph mark had yet to be beaten and he had no wish to risk his life again until it was. Relinquishing the week, however, meant giving the time to Craig Breedlove. Art therefore got busy running out the clock on the Bonneville season.

He started with his *Cyclops* jet dragster, putting Betty Skelton in the cockpit to go after the women's land speed record. Goodyear—derided by Firestone as "Brand X"—had initiated the competition the previous year when Paula Murphy went 226 mph in Walt Arfons's *Avenger* jet dragster. This prompted Firestone—derided in turn by Goodyear as "Flintstone Tire"—to want the women's record for itself. They paid Art to set Betty up in a jet car and get the job done. And she did, pushing *Cyclops* to a new mark of 277 mph. Art closed out the week with quarter-mile runs from a standing start in *Green Monster*, using full afterburner for the first time to set a new record of 258 mph. He then hauled his racer to Salt Lake City two hours away. He wanted to keep it close by so that he could respond quickly if Craig broke his record.

Craig invited Lee to accompany him that year to Bonneville for his land speed attempt. He hoped it would help bring them closer together and rekindle their marriage. His dad Norm went along as well, taking some time off from Hollywood, where he had just finished modifying the eponymous automobile for the new TV series *My Mother the Car*.

The crew arrived in Wendover on October 3. They went out for dinner that evening at a café alongside the freight train tracks on the south side of town. When they came out afterward, George Boskoff remembers a hobo standing by the tracks, waiting to hop on the next freight, and Connie Swingle slipping him twenty bucks and getting him something to eat. "All those guys," says Craig, looking back fondly, "the whole group that runs hot rods, they're all pretty damn good guys."

There were only four and a half miles of usable course out on the salt. It was sufficient to get started with preliminary testing, however, and the flooded south end was rapidly drying. Hopefully, after the first of Craig's two booked weeks, there would be enough room for a record attempt.

The team got down to work. After a year out of the cockpit Craig was dreading this moment. It was a big reason why he had been so tense, struggling with the memory of his 1964 crash. The worry had kept him awake at night and driven him to a reliance on sleeping pills, which was now an addiction. He had tried talking to a psychiatrist like his dad suggested but it didn't help.

George Klass had been living with Craig for the past several months and knew better than most what he was feeling. "Craig had lots of concerns about dying in that car. There was this doctor who came by the shop to look at the car when it was being constructed. We were showing him where the roll bars were, the cage around the cockpit, all the safety features, and he said, 'It doesn't matter. You turn this thing over and roll it around a few times at the speed you guys are shooting for and all your internal organs will come loose inside your body. Too many Gs.' I know that upset Craig. I know that he had concerns about his life." He did a good job never showing it, however. George continues: "Craig never exhibited fear. He was always cool and collected pretty much about everything. He seemed above it all. Very calm."

Sonic I handled like a dream when Craig made his first passes. The *Deseret News* described him afterward as being "elated." It weathered the bumps better than his three-wheeler and didn't have the same tendency of tramming along in ruts. It also handled better, its two front wheels allowing for ten degrees of steering as opposed to the original *Spirit*'s two. The position of the cockpit up in the nose was somewhat awkward but that was par for the course in land speed racing. The sport was all about acclimation, about getting used to your racer and used to the speed.

The problems began presenting themselves. They always did with an experimental vehicle built from scratch. The first major issue had to do with the new ribbon chutes provided by Goodyear's aerospace division. They were intended for extreme high-speed deployment on rocket sleds and on the Gemini spacecraft and had a tendency to not open fully when Craig started using them at 400 mph. They were flown to Akron for modifications and quickly sent back. Walt Sheehan's onboard load sensors were also revealing that the racer's front end was getting lighter the faster Craig went. To counter this, the little winglets at the front were angled down to give the car negative lift and press the nose back onto the salt. When the problem persisted, they were angled down further.

An even bigger concern materialized when Craig pushed into the low 500s: *Sonic I* was not hitting the speeds he expected. He had planned on bagging the record in full military power and saving the afterburner for later—hopefully much later—but even with the throttle open all the way he was coming up short. "How about getting some power out of this thing?" he snapped at Walt Sheehan, momentarily losing his cool.

Fortunately, there was a J-79 specialist on the crew, forty-three-year-old Bob Koken—"the old guy" to the rest of the crew, all of them still in their twenties. Bob had been sent out to Bonneville by his employer General Electric to make sure Craig didn't kill himself using one of their engines. He and Walt Sheehan adjusted the control valve to deliver more fuel to the 79 and in turn generate more power. Then Craig tried again.

KA-BOOM!

A massive explosion shook the racer when Craig throttled down after exiting the mile on his next run. "It was so loud my ears were

ringing," he says. "It just totally rang my bell. I thought the whole frigging car blew up." He released the chutes—thankfully they worked—and
pulled to a stop and scrambled out of the cockpit.

"What in the hell was *that*?" he said when Walt drove up.

"Oh, just a decel stall," said Walt nonchalantly. A deceleration stall.
They occurred when the engine was abruptly throttled back and the
compressed inferno of air inside blasted forward out the air duct instead
of backward out the tailpipe—like a fiery and very loud burp.

"'Just a decel stall?'" said Craig. "Well, it scared the piss out of me!"

Walt shrugged. "We went a bit too far with the fuel control adjustment."

J-79s were rugged enough to handle decel stalls. But *Sonic I* wasn't.
The force of the blast had severely cracked the front end of the air duct
and jolted it loose, buckled body panels all around, and bent the hatch
door of the cockpit. The panels along the top of the racer had also been
crinkled. This was a separate problem, caused by the pressure differential
between outside air and air inside the chassis. At 500-plus mph, the
aerodynamic forces on *Sonic I* were so great they had dented its skin.

The car was taken to Wendover Air Force Base for repairs. The
crinkled top was repaired and strengthened with flanges and George
Boskoff punched louvers through the aluminum to vent the interior air.
Bob Davids meanwhile went to work on the air duct. "I had a shitload of
problems fixing that duct," Bob recalls. He ground it down to structurally
sound material, then built it back up, then painted it with flat black primer,
cutting away or painting over most of Craig's name behind the cockpit in
the process. "Craig hated that," says Bob with a chuckle. "It bothered him
a lot. And he was furious that we didn't have any blue paint."

By working almost round the clock, the crew got all the work done
by the end of Craig's second booked week on the salt. He was out of
time but he wasn't worried, for the following week had been reserved
by Goodyear. Craig assumed he would be able to keep running, sharing the course with Walt Arfons, who had now finished adding more
rockets to *Wingfoot Express*.

He was wrong. When he got to the road leading onto the salt flats,
hauling *Sonic I* on its trailer, Bob Lane's underling Howard Babcock

turned him away. "I'm sorry, Craig," Howard said, looking sheepish. "Lane has ordered that your car is not allowed on the salt until after Walt's time is up."

Craig hauled the car back to Wendover and waited, fuming over what he knew was more payback from Lane. "Bob's intention was that Walt's rocket car would break the sound barrier," he says, "and set the record so high that we wouldn't be able to get it. So we found ourselves in competition with Goodyear. Our own sponsor was trying to knock us out because I didn't immediately fold under to Bob and put Goodyear's name on the tail above the American flag."

Craig and the crew returned to the salt a few days later to watch *Wingfoot Express* make its record attempt. The arrowhead-shaped racer, bristling now with 25 JATO rockets, the Goodyear logo prominent on its tailfin, was positioned a mere nine-tenths of a mile from the clocks. With the JATOs having such a short burn time, the run would be all about massive acceleration, the rockets set off in two stages for a total blast duration of twenty-one seconds. The *Sonic I* guys marveled at the car, wished Bobby Tatroe good luck, then stepped back. Way back.

"I wouldn't have even sat in that car," says George Klass. "What they did to make those rockets 'throttleable' was they fastened dynamite caps to the front, so if Bobby had to cut the run short he could blow off the front and have thrust blowing in both directions. How would you like to sit in front of that? There was just a ¾-inch piece of plate between those rockets and Bobby Tatroe. Poor bastard."

What happened next was quite a show. One of *Wingfoot's* JATOs tore loose as it blasted off in a sea of flame, sending observers scattering back. The racer disappeared down the course gathering tremendous speed, then a second JATO tore off and went arcing up into the air. Then the retro charges on some of the rockets ignited prematurely, blowing the front ends off the bottles, releasing thrust front and aft and setting the racer on fire. *Wingfoot* was a truly impressive sight now, a flaming comet as it streaked into the mile. Then its rockets burned out and it coasted to a stop, Walt Arfons chasing wild-eyed behind, frantic to the point of heart seizure. He came screaming up and leaped out of his car and seized Bobby, stunned but unhurt, and they both burst into tears. Their rocket car, which had done a disappointing 438 mph through the clocks, had most of its Goodyear paint burned off. It looked like a charred ruin.

"So the *Wingfoot Express* burned up," says Craig. "And then here comes Howard Babcock and the other guys from Goodyear PR. They come shuffling up, their heads down, kind of embarrassed, and Howard says, 'Craig, we just talked to Akron. Walt won't be running again for a while, so Bob Lane says it's OK for you to run now.'"

For Craig, it was a moment of immense satisfaction, the thought of Bob Lane smashing his fist on his desk making him smile. "Gee, I don't know," he said. "Are you sure it's all right?"

"No, no, it's OK," Howard stammered. "Lane said you can start. You have the salt."

Craig geared up for his own record attempt the next day, October 20. He had come to the realization that full military power wasn't going to do it, for *Sonic I* was proving not as aerodynamically slippery as his original *Spirit*. To push past the low 500s and beat Art Arfons's record, Craig would have to use afterburner.

The car was towed to the north end of the course and turned around to point south toward base camp and the highway. Craig wanted to save the northbound direction for his return trip, which would be faster, so he would have miles and miles of white desert in which to slow down. He was nervous when he climbed into the cockpit, for he had never used afterburner before. What would it feel like? Would he experience tunnel vision or even momentary blindness, as he had heard was possible during extreme acceleration? Would it put so much strain on his racer that it would blow a tire like Art's *Green Monster*?

He blasted off in full mil power and immediately throttled up into first-stage burner. "And man, I was gone," he would write in his autobiography six years later. "I could see why Walt and Art had used the burner all along. The burner gets you to the moment of truth in a hurry.

I liked that because I wanted to get the record over with. By the time I got to the measured mile I was going like Jack the Bear."

Craig was on his way to blowing Art Arfons out of the water. Suddenly 600 mph was no longer a goal for somewhere down the road. He was doing 600 *right now*. He hung on as the green marker at the entrance to the mile swept past, his mind working in overdrive, that peak of ferocious intensity that the ultimate LSR demanded. And then the horizon was falling away. Craig thought at first it was some kind of acceleration-induced illusion, the flip side of the weird sensation of driving down a cliff when the chutes came out. Then it hit him: *Sonic I*'s nose was lifting. *He was starting to fly.*

He was veering off course. He turned the steering yoke to correct. With his front wheels up off the ground he got no response. He slammed his hand down on the engine-kill switch on the yoke and immediately released the braking chutes.

Too soon. The tow line couldn't take the strain when the canopy blossomed and caught the air. It tore off the back of the car. Craig was leaving the course now, the black line veering away to the left. He forced himself to wait, thumb poised over the backup chute button. One second. Two seconds.

He pushed the button. Nothing happened. The backup chute must have torn away with the main. With a feeling of sick dread he realized that he was reliving his crash of the previous year, both chutes gone, no way to stop, hurtling across the desert out of control. He was even going in the same direction, south, straight for the brine pond. All that remained was for his brakes to burn up so that he could head to his doom pumping a useless pedal.

Sonic I had much better brakes than the three-wheeler. They were not intended for use at anywhere near 500-plus but when Craig ever so lightly touched the pedal, they held. He touched it again. They held. The front wheels had now dropped back down onto the salt. Craig was able to steer. He continued gently applying the brakes, press and release, press and release, giving the discs a few seconds to cool between each application. He had gotten his racer down below 300 mph when the mile 0 marker passed, the end of the graded course well off to the left. He plowed into the rough salt beyond, working the brakes, slowing, slowing, and rolled to a stop barely two hundred yards from the embankment and brine pond where he had nearly drowned twelve months before.

Craig appeared remarkably calm when the crew and reporters arrived. Walt Arfons, who had been on hand to watch, came up and gave him a hug and told him he had gone overboard with the burner. "Gee whiz," he said, "you should have let up after the first couple of miles and then hit it again." Craig smiled and laughed and didn't seem at all rattled. Inside, however, he was shaking. "This run had scared me so badly," he later revealed, "that I knew I must get back in the car as quickly as possible or I might never run again." But *Sonic I* was out of commission. The brakes were shot, the discs fused to the wheels. The heat had been so intense that the paint on the chassis was charred six inches away. And then there was the more serious matter of the car almost flying. Something had to be done about that.

"We're going to make some changes," project manager Stan Goldstein announced to the press later that morning. "We're going to try to do it right, and make sure it is right."

Walt Arfons and Bobby Tatroe, defying all expectations, had *Wingfoot Express* repaired and ready to run just three days after Craig vacated the course. The damage from Bobby's fireball ride had turned out to be largely cosmetic.

"Five eighty!" Bobby exulted after his first run. "My airspeed was 580. Change the rockets! Let's go!" Five eighty may have been Bobby's terminal velocity coming out of the clocks but it wasn't his speed through the mile. Joe Petrali measured that as being only 476 mph. "Leave it go. It's no use," Walt said dejectedly when he caught up. They could have snagged the record with another five seconds of thrust but *Wingfoot* didn't have it. The rocket racer would not run again.

Two hours' drive east in Salt Lake City, *Sonic I* was sitting in an Air National Guard workshop at Hill Air Force Base. The Air Guard had been generous with its assistance to the *Spirit of America* project going back to 1961 and once again had come through when Craig reached out for help. Craig now realized that his racer was not nearly as aerodynamically sound as he had intended. It was the cause of the crinkled top body panels. It was why he needed to use burner sooner than planned. It was why the nose lifted up. The problems were inherent in the design—not surprising, considering how quickly he had thrown it together—and could not be fixed short of a complete reconfiguration and rebuild and six months of labor. And he didn't have six months. He scarcely had seven days. All he could do was cobble together a short-term fix and pray it wouldn't kill him.

The fused-on disc brakes were cut away from the wheels and the braking system rebuilt. The heat-damaged wheels also needed replacing, as did the tires. "The wheel wells were so tight around the wheels," says Stan Goldstein, "that at the speed they were turning, it was like an air pump and created this vacuum that sucked the aluminum into the tires. It was like pulling a cheese grater in on top of the tires." It was part of the larger air pressure imbalance problem that had caused the crinkling. It seemed to be affecting the whole racer. When *Sonic I* traveled at high speed, an envelope of negative pressure built up around it that sucked up on the body hard enough to bend the aluminum skin. To vent interior air and relieve this pressure imbalance, Wayne Ewing and several Air National Guard mechanics punched additional louvers into the aluminum body by hand, dozens of them along the sides, on the bottom, and inside the wheel wells. Stiffening flanges were also welded all over the inside of the body to help it better withstand the pressure of the wind.

That still left the most serious problem: *Sonic I*'s desire to fly. Craig had contacted aerodynamicists about it but had gotten no satisfaction. "Friend, when you get over 150 mph on the ground," he recalled being told, "you're on your own." In a bid to keep his car locked on the ground, Craig had larger front wings fabricated from cast aluminum, roughly two feet across, double the size of the original winglets. Ballast was also added to the nose.

14

RUSSIAN ROULETTE WITH JETS

SONIC I WAS NO LONGER PRISTINE and pretty when it was hauled back to the salt on the first day of November. It was a battle-scarred veteran, cut up, punched full of louvers. So was Craig, figuratively speaking. The teenage fun of hot-rodding was a million miles away. This was deadly serious war—superficially with record holder Art Arfons but really with himself, the design shortcomings of his racer, and the unforgiving hardness of the Bonneville Salt Flats.

Craig made three runs on his first day to see how the car stood up to the wind blast with its new venting louvers. Minor denting in the skin over one of the rear wheels revealed a lingering problem. To redirect airflow and ease the pressure at this point on the car, vertical flanges were welded to the body fore and aft the rear wheels. It was a quick and dirty fix and the opposite of streamlining—like rolling down the window and sticking out your hand.

Craig decided to go for the record the next day. He went out for a solitary stroll the evening before, after dinner. He often did in Wendover at the end of the day, taking a walk to escape the intensity of everything and relax for a bit. He headed down Main Street toward the giant cowboy statue of Wendover Will, its arm slowly waving, and cut through the parking lot of the Stateline Casino. There was a quiet side road behind the casino that would take him back to the motel.

"Hey, Craig."

A figure approached in the twilight. It was Art Arfons. He was in town for Craig's record attempt. He had his *Green Monster* parked in Las Vegas, ready to return to the salt at a day's notice. "Now that you've got your car straightened out," he said, "I guess you'll break the record again."

"That's right," Craig replied, trying to sound more certain than he felt. "I'm going to break the record tomorrow."

Art didn't respond. Craig filled the silence. "You were right about the J-79. It really is powerful."

Art kicked the dirt. He seemed to have something on his mind. Finally he said, "So what's going to happen here? If you break my record, am I going to come back and then you come back and we just keep going back and forth until one of us gets killed?"

Nice question. Thanks, Arthur. The thought of getting killed was why Craig was out here in the first place taking a walk to settle his nerves. "Well," he said, "I really hadn't looked at it that way, but I guess that's a possibility."

"So it'll be like a game of Russian roulette."

"Yeah, I guess so."

Art thoughtfully nodded. "Well OK, I just wanted to know."

———

Craig was in the cockpit and ready to go at eight forty-five the next morning, November 2, 1965. To prevent his speed from getting away from him in afterburner like it had two weeks before, he started just three and a half miles out from the clocks instead of the usual five. The first run went smoothly, Craig more confident now using burner, the queasiness in his stomach when it kicked in soon passing as he thundered along. The result was just about perfect, 544 mph, enough to put Craig past Art's mark without getting into the zone where *Sonic I* wanted to fly.

"That was a great run," he said, climbing out at the far end.

Nye Frank, meeting him with a pained look, said, "Take a look at your car."

One of the top body panels behind the cockpit had been squashed by the air pressure. At first it looked like the record bid was a bust. After examining the damage, however, Walt Sheehan concluded that the car could probably stand up to one more trip, for there were no sucked-up humps in the aluminum to impede the airflow. The louvers had solved that problem by venting the interior air and relieving negative pressure. This time the skin had only been flattened, pressed down into a configuration that the aerodynamic forces acting on the car seemed to want.

The edge of the damaged panel was taped down and Craig was off before his hour expired. It was another good run, no mishaps or surprises . . . until he got through the mile and hit the chute release button and nothing happened. The Goodyear Aerospace chute had failed again. The drogue chute had come out but the full eight-foot-wide canopy hadn't followed. Fortunately, Craig had prepared for this. He had brought drag chute maker Jack Carter back on board during the downtime to make him a backup. Big beefy Jack, a working stiff with a high school education, didn't have an impressive operation. When he was on the salt he worked on a sewing machine set up on the tailgate of his old station wagon. But he made reliable chutes. When Craig hit the button to release his backup after a few heart-pounding moments, Jack's handcrafted creation came out and blossomed exactly to order, throwing Craig hard against his harness, slowing him down.

Craig was clocked at 566 mph on the return, giving him a two-way average of 555.127 mph. He had just broken the land speed record for the fourth time. "I've never had to work so hard for a record in my life," he said after, giving Lee a big kiss and his dad a hug.

"I was sure Craig had the record," Norm said, relieved and delighted. "I'm wearing my lucky shirt, the one I wore when he set his last record."

Back at the Western Motel in Wendover, after the celebrations subsided that evening, Walt Sheehan developed the photographic strips from *Sonic I*'s data recorder and hung them from headboards and lampshades to dry. They told a frightening story. On Craig's return run, when he hit his top speed, there had been a load of only 200 pounds on the 8,000-pound racer's front wheels.

Even with its stabilizing winglets doubled in size and set at a sharp downward angle, even with ballast added to the nose, *Sonic I* wanted to fly.

It was still only Tuesday of Craig's week on the salt. He couldn't just pack up and go home, for that would leave the course open for Art Arfons to come back and break his record. But he couldn't just hang around and do nothing either. The Speedway Association took a dim view of salt-hogging and would boot him off the course.

The name of the game now was therefore to make a show of looking busy to run out the clock. With winter weather expected to hit any day, tying up the salt for the rest of the week would put Art off until November 7, so late in the year that he wouldn't stand much of a chance. Craig would hold the record at the end of the season, with nearly twelve months of promotional opportunity ahead. "They've heard there's a cold front coming on Sunday," a member of Art Arfons's crew complained, "and they think the snow'll shut us down." Yeah, that was about the size of it. There was a lot of money involved in this game and sometimes the big boys played rough.

The first time-killer was to put Lee in the car to go after the women's LSR. George Klass chuckles about it now, looking back. "We didn't give a shit about the women's record," he says. "Strictly a con to hold on to the salt." Goodyear was hot for the record, however. They had been ever since Betty Skelton took it away the previous year in Art Arfons's dragster driving on Firestone tires. They also liked the marketing angle: "Craig and Lee Breedlove, World's Fastest Couple."

Lee needed no convincing. She agreed as soon as Craig made the suggestion. "You have to realize that Lee was no prissy lady," says Stan Goldstein. "She was a tough chick—a very attractive one, but nevertheless a tough chick. She didn't walk around in crinoline dresses, I'll tell you." Lee had in fact wanted to try for the record going back to the original *Spirit* but Shell had nixed the idea, horrified by the thought of a woman getting killed in a vehicle bearing their name. Now, when she was needed, Goodyear proved much less squeamish.

Despite having never driven competitively before, Lee climbed into the cockpit without hesitation and went for the record after practicing for only one day. Craig, the epitome of self-control when behind the wheel himself, almost lost it watching helpless from the sidelines. "I aged ten years," he would later write. "After we saw the chute come out and the car begin to slow down, Stan Goldstein came over to me and said, 'Look, Champ, you're not going to make it. Calm down.'" Lee easily blew past Betty Skelton's mark that day with a two-way average of 308.56 mph. Her record would stand for eleven years, until 1976.

Craig filled out the rest of the week setting endurance records on the ten-mile oval. He had had the idea of running a Mustang like the one he now owned, but when the request was made to Ford they sent out one of Carroll Shelby's Daytona Cobras instead. On November 6, Craig's last day on the salt, he and Bobby Tatroe ran the hell out of the Cobra for twelve straight hours, taking two-hour shifts at the wheel to set a total of twenty-three endurance records. The salt was pretty cut up when they were done, prompting the waiting *Green Monster* crew to grumble that it had been damaged on purpose. "It was not!" an outraged Goodyear man replied to the accusation. "I felt awful when I heard that we'd damaged the course."

Craig, basking in the glow of being back on top, immediately flew east with Lee to begin a publicity tour. "Breedlove Does It Again!" read the full-page ad Goodyear ran in the *Akron Beacon Journal* on November 5. "Sets New World's Land Speed Record on Goodyear Tires!" The Akron paper always got the biggest ads. It was like shoving them right in Firestone's face.

Craig and Lee had only just arrived in New York to appear on the game show *To Tell the Truth* when the Goodyear handler picking them up at the airport brought everything crashing down. "Craig," he said, "I've got some bad news for you. Art just went 576. The weather cleared for a moment, and he was right there."

Arfons had done it again. He had broken Craig's record on his very first day on the salt, within just a few hours of unloading his car.

It had ended with another white-knuckle return run, *Green Monster* blowing its right rear tire again, the explosion this time so catastrophic that it did massive damage to the back of the car. Art emerged from the cockpit this time kicking and swearing. He was getting damn tired of ultra-high-speed Bonneville blowouts. This was his third.

Craig's TV appearances were canceled, along with everything else. Later that day, as he sat dejected in his hotel room, the phone rang. It was Bob Lane. He hadn't spoken to Craig since the dustup over the Goodyear logo on the tail. After some stammering preliminaries he got to the point.

"Yeah, well, so, you've done everything to fulfill your contract with Goodyear. We owe you the money for breaking the record. You're not obligated to do anything else. But now that Art's got the record . . . well, what do you think about that?"

"I'm not too happy about it, Bob. I'd like it back."

"So, you're willing to go back out and run the car again? How much would we have to pay you?"

It was a perfect opening to squeeze more money from Goodyear. But Craig didn't take it. He used it instead to mend fences with Lane. "In that presentation I gave when you agreed to sponsor the car," he replied, "I said I'd go 600 mph. Well, I haven't done it yet, have I?"

"No, but no one's going to hold you to that."

"Well, I said I'd go 600 and I have every intention of keeping my word."

"So . . . you don't want any more money?"

"No. I'll need Goodyear to pay expenses but I'll do the driving for free."

After finishing the call Craig phoned George Klass, who had stayed behind in Wendover with *Sonic I*, and told him to reassemble the team. Craig and Lee flew back to Salt Lake City the next day. Smoke was billowing up from one of the runways when they landed. A Boeing 727, the same aircraft they were in, flying the same route, had crashed an hour before, killing half the people on board.

It was now Craig's turn to pace the sidelines while "Flintstone Tire" tied up the salt. Art was done for the year—*Green Monster* would take months to repair—but Firestone had another car in the wings, Bill and Bob Summers's *Goldenrod*, running for the wheel-driven record. The brothers finally succeeded toward the end of the week in pushing their pencil-shaped racer to a new record of 409 mph, surpassing by six miles an hour the mark Donald Campbell had set the year before in Australia. The achievement was widely reported in the papers but didn't attract nearly as much attention as the fight between Craig and Art for the ultimate record. The Big Number, and the publicity that went with it, was now owned by the jets.

Finally, on November 13, Firestone packed up and went home, vacating the salt for the *Sonic I* team to take over. It was now desperately late in the season, well past the usual time when the desert flooded out for the year. It already seemed on the verge, with a light rain falling and puddles forming on the course, the water table hovering just beneath the surface. In these conditions test runs were out of the question. The most Craig could hope for was a single shot at the record—a break in the weather long enough for him to climb into his racer, kick into burner, and go.

It was hailing at dawn the next morning. Craig and the crew headed out to the salt and huddled in the trailer, shivering in winter coats as they drank coffee and played cards and watched the awning sheltering the racer snap in the wind. Up the course at the measured mile, Joe Petrali and his fellow timing officials were camped out in the USAC shack, similarly trying to stay warm as they monitored course conditions.

The wind abated. Petrali got on the field telephone and called down to base camp. *It's calm in the mile*, he said.

Craig decided to go. Nye Frank, looking up at the iron-gray sky, didn't feel good about it. He said, "Are you sure you want to go?" No, Craig didn't want to go. He *had* to go. He said, "I don't have a choice."

The crew got *Sonic I* prepped and Craig climbed into the cockpit. The engine was started. Craig had advanced the throttle to full military power, about to go into burner, when USAC official Ben Torres ran forward waving his arms, signaling him to abort. Word had just come in of strong gusts of wind sweeping across the course in the mile. They had knocked over the markers and damaged the clocks.

Craig killed the engine and got out, deeply frustrated. A minute later the wind hit base camp. It was so powerful that the crew had to take down the awning to keep it from tearing. It was followed by more hail, then more rain. That was it for the first day.

The crew was back on the salt at dawn the next morning, November 15. It was more of the same—overcast sky, gusting wind, drizzling rain. More waiting in the trailer, praying for a break in the weather, *Sonic I* parked nearby under its red-and-white awning. All they needed was an hour, just one lousy hour.

Craig tried to stay focused but it wasn't easy. He knew that his racer wanted to fly and there was nothing he could do about it. The nose was already loaded with weight. The enlarged front wings were already set at the absolute maximum angle for downforce, a whopping 14 degrees. The problem, he now realized, was inherent in the design, starting with the tailfin, which was too high, and continuing with the rear wheels, which were too far forward in the chassis. Up around 600 mph, the drag generated by the tailfin was pulling back on the car high up at the rear while the thrust of the engine was pushing forward down close to the ground. The result, says Craig, "was the car was teeter-tottering over the back wheels and lifting the nose into the air. It was doing a wheelie. I knew now the tailfin was a big problem but we didn't have time to change it. We had to run what we brung."

Eight o'clock. The drizzle subsided. The heavy overcast lightened. Then, like a scene in a religious painting, the clouds opened up and shafts of sunlight broke through.

With rising hope, the crew got *Sonic I* ready at the head of the black line, pointing north. Walt Sheehan got under the car and set the throttle linkage to give Craig a speed of just under 600 mph. If he had to contend with his racer flying and very possibly crashing, Craig wanted to do it on his return run, not on his first. He already had his helmet on. He was pacing around, trying to block out everything extraneous and focus on the task at hand. Concentration on the moment—when you were putting your life on the line, it amounted to the same thing as courage.

The crew waited for word from the USAC shack on the wind. It came at eight thirty. "Joe says it's great in the mile," said Nye Frank, running over. "Let's get it running."

Craig took off his winter coat and climbed into the freezing cold cockpit. He buckled into his harness and snapped his air mask onto his helmet. The J-79 jet engine was started. Craig advanced the throttle to idle, brakes on to lock *Sonic I* in position. Bob Koken took his usual position directly behind the tailpipe and a hundred feet back. He was checking to make sure the pilot light for the afterburner was on. This step had been added to the pre-run checklist after the trouble back in October getting the burner to light.

Bob saw the telltale flicker of flame. He raised his hand high, giving the "OK" sign. Nye, standing in front of the car where Craig could see him, relayed the message with a thumbs-up. Then he held up two fingers for the final two steps: turn on the onboard camera and data recorder.

Craig flicked on the toggle switches and flashed Nye back two fingers. He took his foot off the brake and advanced the throttle to full military power, then on into minimum burner. *Sonic I* took off in a spray of water and salt, flames shooting out the back.

Craig took the full five miles to build up his speed going into the clocks. The mist was now clearing, Floating Mountain visible in the distance, ablaze in an ethereal column of sunlight. The racer's nose became extremely light in the mile but the vibrations coming up through the steering told Craig his front wheels were still on the ground. He was now getting that skating-on-ice feeling, the sense of being just barely in control that he was coming to associate with ultimate speed. It was like "walking out on a limb to see how far you can go without breaking it," he said, "and then retreating just in time."

The limb didn't break. He streaked out of the mile, killed the engine, waited for the appropriate moment, and released the chutes. Hard deceleration. But not hard enough. The canopy collapsed after opening, weighed down by the spray of salt and water coming off the rear wheels. Thankfully, the drag was sufficient to slow him down.

Craig came to a stop at the north end of the course, mile 0. He climbed out and walked around his racer. Extensive wear and tear was visible beneath the salt spatter: in the sandblasted look of the paint, in the bits of white cord showing through black tires, in the dents in the body left by bits of cord flying off. The aluminum skin appeared fundamentally undamaged, however, and the tires had another run left in them. They could withstand titanic forces, even with the thin rubber surface coming off.

The crew was already well into the turnaround when the verdict arrived from Joe Petrali: 593 mph. That was just about perfect. Now came the hard part: making the return run and topping 600 mph without getting killed.

Craig went over to Walt Sheehan. "Walt, give me enough power to go 610. Not a mile an hour faster. This thing is about to fly and I really don't want to take off."

Walt opened up the engine access panel and reset the throttle linkage. He thought about it for a moment and reset it again, then thought some more and reset it a third time.

The weather was holding, whiffs of breeze below the maximum permissible six knots according to USAC observers stationed at mile intervals down the course. Craig, helmet on throughout, squeezed back into the cockpit. He was about to entrust his life once again to a whole lot of people: to the men at Goodyear who had made the tires, to the fabricators who had built the car back in L.A., to the crew out here helping him run it, to Walt Sheehan and his throttle setting, which at the moment was foremost in Craig's mind.

He waved Nye Frank over. "Ask Walt if he really knows what he's doing."

Nye went over to the Lockheed engineer. "The boss wants to know if you know what you're doing."

"I don't have the faintest idea," Walt snapped, trying to rub some warmth back into his fingers. "Just tell him to get ready and make his run and not to worry."

Not to worry? "I was sweating bullets," Craig says.

He was away at nine o'clock on his return run, the turnaround having taken only thirty minutes. He was heading south now, back toward base camp and the flooded part of the desert where he had almost drowned the previous year. It was a rough ride, the racer buffeted about, Craig aware of a sensation like the chassis was flexing.

He was approaching the clocks now, a green speck far up ahead. *Whoosh.* The eight-foot board swept past.

One second . . .

The vibrations coming up through the steering yoke were subsiding. That wasn't good.

Two seconds . . .

The vibrations stopped. The front wheels were no longer touching the ground.

Three seconds . . .

Craig hung on, all steering gone. *Sonic I* was poised for takeoff.

Four seconds . . .

Craig was now deep into the place he dreaded, the psychedelic netherworld of ultimate racing, the unique experience of what he would call "ecstasy mixed with stark terror." It all came down to this moment and his nerve in keeping his foot on the throttle all the way through.

Five seconds . . .

Craig kept his foot pressed to the floor. A red speck in the distance. *Whoosh.* It streaked by in almost the same instant he saw it. He was out of the clocks. He hit the button killing the engine. One. Two. Three. Four. Five. He hit the chute release button. Ten full Gs of deceleration slammed him forward against his harness, so hard his goggles lifted off his face. The world tipped over and he was hurtling straight down a cliff, then it righted itself and he was slowing, slowing. As he neared the end of the course, base camp in view up ahead, the tremendous load of anxiety he had been carrying around began falling away and he remembered something Nye had jokingly said earlier that morning: "How about parking the car in the garage so we don't have to get our feet wet?" No sooner had the thought entered his head than Craig was giddily steering off the course, giving the waiting crew a pang of alarm that he was out of control. He brought *Sonic I* around in a big arc and came to a stop alongside its trailer. "I just wanted to park it in the garage," he said as he climbed out and the celebrations began.

ABOVE LEFT: Craig with his dad, Norm, at their house on Marcasel Avenue. ABOVE RIGHT: Craig with his mom, Portia. BELOW LEFT: Craig (second from right) at the beach with Gene and Roger Rourke (left). BELOW RIGHT: Craig at thirteen, around the time he got into hot rods. *(All courtesy of Craig Breedlove)*

Labels in photo: GARY DAVIS · DENNIS BOWMAN (SHORTY) · STAN GOLDSTEIN · BILL MOORE · MIKE FREEBARIN · BILL TURNER · RICHARD KRAUSE · ROLAND DOVE · CRAIG BOWMAN "BREEDLOVE" · DON WOMACK · ARDEN BLEM

ABOVE: Craig, around age sixteen, at a Bay City Timing Association show in the early 1950s. *(William A. Moore)* BELOW LEFT: Craig looking cool in a leather jacket, age sixteen. *(Cynthia Bowman)* BELOW RIGHT: Craig's high school graduation photo, 1955. *(Craig Breedlove)*

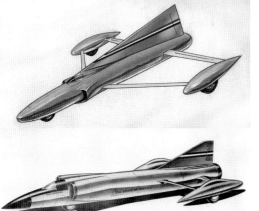

ABOVE: Craig and his first wife Marge at Wendover in the late 1950s, washing his '34 Ford coupe. *(Marge Kastler)* LEFT AND BELOW: Bill Moore's concept drawings showing the evolution of the *Spirit of America* jet car. *(William A. Moore)*

Top: Craig with the belly tank racer he built and raced with the Rourke brothers. Right: One of the flip charts Craig used in his presentation to Shell district manager Bill Lawler. Below: Craig with his original pointy-nose model of *Spirit*, in his dad's garage in front of the wooden mock-up. You can just make out "Firestone" painted on the mock-up's front wheel. *(All Craig Breedlove)*

COST TO COMPLETE/OPERATE

CHASSIS & BODY		SUPPORT EQUIPMENT		PER DAY - RECORD RUNS	
SEAT	50.	FIRE EQUIP.	60.	8 MEN $45 PER DAY	360.
CONTROLS	60.	AC POWER SUPPLY	350.	PARACHUTE EXPLOSIVES	25.
WINDSHIELD	30.	DC POWER SUPPLY	250.	AMBULANCE SERVICE	150.
CANOPY GLASS	80.	PUMPS	150.	TIMING CHARGES	200.
HIGH SPEED CONTROL	100.	LIGHTS	300.	MISC.	65.
LOW SPEED CONTROL	400.	PLATFORMS	100.	TOTAL $	800.°°
DECELERATION SYSTEM	600.	TENT	50.		
REAR SUSPENSION	150.	VAN	500.		
FRONT SUSPENSION	200.	TRAILER	1,000.		
BODY SUPPORTS	50.	SPARE ENGINE	1,500.	GRAND TOTALS	
PARACHUTE FAIRINGS	200.	AFTER BURNER	300.	CHASSIS & BODY ~ $ 9,870.00	
BODY FORMING	2500.	TOTAL $ 4,560.°°		SUPPORT EQUIP. ~ $ 4,560.00	
RACING WHEELS	4,000.	LABOR		LABOR ——— $ 15,800.00	
TRANSPORT TIRES	250.	THREE MEN @ 3./HR.	10,800.	$ 30,230.00	
FUEL TANKS	400.	ENGINEERING	5,000.		
PAINT	100.	TOTAL $ 15,800.°°			
TOTAL $ 9,870.°°					

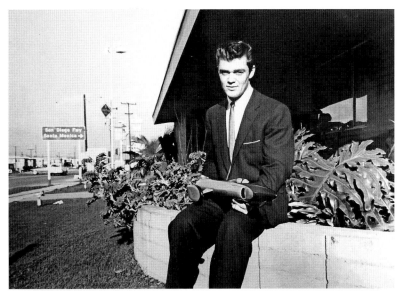

ABOVE: Craig with his *Spirit* model in front of Lawler's office after getting sponsorship from Shell. LEFT: *Spirit* being moved from the garage, en route to Quin Epperley's shop for completion, Craig in the foreground. *(Both Craig Breedlove)* BELOW: *Spirit of America*, 1962. *(Photo by Tom Carroll, courtesy of Bob Davids)*

August 1962. Top Left: *Spirit* arriving in Wendover. Top Right: Testing the engine at Wendover Air Force Base. Above Left: Arriving on the salt. Above Right: Base camp. Below Left: Craig and his second wife, Lee. Below Right: Nye Frank. Bottom left: Craig and *Spirit* on the salt. Bottom Right: Craig in the cockpit.

(All photos by Tom Carroll, courtesy of Bob Davids)

ABOVE: Craig with Rod Schapel, August 1963. *(Craig Breedlove)* LEFT: Stills from the film *Spirit of America* of Craig setting his first record, 407.447 mph, on August 5, 1963. *(Goodyear Tire and Rubber)* BELOW: Craig in front of the Bonneville sign, where the crew has painted over John Cobb's speed with Craig's fastest pass of 428.37 mph. *(Craig Breedlove)*

ABOVE: Craig in 1963, after setting the record. Beside him (left to right): wife Lee, mother Portia, stepdad Ken Bowman, half sister Cynthia. RIGHT AND BELOW: Craig and his *Spirit II* dragster, 1964. *(All Craig Breedlove)*

ABOVE: Craig releases his chute coming out of the mile, October 13, 1964. It's a new record: 468.719 mph. LEFT: Art Russell repairs the canopy after Craig's helmet smashed through the glass, Quin Epperley (left) looking on. BELOW: Craig and his dad Norm.

(All Craig Breedlove)

ABOVE: Craig and land speed rival Art Arfons. *(William A. Moore)*
RIGHT: Craig in the cockpit, a seat cushion shading him from the sun.
BELOW: Craig and *Spirit* on the salt, October 1964. *(Both Craig Breedlove)*

ABOVE: *Spirit's* tracks after careening off course, October 15, 1964. *(Craig Breedlove)* LEFT AND BELOW: Stills from the film *The Wildest Ride*: footage captured by *Spirit's* onboard camera (left); Craig hugs Bill Moore after his lucky escape (below); everyone laughing about it afterward—except Norm Breedlove, still visibly shaken (bottom). Craig's new record: 526.277 mph. *(Goodyear Tire and Rubber)*

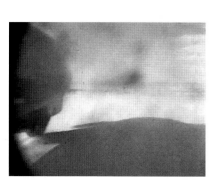

ABOVE: *Spirit* is hauled out of the brine pond, Craig in the foreground, Nye Frank in T-shirt on right. BELOW: *Spirit*, its tail removed, sits on dry land. *(Both Craig Breedlove)*

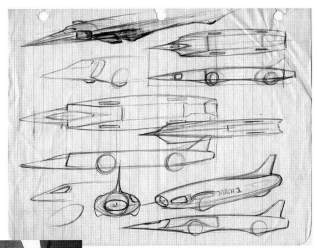

Above: Craig's rough sketches for possible *Sonic I* designs. *(William A. Moore)* Left: *Sonic I* under construction, Craig trying out the cockpit space, Nye Frank looking on. Below: *Sonic I* fabrication in the warehouse in Watts, Nye (right), Bob Davids (left). *(Both Craig Breedlove)*

ABOVE: *Sonic I* in pristine condition on the salt, October 1965. *(Craig Breedlove)*
RIGHT: Blastoff! *Sonic I* going into afterburner. *(Goodyear Tire and Rubber)*
BELOW: Craig in the cockpit. *(Bob Davids)*

ABOVE: *Sonic I* base camp, October 1965. *(Bob Davids)* LEFT: Craig with Walt Sheehan. BELOW: November 15, 1965. Craig goes 600.601 mph to reclaim the record. Note the louvers cut in the body, the flanges attached to the side, and the repair work around the air duct. *(Both Craig Breedlove)*

ABOVE: Celebrating the 600.601 mph record, November 15, 1965. RIGHT: An ad soliciting bookings for *Sonic I*, 1966. BELOW: Bill Moore concept drawing of the turbo car Craig designed for the 1968 Indianapolis 500. (*All Craig Breedlove*)

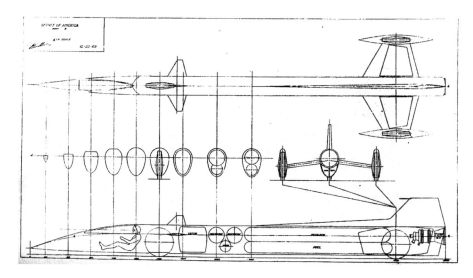

ABOVE: Craig's design for a land speed rocket car, *Sonic II*, dated December 22, 1969. LEFT AND BELOW: Craig with his rocket dragster in its English Leather paint job, 1973. *(All Craig Breedlove)*

ABOVE: Craig and his third wife, Peggy, 1974. RIGHT: Mock-up of the *Spirit of America* rocket car, parked in Craig's shop in the 1980s. BELOW: Craig and his son Norman pose with the rocket car mock-up in front of the *Queen Mary*, 1980s. *(All Craig Breedlove)*

ABOVE: Craig and his family at Norman's high school graduation, 1977. Left to right: Dawn, Norman, Marge, Craig, and Chris. *(Marge Kastler)* LEFT: Craig and land speed rival Art Arfons, 1990. *(Tina Trefethen)* BELOW: Craig at his drafting table in Rio Vista, designing *Sonic Arrow*, early 1990s. *(Craig Breedlove)*

ABOVE: Craig with a model of *Sonic Arrow* in front of the real thing under construction, early 1990s. RIGHT: *Sonic Arrow* team logo. *(Both Craig Breedlove)* BELOW: Craig poses in laminate cockpit capsule with fabricators Tina and Tom Trefethen. *(Tina Trefethen)*

WORLD SPEED • RECORD TEAM
SPIRIT OF AMERICA
CRAIG BREEDLOVE
USA RIO VISTA, CA.
ARE YOU READY TO RUMBLE!

LEFT: Craig testing his "Fred Flintstone" ski brake at Black Rock. *(Craig Breedlove)* BELOW: *Sonic Arrow* arrives at Bonneville for testing, September 1996. Background left to right: Kevin Binkert (in sunglasses), Alyson Kimball, Marilyn Breedlove, Dennis Craig, and Dezsö Molnar (in sunglasses). Foreground left to right: Harry Weiser, Ely Plaughter, and Craig. *(Chuck Lyford)* BOTTOM: *Sonic Arrow* on the salt, Craig in the cockpit, a film crew and Dezsö Molnar (in Shell shirt) looking on. *(Chris Rossi)*

ABOVE: Craig in *Sonic Arrow* at Bonneville, September 1996. *(Chris Rossi)* RIGHT: Craig at Black Rock in October 1996 with his grandchildren Thomas and Leona, his dog Muffin behind. *(Craig Breedlove)* BELOW: Craig suited up at Black Rock, October 1996. *(Chuck Lyford)*

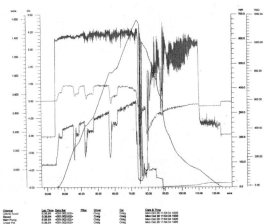

ABOVE: *Sonic Arrow* at Black Rock, October 23, 1996. *(Chuck Lyford)* LEFT: Onboard data recorder printout from Craig's crash, October 28, 1996. The inverted *V* is Craig's speed, peaking at 675 mph. *(Craig Breedlove)* BELOW: Craig and Dezsö Molnar (right) congratulate Andy Green (left) on becoming the first to reach Mach 1, October 15, 1997. *(Chuck Lyford)*

LEFT: Craig with his current wife, Yadira. *(Craig Breedlove)* BELOW: Craig at his drafting table in 2016 with plans for his latest extreme machine, a land speed rocket car. *(Samuel Hawley)* BOTTOM: Model of Craig's twin-engine jet car. *(Model photo by Craig Breedlove, composite image by Samuel Hawley)*

Craig knew he had the record. The needle on the speedometer had been comfortably over 600 through the mile on his return. But had he gone fast enough to get 600 on the two-way? If he hadn't, he might be running again.

He waited. Nye and the others straggled into base camp from the north end of the course. Finally Joe Petrali arrived. He handed Craig a piece of paper with "600.601" penciled on it. Craig's heart sank, for with his first run of 593 this gave him a two-way average only in the high 590s. Then, seeing Petrali's funny look, he wasn't so sure.

"Joe, is this the run speed or the average?"

Petrali broke into a smile and handed over a second piece of paper. This one said "608.211." The 600.601 was Craig's two-way average and official new mark. He had just broken the land speed record for the fifth time and become the first person to drive faster than 400, 500, and now 600 mph.

Craig started laughing. Pure delight. "I'm so happy I could kiss you, Joe," he exulted, giving Petrali a bear hug. "Man, this is a thousand times better than 599!"

Craig stopped off in Las Vegas on his way home from the salt flats to exhibit *Sonic I* for a few days at the Stardust Casino. Muhammad Ali, then still going by the name Cassius Clay, was there as well, training for his upcoming title defense against Floyd Patterson, and welcomed Craig into his entourage. "Ali and his trainer Angelo Dundee really took me right in," says Craig. "The biggest thing for me, though, was that Joe Louis was there too. When I was growing up, I remember going across the street to the Rourkes' to listen to Louis fight Billy Caan. Joe Louis was a big thing for me back then.

"So I was at dinner with these guys and I was talking to Joe Louis, and something came up and I said, 'Well, I hold the world speed record.' And he said, 'I know who you are. You set the 600 mph record. I've read all about you.'"

For Craig, it couldn't get any better than this. His childhood hero Joe Louis—*Joe Louis!*—knew who he was.

15

CUTTHROAT

CRAIG WAS EXHAUSTED WHEN HE GOT BACK HOME TO L.A. He badly needed a break but couldn't afford to take one. He had to make the most of his 600 mph record while *Sonic I* was still a hot item and he still had possession of the car.

At least his future seemed secure. The performance bonuses he had coming from sponsors totaled more than $100,000. After seeing most of his newfound wealth slip away the previous year, Craig was anxious to put the money into something substantial, something that would set him up for the rest of his life. He was therefore excited when Bob Lane invited him home for dinner during a visit to Akron and presented him with the opportunity to invest in a Goodyear franchise store.

"I was not very knowledgeable businesswise," he says, looking back. "My attorney at the time told me, 'Craig, the thing with franchises is, they get people into these stores to pay all the start-up costs, because the store doesn't make money for two, three, four years, not until you've built a clientele.' But I said, 'I don't think Goodyear is going to screw me on this. A. J. Foyt and Roger McCluskey have Goodyear stores, and Parnelli Jones has like twenty Firestone stores, and they're doing well.' I was optimistic." Craig agreed to have his Goodyear bonus, the lion's share of his record money, put into escrow to fund the start-up for his very own Goodyear store.

In the meantime *Sonic I* was cleaned up and repainted and a tractor-trailer was customized to take it on tour, GOODYEAR and SPIRIT OF AMERICA emblazoned on the sides. And on the back, as a little joke to folks on the highway, YOU ARE NOW PASSING THE WORLD'S FASTEST CAR! Craig had already received several requests from around the country to exhibit the car, most notably at the New York International Automobile Show, and expected many more bookings from Goodyear—bookings for which the company had contracted to pay him commercial trucking rates. This was where Craig expected to really clean up. When he met with Bob Lane to work out a touring schedule, however, everything changed.

"We don't want to use the car," Lane told him.

"You don't want it? But we had an agreement."

"Well, we've decided we're not going to tour it around."

"But I already bought a truck and have it all painted. I've paid for the whole thing."

Lane just shrugged. "We don't want it. That's it."

Craig knew exactly what this was about. It was tit for tat from Lane for Craig's refusal to put Goodyear's name on *Sonic I*'s tail. He had thought doing the 600 mph record for free had put things right with Lane. Apparently it hadn't.

"Well," he said, "I'm just going to have to leave the car at home then, because I can't afford to leave it idle and pay a driver to just sit around between car shows. I won't make any profit."

"So, your problem is that you need something to pay your costs between the shows you have booked, right?"

"Well, yeah. It's not profitable otherwise."

Lane moved in for the kill. "OK, I'll tell you what. We will use the car at your cost. We'll reimburse you for gas, for your driver's salary, and out-of-pocket expenses. That way you won't lose any money. How's that?"

Thinking about that meeting today still makes Craig burn. "I had literally risked my life for Goodyear to get the record. They were running all these ads and would be the big benefactor for all these shows, and Lane just screwed me. I've never seen a guy so nuts."

Craig, with another lesson under his belt in how ruthless big business could be, hired George Klass to drive the truck and sent him on tour with *Sonic I*. "I left on New Year's Eve to go to Connecticut, the first place we were having a show," George remembers. "From that point on I was pretty much on my own until I guess about May, crisscrossing the country. Craig would show up at the important gigs where they paid him to be there, but they didn't always do that because I think we were trying to get a thousand a day to have him appear. It seemed like a lot in those days."

Around the time *Sonic I* was being exhibited at the Des Moines Car Show in the middle of March, Craig received a notice informing him that he was being sued by Rod Schapel. "I think the publicity from the 600 mph record was what encouraged Rod to sue me. I guess he thought there was a big pile of money to go after. What he sued me for was the time he had put into the car in 1961 and '62, prior to us getting sponsored. Once we got sponsored he was paid very well. But initially, when we did the wind tunnel tests and what have you, Rod volunteered his time, like everyone else.

"His lawsuit was for $30,000 for the actual work he had done, plus 30 percent of my income for the rest of my life, retroactive from the first record I set in August 1963. The 30 percent was based on the theory that I would never have been smart enough to design the *Sonic I* car without the things he had taught me, without his mentoring on the three-wheeler, which is probably true. But I mean, everybody goes to school, everybody learns from somebody."

Craig would subsequently discover that Rod had tried to get Walt Sheehan to join him in a suit. Walt refused and urged Rod to drop the whole thing. "I thought the idea was so dumb that he just forgot about it," Craig remembers Walt saying. Rod hadn't. He hired a lawyer and went ahead on his own.

The trial took place in Los Angeles in August 1966. Craig's attorney Lowell Dryden mounted a vigorous defense, eliciting testimony from a number of former *Spirit of America* team members that they had knowingly participated in the project as volunteers, without any expectation of payment. "I said that I wasn't promised any money," says Art Russell, "and that as far as I knew nobody else was either. I wasn't paid anything until Shell and Goodyear came into it. Everybody was just helping on a volunteer basis." The most telling moment, however, came when Rod Schapel took the stand and Dryden started grilling him over his employment records subpoenaed from Task Corporation. "There were just huge conflicts," says Craig, "where Rod was saying he was working for us and he was actually working at Task. When the jury saw that he had falsified the time he was claiming to have put into the car, he was a dead Indian."

Schapel lost the suit. He would remain bitter about it for the rest of his life. Craig, looking back on the experience, is philosophical today. "Rod and I had our differences but I still respect him. I care for all of the things he brought to me and the mentoring he gave me. He was a really smart guy and an important person in my life. Yeah, he sued me, but that was ego shit. He even told me in later years, 'That was the worst thing I ever did.' He was just a very strong-minded guy."

The Rod Schapel lawsuit left Craig emotionally and physically exhausted. He was therefore grateful for an invitation from Goodyear to attend Nassau Speed Week later that year. A weeklong getaway in the sun was just what he needed. It would also be a chance to reconnect with Lee and hopefully shore up their marriage.

It was at a dinner at the Nassau Beach Lodge that Craig stumbled on the next opportunity he would pursue. It came from Carroll Shelby, one of Craig's racing heroes from his days working under Sam Hanks at Bill Murphy Buick. Shelby was seated at the table next to Goodyear racing division head Tony Webner. And he was complaining. "I don't know why you guys are going into that drag racin' stuff," Craig remembers him saying in his Texan drawl. "I don't want to handle those drag racin' tires and deal with those drag racin' people." Goodyear's entry into the drag tire market meant that Shelby, the company's western distributor, would be put to a lot of extra trouble for what he expected to be minimal return. "This drag tire thing," he kept on, "means I'm going to have to spend money to stock all these shitty new drag tires and I'll have to send a truck to the damn drag races. I just don't need the hassle."

Goodyear's recently developed drag slicks were indeed shitty, as Craig well knew. He had tested them on his *Spirit II* dragster in 1964 and found them nowhere near as good as the M&H Racemaster slicks then dominating the market. But he also recognized a ground-floor opening in Shelby's earthy complaint.

"Carroll," he said, "I'd love to take care of the drag tire business . . . that is, if you don't want it."

Shelby liked the idea of unloading the unprofitable sideline. He turned to Webner. "What do you think, Tony? Could we work out a deal with Craig to handle the drag tires?"

That's how Craig became Goodyear's exclusive drag tire distributor for the Western USA, eleven states, operating under Carroll Shelby. He would order tires directly from Goodyear, do all the work of developing the business in return for two-thirds of the 30 percent markup, and kick the remaining 10 percent back to Shelby. Shelby wouldn't even have to look at a drag tire, just cash the checks.

Craig pulled Nye Frank and George Klass into the venture and got down to work in his new fifteen-thousand-square-foot, two-building shop in the L.A. neighborhood of Torrance. They bought a tire profiling machine and began an exhaustive program of testing, identifying which compounds, rubber hardnesses, contours, and tread patterns were most effective. Working from these results, Goodyear turned out a whole series of experimental new tires that Craig then gave to his drag racing friends to test in competition, coding each tire with little brown dots so that performance could be tracked. The result was a vastly improved slick.

In early 1967 Craig talked Connie Kalitta into using a pair of the new tires on his *Bounty Hunter* dragster in the NHRA national championships. Kalitta won. After that the racing world began to take notice. Other prominent drivers started using and winning on

Craig's "brown dot" slicks and the business took off. "All of a sudden," Craig says, "we were selling *hundreds* of these tires a month to the top cars all over the place. Nye Frank and I had brought them to a level of quality where we took over the entire drag racing industry for Goodyear."

Carroll Shelby was noticing too. The bothersome little sideline he had been glad to get rid of was turning into a moneymaker—and he was getting only 10 percent of the action.

"So Shelby wanted the whole thing back," Craig continues, "because it was a gold mine. He told Goodyear—he wouldn't talk to me, that relationship was suddenly dissolved—he told Tony Webner he wanted the drag tires back, that he was the contracted distributor of the tires so they had to go through him, they couldn't send them directly to me. So that meant the tires would be shipped to Shelby from Goodyear and I'd have to order from him.

"I never saw another Goodyear drag tire after that. I tried placing orders through Shelby but they were always 'out of stock.' All the money and all the effort, you can't believe all the effort—we had a truck all set up to go to the drag races and do the servicing on the tires, we went to all the major meets—all of it was gone. We just had to shut down. Shelby put me out of business. He was actually kind of notorious for that. He was a sharp, tough business guy and would take advantage of any situation. That's how he built his empire. I was younger and more naive—and boy, he sure took advantage of me."

At the same time that Craig was building up his drag tire business and watching the construction of his Goodyear store in Torrance, he was also pursuing a renewed interest in Indy car racing. It went back to early 1963, when he had been sitting in Quin Epperly's shop with Parnelli Jones, contemplating the car nicknamed "Old Calhoun" that Parnelli drove for J. C. Agajanian. Parnelli asked Craig if he had any ideas how they could make the racer go faster that wouldn't cost much. "Because Aggie wouldn't spend any money," says Craig with a laugh. "He was cheaper than shit.

"So I said, 'Well, we could build a duct in the top of the nose for ram air, tunnel that air back to the fuel injectors, and build a plenum box over the injectors to pressurize the whole thing. That would give you some boost on the straightaways. We could also make some little fairings to go over the torsion bars where they're all sticking out of the nose. And the oil tank, we could slim it out and make it longer and more streamlined.'

"So we went around the car with stuff like that and did all these modifications to Old Calhoun. And Parnelli took that car to Indy, it was just an average runner basically, and he put it on the pole, broke the 150 barrier, and led the damn race almost from start to finish and won it. And that was just because we clipped on some cheap shit, made the thing a little more streamlined. That was an era when that stuff was just starting to catch on."

His behind-the-scenes contribution to Parnelli's victory led Craig to realize that he had something meaningful to offer to Indy, not just as a driver but as a designer and builder. This was very much in his mind when he agreed to drive for Lindsey Hopkins in 1964. That plan fell apart when Hopkins's driver Bobby Marshman was killed just weeks before he was to start training Craig. Craig's Indy dream went into limbo after that, then was rekindled by the sight of Parnelli Jones tearing away from the competition at the Indianapolis 500 in May 1967. Parnelli was driving an Andy Granatelli–owned racer powered by a turbine engine like the one in Donald Campbell's *Bluebird*. It was a variation of the jet engine that Craig used in his land speed racers, sucking air into a compression chamber and igniting it with fuel to generate power. The difference was that instead of this power being blasted out the back as thrust, it was used to drive a turbine wheel connected to a driveshaft that rotated the wheels. The result was more juice than any other car on the track—so much that on the straightaways Parnelli was whooshing past the competition at will. He was on his way to a shockingly easy victory, three laps from the finish, when the failure of a transmission bearing sent him coasting into the pits.

Right then and there, watching Parnelli burn up the track, Craig knew what he would do next. He would design and build his own turbine car and drive it himself at next year's Indianapolis 500. It made perfect sense, for with his jet car background he knew more about turbine engines than just about anyone at Indy. "Craig Breedlove, car builder and star driver" would also make an irresistible marketing package.

Craig spent the summer of 1967 designing a car and acquiring a pair of General Electric T-58 turbine engines used in helicopters, 1,250-horsepower monsters that would blow the competition away. He then landed a sponsorship deal with ceramic turbine blade manufacturer Fansteel to build two cars, one for Craig and a backup to be driven by Danny Ongais. The deal was that Fansteel would give Craig the use of its manufacturing facilities and shoulder the cost of building the cars, but not front any cash. Craig would have to find a secondary sponsor for that, one to pay him a salary and cover the cost of testing and running at Indy. That suited Craig fine, for this was where Goodyear came in. Goodyear was sure to jump at the chance of backing a racer to go against the Granatelli-Jones turbine car, which ran on Firestone tires.

Craig bypassed Bob Lane this time—he never wanted to deal with Lane again as long as he lived—and submitted his proposal to Larry Truesdale, head of Goodyear's racing division. Then he waited. And waited. Finally he phoned Truesdale to ask if a decision had been made. They still hadn't heard anything from Goodyear president Vic Holt, Truesdale told him. Craig waited some more, then tried Truesdale again. Still no decision from Holt, Truesdale said.

The news then broke that Goodyear was sponsoring Carroll Shelby for a turbine car to the tune of $1.7 million. *OK*, Craig thought, *this can still work.* Goodyear will want to hedge its turbine car bet just like it did in land speed racing by sponsoring both *Spirit of America* and Walt Arfons's *Wingfoot*. All he needed was a couple hundred thousand dollars, peanuts compared to what the company was giving to Shelby. He was therefore hopeful when he phoned Truesdale yet again. Truesdale, however, gave him the same excuse. Craig's proposal was still parked on Holt's desk.

Craig was still waiting on a decision from Goodyear when USAC announced that it was restricting the air inlet size on turbines. It was an unprecedented step, flouting USAC's long-standing practice of giving three years' notice before imposing any new restriction on engines. The intent was obviously to prevent turbines from running away with the game by limiting their oxygen supply and thus their performance. To Craig's amazement, however, the wording of the rule left a gigantic loophole: it specified only the maximum dimensions of the visible exterior compressor case and totally overlooked the inner workings of the engine.

Craig talked the rule over with his friend Ken Wallis, who had been previously employed by Andy Granatelli to build Parnelli Jones's turbine car and was now building Carroll Shelby's racer. Ken had seen the loophole too and shared his delight. All they had to do was make a relatively small change to their engines and they would be in full compliance with USAC.

Not so fast, Walt Sheehan said when Craig excitedly told him his plans. Check with USAC first before you go to the effort and expense of building a car, he cautioned. Otherwise they might say you can't run.

Craig phoned up USAC and was put in touch with one of their turbine engine experts. "I have two T-58s," he said, "and I want to comply with the new turbine inlet size rule. What I plan to do is machine the outside tip diameter of the first moving stage of the compressor down to 15½ inches."

"OK, that sounds fine," came the reply.

"So you understand that I'm making no further modifications to these engines."

"Yeah, sounds fine."

"No further modifications whatsoever."

"Yep . . . oh, wait a minute, what about the . . ." A pause. Then: "Oh shit. OK, so we're going to have to rewrite the rule."

"But you can't just rewrite the rule," said Craig. "Rules can't be changed for at least a year after they're passed. That's right in USAC's own bylaws."

USAC rewrote the rule.

Ken Wallis was upset with Craig when he found out what happened but admitted that it was for the best, that USAC probably would have just shut them down later on.

"I guess that pretty well kills the whole deal," Craig sighed.

"Well, not really," said Ken.

Craig gave him a questioning look.

Ken smiled. "You cheat." He showed Craig a sketch of what he had in mind, a secret chamber hidden behind a sliding panel to increase airflow.

"Too obvious," Craig said. "You'll get busted. With all the publicity these cars are getting they'll be going over them with a fine-tooth comb."

Ken didn't think so. "USAC doesn't know what the hell they're doing. They don't know a damn thing about turbines."

Craig kept mulling over the problem back at his shop, contemplating one of his T-58 engines. If he were to cheat, how would he do it? What would be a smart way to—

That's when it hit him, an undetectable way to increase airflow and return the turbine to full power. And USAC wouldn't spot it in a million years.

Craig returned to Ken Wallis's shop with his idea. "Jesus," Ken marveled, perusing Craig's sketch. "This is beautiful. Fantastic." There, hidden inside the starter motor, was a hydraulic cylinder actuated by the engine's oil pressure. It remained retracted when the engine was running below 80 percent RPMs, everything in perfect compliance. Above 80 percent, however, the cylinder began to extend, moving the air inlet restriction fairing forward, opening it up to restore the engine to full power.

Fansteel by this time was starting to get anxious about its sponsorship deal with Craig. What was taking him so long to settle things with Goodyear and get started on building? When Craig expressed his frustration to Ken, saying that his proposal had been sitting on Vic Holt's desk for months, Ken shocked him by explaining the likely reason. "Your proposal never had a chance," he said. "You weren't paying anybody."

"What do you mean, 'I wasn't paying anybody'?"

"Look, I have a deal to build these turbine cars for Carroll Shelby, right? So Shelby gets $1.7 million from Goodyear, he keeps $300,000 for putting the deal together and he pays me $1.2 million to build them."

"OK . . . so what happened to the other $200,000?"

"It went back to the people at Goodyear. That's how these deals work."

Craig was dumbfounded. He had never given a kickback. All his business dealings so far had been aboveboard.

He got on the phone to Goodyear and this time asked to speak with President Vic Holt directly. It was just as Ken had said. Holt had never seen Craig's proposal and knew nothing of his turbine car project. When Craig flew to Akron for a personal meeting, Holt called Truesdale into his office and demanded an explanation. "We-we-we got the Shelby deal," Craig remembers Truesdale stammering to his boss, deeply embarrassed. "We-we just can't do Craig's thing and Shelby's thing at the same time. Look, I'll take care of Craig. We'll work something out."

Craig remembers Truesdale being furious with him after leaving Holt's office. "He was going down the hall hunched over and holding his head and saying, 'Jesus Christ! Why did you call Vic Holt? Why? Why?' Anyway, he took me downstairs and offered me a brand-new Dan Gurney Eagle with a Ford turbocharged engine. It was a phenomenal thing, a free car to go to Indy with, but it cut out my turbine car."

Craig had his heart set on a cutting-edge turbine car to revolutionize Indy. He therefore declined, opting instead to pursue an offer he had received from Ken Wallis's former boss, Andy Granatelli, who had been calling him almost weekly. Granatelli promised to build Craig a turbine car to his specifications, a car that he would not just drive at Indy—on Firestone tires—but actually own. He would also get him a full sponsorship package with his company, STP. All Craig had to do in return was reveal the USAC rule-busting secret he had figured out.

"OK," said Craig, seated in Granatelli's Chicago office, "if I reveal how to do this thing, I get my own turbine car and STP is going to sponsor me, right?"

"Absolutely," Granatelli assured him. "That's the deal. But first you need to tell me just how you plan on doing it."

"OK," said Craig, laying his cards on the table. "There are two ways of doing this. One is legal and one is illegal." He first sketched out a legal way he had come up with to optimize a turbine. It involved using ram air to increase airflow and installing Fansteel's ceramic turbine blades so the engine could be run hotter. It wouldn't return an air inlet–restricted T-58 to anything like full power but it would make it very competitive alongside turbo Fords.

"OK, that's interesting," said Granatelli. "We can use this with our Pratt & Whitney turbine. But what about the illegal way? Is anybody going to be able to spot it?"

"No. It's virtually undetectable."

"OK, show me."

Craig did. Granatelli soaked it all in. "This is phenomenal," he said. "But Ken Wallis is a smart guy. He's going to figure it out. He'll know something's up."

Craig shook his head. "You don't have to worry about Ken. I already showed this to him. He's doing the exact same thing."

"You're sure?"

"Yeah, I'm sure. This is what he's doing."

"Well, I'm going to need some proof." Granatelli thought for a bit. "OK, what I want you to do is go over to Ken's shop and take some photographs and—"

"Whoa, you want me to take spy photos? Come on, that wasn't part of the deal." Craig's heart was already sinking. If Granatelli was willing to engage in espionage against his former racing partner, there was no way he was going to play straight with Craig.

"Well," said Granatelli, settling back in his chair, "I guess I'll have to think this over."

Craig left the office knowing he would never get a turbine car or STP sponsorship out of Andy Granatelli. "Craig is too open and trusting," his business manager Lynn Garrison would say a couple years later. Life at the heights of motor racing was just too cutthroat for him.

———————

That was the end of Craig's turbine car dream but not quite the end of the story. The final chapter began in the lead-up to the 1968 Indy, when he was invited to the unveiling of the new turbine racers that Ken Wallis had built for Carroll Shelby. The hoods were up and he had a good look at the T-58 engines and wistfully recognized his inlet design. Ken and the Shelby team had indeed gone the illegal route, as Craig knew they would, using his hidden hydraulic cylinder to increase airflow.

Practice runs commenced at the Brickyard. Craig followed the action in the news and was struck by something: Andy Granatelli's cars weren't using T-58s, the engine for which Craig had developed the illegal modification. They were running smaller Pratt & Whitneys, the same turbine engine they had used the previous year. Now, why would a tricky son of a bitch like Granatelli have passed up a completely undetectable way to—

A terrible thought suddenly occurred to Craig. Granatelli had gone the legal route, optimizing his Pratt & Whitneys with ram air and ceramic blades to run hotter, because he knew that Shelby's T-58s were illegal. He knew exactly where to point the finger. He was going to rat Shelby out!

Craig struggled with this realization for two weeks. "I'm thinking, *Oh man, this is going to be really bad.*" He didn't want to see Ken Wallis exposed or Carroll Shelby hurt. Shelby had screwed him out of the drag tire business but Craig still looked up to him as a racing hero. Besides, he probably didn't even know the engines were illegal. "I think Ken probably held it to his vest." Craig didn't want Goodyear hurt either. The company had been good to him. It had helped make him, Bob Lane and everything else notwithstanding.

He ended up calling Larry Truesdale at his Indianapolis hotel—Larry who had spent a fortune of Goodyear's money on Shelby. "You've got a big problem brewing out there," he said. "Are you sitting down?"

"Yeah," Truesdale replied warily. "I'm sitting on the bed. Why?"

"Are you aware that the engines in your turbine cars are illegal?"

A long silence from Truesdale. "There've been some rumors, mostly out of Granatelli's camp. But we spoke to Ken Wallis and he's assured us everything is OK."

"Well, they're illegal. Granatelli knows it too."

Truesdale put the phone down and got Phil Remington, Shelby's top mechanic. He came back on the line a few minutes later. "OK, tell Phil what's been done to those engines."

Craig explained. Phil said, "The garage is locked up right now but we have a key. I'll go over there and tear down the front of the engine and see what's inside."

Carroll Shelby pulled his turbine cars out of the Indianapolis 500 the next day, citing safety concerns in the wake of the death of Granatelli backup driver Mike Spence during practice. One of Granatelli's two remaining turbine cars went on to qualify for the pole position and led for much of the race, only to be knocked out by a blown fuel pump in the final few laps. USAC subsequently imposed further restrictions on turbine engines and eventually banned them altogether.

———————

Craig's Indy disappointment and the loss of his drag tire business were not the only knocks he experienced in what was becoming a rough year. Up next was the failure of his Goodyear store. It had opened the previous fall in Torrance on the Pacific Coast Highway, a sparkling new business consisting of multiple servicing bays and an attached retail outlet selling Goodyear tires and automotive products. Craig proudly cut the ribbon as the mayor of Torrance and a bevy of Goodyear executives looked on. The doors were thrown open . . . and the place started losing money. The problem was that Craig's franchise agreement committed him to buying his merchandise exclusively from Goodyear at hefty wholesale prices that made it impossible to compete. It wasn't just the inherent constraints of a franchise business. Craig believes he was purposefully set up by Bob Lane to fail.

"I remember talking to Parnelli Jones about what was going on. He said, 'Craig, if I needed help, Firestone would send me literally boxcars full of tires and *give* them to me to get me through. Anything it took. I just can't believe Goodyear is doing this to you.' And I said, 'Well, I guess I learned my lesson.' The thing was, there were a number of Goodyear outlets in the area that were independently owned, not franchise dealerships like mine, and they were selling product cheaper than the wholesale price I was paying to Goodyear. So after I'd been in business for twelve months, they'd gone through all the money I had coming for setting the record. So they took the store over and kicked me out."

That was the end of Craig's Goodyear franchise and most of his money. "I was broke," he says. "They cleaned me out."

In fact he still had more to lose. He was about to sink even deeper into hard times.

16

HARD TIMES

CRAIG STILL HELD THE LAND SPEED RECORD. He ruled the ultimate speed game in the late 1960s. Unfortunately, it was a game that was no longer played. Art Arfons, his sole remaining competitor, had dropped out.

Art made his last bid to recapture the title in November 1966, *Green Monster* now equipped with double rear wheels to withstand the tremendous downforce of the engine and hopefully prevent another blowout. "When I heard about what he was doing," Craig would write, "I knew that my record wasn't in jeopardy because the extra wheels were to be *exposed*. I was confident that they would add so much air drag that the car wouldn't even go as fast as before." This time Art didn't suffer a rear tire blowout. Instead a front wheel bearing seized up, the wheel tore off, and *Monster* cartwheeled to oblivion at 600 mph, scattering wreckage over four miles of salt. The scene, remembers Firestone's Humpy Wheeler, "was like an airplane wreck. You could see the engine, because it was the biggest part of the car. But the rest of it . . . the car had disintegrated. There was sheet metal and tires all over, a piece here, a piece there. We were looking over a long piece of real estate trying to find where everything was."

It was the fastest crash in motorsport history. Unsurvivable. Yet Art somehow survived. He was back home that weekend, enjoying Thanksgiving dinner with his family and watching football on TV, the only lingering effect scratched corneas from the salt blasted into his eyes.

Art would build a new *Green Monster* the following year but Firestone, shaken by the crash, declined to sponsor it. The company wanted nothing more to do with the land speed record. The field was thus conceded to Goodyear and Craig with their record of 600.601 mph.

So that was the end. Craig was out of the LSR business. Goodyear assured him of sponsorship for a new supersonic jet car if his record was ever broken, but until that happened he was expected to rest on his laurels. "Any time we want to publicize or talk about the land speed record," said company PR man Bill Newkirk, "we can do it already. Why do we need a new record?" George Klass puts it this way: "When Craig set his last record, Goodyear ran these full-page ads in magazines like *Life* and *Look* that said, 'We test our tires at 600 so yours will be safe at 60.' What are they going to do with a new record, say: 'We test our tires at 630 so yours will be safe at 63'? I mean, it's just pragmatic. The idea of going 630 mph or whatever had no benefit to them."

With the LSR not a viable pursuit for the time being, Craig turned to the water speed record (WSR), designing a twin-engine jet boat called *Aqua America* in early 1966. In the end he was unable to attract sufficient sponsorship to get the craft built. It was perhaps just as well, for going after the speed mark on water was incredibly risky. It had claimed the life of John Cobb in 1952, and in January 1967 it took Donald Campbell, his jet boat *Bluebird K7* flipping at 300 mph as he attempted to break his own record. Campbell's death hit Craig hard, for they had become good friends. Lee Taylor, after recovering from his own near-fatal crash, went on to break Campbell's WSR later that year in June, bringing it back to the United States for the first time in fifteen years. Craig's *Aqua America* project petered out after that.

That was not the end of Craig's flirtation with boats. He subsequently did some racing on water, starting at the World Outboard Motor Championships on Lake Havasu in November 1967. It was intended mainly as a publicity stunt, Craig being teamed up with water speed record holder Lee Taylor and air speed record holder Pete Knight. They were there to lend their names to the event, not to risk their lives trying to win—which of course the highly competitive trio did, nearly giving meet organizer Larry Laurie a heart attack in the process. "Let's go tell

Larry that Pete flipped and we need another boat," Craig said to Taylor during practice. "It'll drive him up the wall." It was instead Craig who flipped the boat on the second day of the race. It dumped him into the water, did a complete turn in the air, and landed right side up. Craig, bruised and half-frozen, swam over and climbed back in but was unable to continue. The steering was jammed.

Craig returned to the Lake Havasu race in November 1968 and flipped his boat again, this time in practice. "It blew over backwards and dropped me out something like twenty feet in the air. I went into the water face-first and the boat landed on top and the steering rod that goes between the two outboard engines got me right across the small of the back and drove me down deep into the water. That was a bad crash. I mean, I was peeing pure blood when I got hauled out. It took me a while to get over that one. My back was killing me. Oh God, there was a lot of pain."

Craig was taken to the hospital in Needles, California—where a doctor promptly produced a huge needle. "If you think you're putting that into me," Craig said, blanching, "you've got another thing coming." It contained dye, the doctor explained, for taking X-rays of his insides. Craig didn't care what was in it. It was too damn big.

So he left.

———————

Craig was struggling in 1968. His drag tire business had been appropriated by Carroll Shelby, his Indy turbine car project was dead, the drag chute company he started with Jack Carter hadn't panned out, and his unprofitable Goodyear store was burning through what was left of his money. What had seemed like a secure financial future just two years before was falling to pieces. Behind the big house and flashy cars and nice clothes, behind the public appearance of success and wealth, Craig was becoming desperate. He needed money.

His association with the American Motors Corporation was therefore a godsend. It sprang from a proposal he had been shopping around Detroit for a while to use a Ford Mustang or Chevy Camaro to break speed records to enhance the vehicle's muscle car image. American Motors eventually bought the idea in December 1967 and sent Craig two of their new AMXs, which they were planning to introduce to the public the following year. This was what Craig threw himself into after shelving his turbine car prior to the 1968 Indy. He prepped the AMXs and took them to Goodyear's five-mile oval in San Angelo, Texas, to break a whole slew of records, his wife Lee serving as one of his co-drivers. He then sold AMC on a follow-up idea, a streamliner to be called *American Spirit* that he would run at Bonneville for the wheel-driven speed record in three engine classes. It was by now already well into 1968, so yet another crash program was required to get the racer ready before the end of the Bonneville season. Craig hired fabricators and got down to work in his Torrance shop, giving little thought to the budget in the rush to get the car built.

While all this was going on, Craig was running around the country trying to make money to keep his head above water. It was why he made every public appearance that came with a paycheck. It was why he did the Lake Havasu motorboat races and endorsed everything from spark plugs to car wax. And it was why he jumped at the chance to do a one-hour TV special when ABC called.

The Racers: Craig and Lee Breedlove, which would be nominated for an Emmy, portrayed Craig and Lee as a happily married couple. They weren't. Just how bad things were, however, didn't fully hit Craig until he got home shortly before the show aired on June 8, 1968. Lee wasn't at the airport to meet him as planned, so he took a taxi to Palos Verdes, unlocked the door, and was shocked to find all his things piled in the entry, with a note from Lee saying she wanted him to move out.

Not knowing what to do, Craig took a walk on the beach nearby to figure things out. It was there that he spotted Lee sprawled on the sand with Nye Frank and the pieces began to fall into place. He secretly watched them for a moment before backing off and driving away. He went over to his dad's house after that, only to be shocked again when Norm confessed that he had known about the affair for almost three years. Back in 1965, when Craig was running for the record, Norm had returned to the motel in Wendover to get his camera bag out of Craig's room. He knocked on the door, got no answer, then used the key Craig had given him. The door was on the chain when he unlocked it but he heard enough to know what was going on inside—bodies scrambling out of the bed and the panic in Lee's voice when she said, "Who is it?" Norm played stupid when she came to the door and thrust out the bag. He decided not to tell Craig.

Craig moved into the loft apartment in his shop in Torrance, sleeping on a mattress on the floor, and concentrated on building *American Spirit*. The red, white, and blue racer was completed in late October—a shorter, lower-to-the-ground version of the original *Spirit of America* jet car but a three-wheeler in appearance only, there being two wheels side by side in the nose. The press unveiling was held at the Century Plaza Hotel in Beverly Hills and went beautifully . . . until Lee's lawyer showed up with divorce papers. Craig was served in front of his sponsors, the press, invited guests, everybody. He tried to hide his embarrassment and smooth things over but the damage was done. Apart from the personal humiliation, he knew his reputation with American Motors had taken a hit. It was like a harbinger of doom. And sure enough, when he got to Bonneville, conditions were terrible, with rain and snow and gusting wind and flooding. Craig was forced to turn around and leave without running the car.

It was when he got back to Torrance that Goodyear lowered the boom and took his store, leaving him effectively broke. And then a letter arrived from AMC informing him he was worse than broke. In his rush to complete *American Spirit*, Craig had gone $36,000 over budget and now had to pay back the money. If there was a silver lining to all this, it was that it left little for Lee's hard-driving divorce lawyer to fight for. When Lee exploded in a meeting, "What happened to all the money?" Craig could honestly say it was gone.

To end the legal battle and hasten a settlement, Craig moved to Las Vegas and got a no-fault divorce. Lee came away from the marriage with the house in Palos Verdes, where she would live with her new husband, Nye Frank. Craig got his shop in Torrance and a whole lot of debt. He went a bit wild during his six weeks in Vegas, trying to escape his loneliness and depression. He took flying lessons and bought a little Cessna Cardinal he couldn't afford, then married a beautiful blond model named Caroline he had only just met. But what happened in Vegas stayed in Vegas. The union was quickly annulled. "It's like the man said after he took off his clothes and jumped into the cactus," Craig would say, quoting Steve McQueen in *The Magnificent Seven*: "'It seemed like a good idea at the time.'"

Then the rains came.

———————

It was California's worst weather-related disaster in the twentieth century, more than a week of deluging rain that caused flooding and landslides that killed ninety-one people. It started on January 18, 1969, the downpour overwhelming L.A.'s sewer system and flooding property all across the city, including in Torrance, where Craig's shop was located. The water rose to a height of four feet inside, carrying in a mass of mud, then receded. Then, on January 25, it happened again.

Craig was out of town at the time, exhibiting *American Spirit* at the Custom Auto, Hot Boat and Speed Show in Seattle. His friend Buster Smith, who was staying at the shop, phoned him with the news. Craig's first reaction was to say, "Buster, is this some kind of a joke? I'm mean, you're kidding, right?"

"It's no joke, buddy. The place is a mess."

"Well, should I come back?"

"No, better stay up there and finish the show. You're going to need every penny you can scrounge to clean this place up."

It was yet another blow. Craig stayed in Seattle to finish the car show, then participated in a twenty-four-hour snowmobile race to pick up extra cash, pounding the hell out of his back in the process. When he finally got home he found his shop in even worse shape than he had imagined, everything not just soaked but covered in mud—the two AMX sports cars, all his tools and books, all his blueprints and papers, the AMC engines that were to go into *American Spirit*, his lathe and his band saw and heli-arc welder and everything else, the whole show. Both buildings of his workshop were a complete disaster.

Restoring the place was going to be a huge job. Fortunately, as so often happened in his life, volunteers gravitated to Craig. Among them was Ed Ballinger, recently back from the Vietnam War and selling used cars in Hermosa Beach. He had heard about Craig's plight and offered to help. "It was heartbreaking," says Ed of his first sight of the shop. "We started to clean things up, Chrysler blocks and heads and all kinds of speed equipment. We just hacked at it, kept working at it and working at it until it was done. I had some friends in college and they volunteered too." The place got pretty cold when the gas company shut off the gas for nonpayment. When Craig and the guys got tired of shivering, they removed the diaphragm from the pipe to get the gas flowing and the shop heated again.

Later that spring, when cleanup was still underway, Craig was informed that AMC was canceling his *American Spirit* sponsorship contract. The mud-choked engines that were to go into the car were taken away and sold, leaving Craig with an empty shell of a racer, no prospects, and debts still to repay. He sold his trucks and the two AMX sports cars and leased out most of his workshop space to get himself out of hock. He was left with just the end of one of the buildings when the downsizing was done, the corner containing his loft apartment. And parked outside, his sole means of transportation: a battered '56 Buick with no reverse gear, a top speed of 50 mph, and flower decals on the doors.

The flowers were a part of the new Craig Breedlove that was emerging. Gone was the clean-cut image that he had cultivated since the start of the 1960s, the all-American-boy look that was attractive to sponsors. What good was it keeping up appearances now that his sponsors were all gone? He was now letting his hair grow long, almost down to his shoulders. Pressed suits and white shirts with button-down collars were out, replaced by far-out colors and bell-bottom jeans. He even started smoking marijuana to cope with life's many pressures but soon gave it up, feeling it was dulling his brain.

It was at the start of this period in his life that Craig started getting serious about rockets.

17

PLAYING WITH FIRE

PUTTING A ROCKET MOTOR in a land speed racer started making a lot of sense to Craig in the late 1960s, the best way forward in his quest for Mach 1. A rocket would give him even more power than a jet, it would be lighter, and it would have no moving parts like the J-79's heavy compressor, which could cause destabilizing torque when spinning at high speed. A rocket motor also didn't require huge amounts of air like a jet. That meant that there was no need for air ducts, one of the most technically demanding parts to fabricate on a jet car, making a rocket car easier and cheaper to build. And no air ducts in turn meant that the design could be made even more aerodynamic—long and thin like a pencil on wheels, slicing through the air with almost no drag. Just as the jet represented a quantum leap forward from the internal combustion engine in land speed racing, the rocket represented a quantum leap forward from the jet.

Craig wasn't interested in light-'em-up-and-pray rockets like the JATO bottles Walt Arfons stuck on his *Wingfoot Express*. He wanted something more sophisticated, a rocket he could control. The US Air Force was using such things, most recently in its X-15 program, where Pete Knight, Craig's Lake Havasu motorboat racing teammate, had recently set an airplane speed record of 4,519 mph that stands to this day. NASA also had throttleable rockets that it was using to send astronauts to the Moon. Neither NASA nor the Air Force, however, was willing to help Craig. Their rocket technology had been developed with government funding, he was told when he started phoning around. The government controlled it and it was top secret. And so Craig's LSR rocket racer remained only a dream.

His first break finally came in the spring of 1969, when he was invited on to a local TV talk show where Donald Campbell's widow, singer Tonia Bern-Campbell, was also appearing. Craig took Tonia out to dinner after and during the course of the meal asked about Donald's mothballed land speed racer *Bluebird*. What had happened to it? Where was it stored?

His interest seemed to surprise Tonia. "Why are you asking about *Bluebird*?" Craig remembers her saying.

"Well, because it never really reached its potential. It's just kind of sad that no one has run it. Frankly, I'd be interested in driving it for the wheel-driven land speed record."

Tonia was now looking completely amazed. "Before Donald died," she explained, "he told me that no one was ever to drive *Bluebird* unless it was Craig Breedlove or Dan Gurney. He came out with that one night out of the blue and I was thinking, *What are you talking about, Donald?*"

A door had just opened. Craig stepped through. With Tonia's blessing and support, he set out to restore *Bluebird* to recapture the wheel-driven record, rechristening it *Bluebird America* and planning to drive it with both his and Donald's names on the side. He would ultimately be unable to attract enough sponsorship interest to get the project off the ground. During the time he spent in England, however, staying at Donald's country house in Surrey, Craig stumbled on something that gave him a way forward with his rocket car idea. He found it in Donald's substantial library up in the attic, in a volume of *Jane's All the World's Aircraft*.

"So I'm up in Donald's library, going through this Jane's almanac. I got to the part that's about rocket engines, and I see that a company called TRW has a plant in Redondo Beach where they build rocket engines using technology they developed with company funds, not government money. And I'm thinking, *Oh my God . . . these guys are three miles down the street from me.*"

Craig phoned TRW as soon as he got back to L.A. and spoke with Gerard "Jerry" Elverum Jr., vice president of the Energy Systems Division. Jerry was intrigued by Craig's rocket car idea and dropped by his shop that very day after work.

Craig had just hit the rocketry jackpot. Jerry was the guy who had designed the rocket motor in the Lunar Excursion Module that Neil Armstrong had just piloted to the surface of the Moon. It ran on hypergolic propellants that spontaneously ignited on contact, using Jerry's patented pintle injector to combine them in the combustion chamber. It could produce a great deal of thrust, substantially more than a jet, and in design was simpler and lighter. It was also extremely reliable—so much so that it was "man-rated," meaning that it was proven safe for vehicles carrying people. And best of all, Jerry was willing to let Craig use it. "Craig, I'll design you a rocket engine," he said, "but I don't have time to do engineering drawings. If I make sketches with all the dimensions, can you guys build the engine off that?"

Craig looked up with a grin from the stack of nondisclosure agreements he was happily signing. "No problem!"

Craig's plan was to convert the *American Spirit* racer sitting abandoned in his shop into a prototype rocket dragster, installing a scaled-down rocket with 8,500 pounds of thrust in the empty cavity where the piston engine had been. This would be a cheap and easy way forward, something he could start on his own. He would get the car built, then spend a year or two running it at drag meets, getting experience with rockets, and earning appearance fees to replenish his bank account, for a rocket would be a huge draw. Then, when someone broke his land speed record and Goodyear stepped up with the sponsorship Craig had been promised to win it back, he would build the full-sized rocket car he already had designed by December 1969, a forty-four-foot-long, shoulder-wide, waist-high arrow that he would call *Spirit of America–Sonic II*. According to his calculations, its 35,000 pounds of thrust would be capable of pushing him to 900 mph in just 32 seconds.

"The dragster rocket I designed for Craig was very simple," recalls Jerry Elverum. "It had to operate for just five or six seconds so it didn't need a lot of fancy throttling or an elaborate cooling system like on

the lunar descent module. It didn't have to meet extremely high performance standards either, because Craig wasn't putting a payload into
orbit. All he needed was a few seconds of controllable thrust. So that's
what I gave him, a simplified version of the central pintle type of engine
that I had developed for the Apollo program."

Working from Jerry's sketches, Craig went to work building the
engine, assisted by Paul Sutherland, Ron Gardner, and Ed Ballinger. Al
Sharp would subsequently join the project as well. They machined the
key components from forged pipe fittings purchased at an oil refinery
supply yard, hauling the parts back to the shop in an old pickup Ed
borrowed from Casey's Used Cars. The nozzle was specially cast out of
stainless steel. The result, after Paul Sutherland heli-arced all the pieces
together, was a compact, beautifully gleaming rocket motor, the combustion chamber about basketball size. Chamber and nozzle were 32 inches
long, compact enough for one guy to pick up and lug around.

It was around this time that Craig lost his land speed title. He had been
hoping that someone would take it. In fact, he had helped.

It began with a call from Dick Keller of Reaction Dynamics, a
Milwaukee-based company that was building a land speed rocket car
called *Blue Flame* in the same tricycle configuration Craig had pioneered
with his original *Spirit*. After giving a bit of background—the rocket
would be fueled by hydrogen peroxide and liquefied natural gas, the
LNG being used to promote the American Gas Association, the project's
primary sponsor—Dick asked if Craig would be interested in signing on
as the driver. Craig declined. He didn't want to drive someone else's car.
When he went after the record it would be in a vehicle he built himself.
He also didn't want to be associated with a project sponsored to run on
Firestone tires, not when he was counting on Goodyear backing for his
own car when the time came.

"So I turned down the offer and suggested that Dick contact Gary
Gabelich instead. I was friends with Gary. When I was trying to clean
up my shop, Gary came by and said, 'You need a break. We're going

water skiing. Just lock the frigging door and we're going to Parker.' Parker, Arizona, was a hangout for all the guys with drag boats and ski boats. I went water skiing there with Gary quite a bit. We had some really good times. Anyway, Gary was a very personable guy, a very nice-looking guy, and I thought he would be perfect for *Blue Flame*. So I told Dick about him."

The *Blue Flame* ride was offered to Gary after Don Garlits, the project's second choice for driver, declined. Gary readily accepted, then became wary when the team started talking about bringing in backup drivers to compete for the right to drive for the record and earn the $10,000 payday. "They're trying to make a contest out of it," he complained to Craig. "I don't think that's fair." Craig, with a decade of hard-won experience with contracts, agreed to accompany Gary to the car's unveiling in Houston and helped him negotiate a deal making him the exclusive driver.

Craig also assisted with the wheels and tires when Dick Keller reached out again seeking help. "I got another call from Keller saying that Firestone had dropped out and the *Blue Flame* had no tires to run on. They didn't know anybody at Goodyear, so I called and suggested that if Goodyear still had the tooling for the 36-inch front tires for *Sonic I*, which I was sure they did, that that would be the ideal size for the *Blue Flame*. So Goodyear agreed to make the tires. No sponsorship money, no wheels, just the tires. I had designed the front wheels for *Sonic I*, so I took the drawings and design specs and everything over to Roy Richter at Cragar and they used them to make a new set. So basically the *Blue Flame* ran on *Sonic I*'s front wheels and tires."

The *Blue Flame* team made its record bid starting in September 1970. They ran into difficulty early on in making the rocket work with the planned combination of hydrogen peroxide and liquid natural gas and so quietly did away with the LNG and ran on peroxide alone. But they couldn't get past Craig's five-year-old mark. Gary got the racer up almost to 600 mph multiple times and came close to breaking the record twice, but couldn't quite do it.

"I was up there with them quite a bit, flying back and forth in my Cessna," says Craig. "They were on the salt almost six weeks and they just couldn't break the record. When they were almost out of time, this guy showed up to watch in this hopped-up pickup truck and I said, 'Why don't we rig that pickup so that it can push *Blue Flame*?' We would get it up to 100 miles an hour on a push start, without burning any fuel, then the guy would honk the horn and pull out from behind and Gary would light the peroxide rocket engine and take off, already going a hundred. The first time we tried it, it worked. We went out the next morning and did two runs with this guy pushing the *Blue Flame* up to a hundred with his pickup before the peroxide motor was lit. And that's how Gary got the record."

Gary's two-way average was 622.407 mph. His first words as he climbed out of the cockpit were, "Plenty boss, man. Plenty boss."

Losing the LSR to Gary Gabelich didn't give Craig's shelved supersonic land speed car the boost he expected. When he took his proposal to Goodyear to secure its promised backing, it was pointed out that while Craig himself no longer held the record, Goodyear still did. Gary had set his mark on Goodyear tires, the same tires as on *Sonic I*, so nothing had changed. It was a disappointment, but Craig was used to that now. He pushed ahead with his rocket dragster project in his Torrance shop, hoping that it would lead to another way forward.

Fifty miles north, in Chatsworth, California, Australian Bill Fredericks was doing much the same thing. Bill had been involved in jet cars going back to his *Valkyrie* in the early 1960s and was now fabricating a compact rocket dragster, *Courage of Australia*, as a first step toward building a full-sized LSR car. Gary Gabelich, who had driven *Valkyrie* back in the day, would drive it. To drum up publicity and funding for the project, Bill and Gary hooked up with motorsport promoter Bob Kachler, who put together a plan for a head-to-head race on the Bonneville Salt Flats between *Courage of Australia* and Craig's *Sonic II*, both of which as yet existed only on paper. Craig agreed to join the venture, attracted by Kachler's beguiling talk of selling the TV rights to the "Race of the Century" to fund construction of the cars and pay a half-million-dollar prize to the winner. Nothing came of the scheme but Kachler stayed in Craig's life, representing him in the hunt for a sponsor.

The rocket dragster was finished by late 1971. Major alterations included replacing the dual wheels up front with a single nose wheel, removing the canopy to give Craig better visibility at drag strips, and installing *Sonic I*–style winglets on the sides. There was still no tailfin. Craig figured he didn't need one. The fin-like fairings on the rear wheels would give him all the stability he needed. "Craig was so specific on everything," says Ed Ballinger of the fabrication. "It had to *be* right, and it had to *look* right. Otherwise it just wouldn't work."

The rocket motor was a bipropellant hypergolic system running on nitrogen tetroxide (NTO) and unsymmetrical dimethylhydrazine (hydrazine or UDMH for short). They were inert when kept apart in their separate tanks behind the cockpit. Brought together in the combustion chamber with Jerry Elverum's pintle injector, they ignited on contact. The system also included a third tank that contained water. This was for the simplified cooling system Jerry developed to prevent the 5,000 degree heat generated during combustion from melting the rocket. "There were seventy-two holes in the chamber and out toward the nozzle that sprayed water against the inside walls to keep them cool," says Jerry. "It cut the performance way down but that didn't matter. Craig wouldn't be burning enough propellant in just a few seconds to make a difference."

Jerry arranged for the rocket to be tested at TRW's facility at Capistrano, the same place the Apollo lunar descent engine was tested. The car was bolted to the gantry and tilted up at a 21 degree angle to shift the hydrazine and NTO to the back of their tanks, simulating the condition of a dragster under hard acceleration. "We fired it three times," says Jerry, "which satisfied me that we had the right injector velocity ratios and that it was running nice and stable. I gave it a man-rating, but by man-rating, Craig had to put an awful lot of faith in what I told him. He understood that we were not pushing that engine to the limit so he had a very high safety factor like the Apollo engine. We were just running it for a few seconds."

Craig continues the story. "We had witnessed all the rocket burns from inside a blockhouse. I wanted to be able to see and feel the thing run when we were standing in close proximity, similar to what we'd be doing at the drag races, so I said to Jerry, 'Would it be OK if we went outside and watched?' They'd never done that before, but Jerry kind of looked around and finally said, 'Well, OK. I guess so.'

"So we go outside and stand maybe twenty feet from the car for the last test. They had a speaker system where they'd count down, 'Five . . . four . . . three . . . two . . . one . . . ignition.' It sounded like a big howitzer on a battleship when that thing went off. It was a big shock. The sound waves when the rocket's running will actually aspirate your lungs in a pulsing manner. And it made the fillings in my teeth tingle, like I had electricity in my mouth. I'm thinking, *Holy shit*.

"They ran it for a five-second burn, then it shut off. And Bob Kachler, who had been out soliciting sponsorship and telling everybody how spectacular this thing would be, his eyes are as big as saucers and he's just speechless. Then he starts stammering and he says, 'Y-y-you guys are playing with fire!' We laughed about that."

Things now started looking up. Kachler lined up a sponsorship deal from Ovaltine for its new popcorn snack, Screaming Yellow Zonkers, which would be sold at concession stands at National Hot Rod Association events. Craig, eagerly awaiting the arrival of a nice big check, went ahead and gave the car a bright yellow paint job, popcorn kernels, and EAT! emblazoned on the rear fairings, and rechristened it *Screaming Yellow Zonker*. He then hauled it to the Orange County International Raceway in the spring of 1972 to demonstrate it to the NHRA and secure a six-month probationary approval to run at their meets.

Jerry Elverum was in the stands that day and vividly remembers the impression the *Zonker* made. "Craig was scheduled to go about nine o'clock at night. Everybody in the stands had been watching these nitromethane dragsters all evening, spinning their tires and rearing up before making a run. Then Craig comes to the starting line and he sits there. There's no *vroom-vroom-vroom* like the other dragsters, no spinning tires and all that stuff. He just sits there. Then *BAM*, that rocket engine went off like a 150-milimeter howitzer and this bright flash lit up the stands and everybody thought the car blew up. By the time the people in the audience got their heads back together, Craig was already crossing the finishing line a quarter mile away. It was pretty spectacular."

The experience was even more memorable inside the cockpit—comparatively little noise but a whole lot of acceleration. "The rocket thing, it takes a little time to get your head around it," says Craig. "Because when that thing launches, there's no buildup of power like with a jet. It takes a matter of milliseconds to reach full power when you hit the button to turn the valves on. It's a real stunning ride. It's like going from being parked to a semitruck hitting you in the rear bumper at 300 miles an hour."

With the sponsorship check from Ovaltine still not forthcoming, Craig went deeper into debt to buy the extremely expensive fuels for the racer and a specially equipped fuel truck to transport them. Ed Ballinger drove the truck when Craig headed east to work the drag strips. When he got to the raceway in Dallas, he went over to the tower and said, "Hey, where's our extra fuel that was supposed to be delivered here?" The track manager handed him a pair of binoculars and pointed to a field out beyond the track. "Look over there. See that bunch of cows? The stuff's over there." Word about Craig's scary fuels had evidently gotten around.

"Man, that's the real shit," Craig remembers Don Garlits exclaiming when he came over to check out the dragster. "You running hydrazine?"

Craig: "Yep. Unsymmetrical, baby. What do you think?"

Garlits: "Hoo-eeee!"

Sharing top billing at the Dallas meet with *Screaming Yellow Zonker* was Bill Fredericks's *Courage of Australia* rocket car, which ran on hydrogen peroxide. They would cross paths again at the raceway in Bristol, Tennessee, the two very different rockets being demonstrated one after the other. According to Craig, Bill didn't like that and took steps to shut him down.

"*Courage of Australia* was a very nice car, really fast, but it didn't put on anywhere near the show that our car did. Its hydrogen peroxide rocket looked like a swizzle stick compared to ours. We were really stealing Bill's thunder, and Bill was an aggressive guy. I mean, his driver John Paxson was instructed not to talk to me. Anyway, Bill wrote a letter to the National Hot Rod Association's insurance company saying that hydrazine was dangerous and shouldn't be allowed at public exhibitions. The insurance company then contacted NHRA, and [NHRA president] Wally Parks phoned me and said that they couldn't let me run the car at their meets anymore, that it would put their insurance at risk. So we lost our golden carrot, so to speak. After that we could only run at fly-by-night drag meets. I had bookings set up all across the country and everything got canceled. It happened in one afternoon in a ten-minute phone call from Wally."

It was a big financial blow. Then came another, when the International Hot Rod Association demanded a kickback from Ovaltine to sell Screaming Yellow Zonkers at the concession stands at its meets. Ovaltine refused to pay and dropped Craig's sponsorship, leaving Craig without a penny to show for the deal. He had painted the car yellow and turned it into a crazy Zonker advertisement for nothing.

And the hits just kept on coming. Next was what Craig calls a "nasty-gram" that arrived from Bob Lane informing him that he was not allowed to run Goodyear tires—the *Sonic I* tires that he himself had designed—on his dragster. Then, to add insult to injury, Goodyear donated *Sonic I* to the Indianapolis Motor Speedway Museum and didn't invite Craig, the man who designed and built it and drove it to two world records. "That really, really got to me," says Craig. "Goodyear had a big dedication ceremony to give the car to the museum and I wasn't invited or even told about it. I had to read about it in *Speed Sport Magazine*. That was the kind of guy Bob Lane was. He was just an absolute turd. I don't know how else to say it." It was around this time, in a dark moment, that Craig confided to Norm Breedlove, "Dad, I absolutely hate racing."

Craig parked the rocket car and waited for a new sponsor to turn up. Finally one did, in the spring of 1973, when Craig's new public relations manager, Bob Perilla, negotiated a contract with the MEM Company for its line of English Leather men's toiletry products. It was to be a 50-50 deal, MEM taking half the sponsorship and the Robert Hall Clothes retail chain the rest. And this time the deal was followed up with hard cash, a preliminary payment from MEM that was enough for Craig to repaint the rocket car in English Leather metallic bronze and to build a mock-up of the full-sized LSR rocket car he had planned. In a nod to Robert Hall Clothes, which Perilla was still working to close, Craig had a leather outfit made to wear at the track during the upcoming season. Good-bye, candy-covered popcorn. Hello, masculine chic.

Craig debuted his renamed *English Leather Special* at an American Hot Rod Association meet in St. Louis on August 3, 1973. "It's safe," he stressed, defending his rocket. "With a bipropellant nothing can happen until both fuels mix. Independently they're pretty darn safe. There's no flywheel spinning around, there's no crankshafts coming out the side of the block, no superchargers exploding. There's relatively no danger unless you were to stand directly in the blast." You definitely didn't want to stand in the blast. It came out the nozzle at Mach 4 and could knock a man over at 100 feet. You also didn't want to breathe in the yellowish fumes coming off the hydrazine or get the stuff on your hands.

Craig's plan for the season was to break all the standing-start records beginning with the quarter-mile mark, recently set by Dave Anderson in the hydrogen peroxide rocket car *Pollution Packer* with a top speed of 322 mph. Craig had hit 302 mph the previous year using a fraction of his rocket's full power and knew that with a little more acclimation he could blow the record away. He started out slow in St. Louis, running the rocket for a two-second burn, then three seconds, then four, getting a feel for the tremendous acceleration in an open cockpit, six times greater than on the steepest drop of the world's highest roller coaster. "When you don't get into anything faster than Cheryl's Volkswagen for a year," he said, "and you get back out to the race track and light 15,000 horsepower, it's going to startle you." Cheryl McDonald, a stewardess with Continental Airlines, had been Craig's girlfriend for the past year.

After hitting 297 mph in the St. Louis warm-up, Craig took the *English Leather Special* to the Bonneville Salt Flats to see how fast he could go when he didn't have to worry about stopping, a major concern when running a thrust car on the strip. For the first time he would use the rocket's full burn time of five and a quarter seconds, the maximum that the *Special*'s eleven-gallon tank of hydrazine and seventeen-gallon tank of NTO allowed. To boost his speed further, the crew also lightened the racer, removing the large rear fairings and affixing the back wheels—Firestones—to simple open struts. Craig figured that the stabilizing influence of the fairings would not be missed over a mere quarter mile.

Ed Ballinger recalls what happened next. "So Craig gets in the car and he launches. Hard. That was the only way to launch in that car. He goes off down the track and gets through the quarter, then we see the nose lift up and the car flies up about twenty feet into the air and starts to spin to the left. The chute came out, of course. Craig was on the job. The chute came out and snapped the car back to the right. That's when we lost track of him. The only thing we could see other than dust was Craig's helmet shooting up into the air. It got pulled right off his head."

The wheel fairings had turned out to be necessary after all. As long as the car was being pushed forward by the rocket, the Mach 4 blast of thrust pressure out the tail kept it going straight and stable. "But when that engine quit," Ed explains, "the moment of pressure went right up to the nose of the car. It was like when you let go of a pencil standing on its end. It falls over."

Craig, strapped in the open cockpit, wind screaming in his ears, was seeing nothing but sky. "The instant the engine shut off, the ass end of the car swung out and it turned a dead 90. The air pressure hitting it sideways caved in the lower side of the nose and lifted it up and the car took off into the air and the chute tore out the back end. It gave a big tug that started the car spinning in the air, a boomerang spin, flat and level. That's why it came down on its wheels. As soon as it touched down, I turned into the slide and recovered and got it stopped. I was OK. It was a miracle I walked away from that one. But the car was just trashed."

Ed and the rest of the crew had jumped into their cars by this time and were racing down the course. They came to Craig's helmet and kept on going, the racer now visible up ahead in the distance, a speck a mile away. When they finally got there Craig was out of the car and had already shut off the valves. "He was leaning up against the car," says

Ed, "just kind of thinking. And he says, 'Well, I guess we better put the wheel pants back on the car.'"

Craig was clocked doing a top speed of 377.754 mph on that run, a stunning new record, his elapsed time in the quarter just 4.65 seconds. He now knew the car was capable of a 400 mph quarter. He took it back to Torrance and began repairing the damage, intent on resuming the drag tour and breaking more records. But then another blow landed: Robert Hall Clothes pulled out of the sponsorship deal. The MEM Company was willing to continue with its 50 percent backing, but that meant that Craig had to come up with the remainder himself and he just couldn't afford it. He was already $80,000 in debt, his taxes had gone unfiled for five years because he didn't have money to pay an accountant, and his shop and everything in it was financed to the hilt.

It was the last straw. At age thirty-six, after a lifetime devoted to cars, Craig decided it was time for a change. He turned his back on motorsports and became a real estate agent.

18

THE RIVER

IT WAS MIKE HUBBARD OF HARBOR REALTY who put the thought of becoming a real estate agent into Craig's mind, telling him on several occasions that he would make a great salesman and could earn a lot of money. Craig didn't think much about it at first. Sales didn't attract him. But as his debts and worries mounted, he began to give the idea serious consideration.

It wasn't just his frustration over the stalled rocket car project that drove him. He was also thinking about his children. His two eldest, Chris and Norman, now in high school, had become a handful for their mother and were living with him in the loft apartment over his shop. He wanted to do right by them, to provide for them and set a good example, and digging himself deeper into debt with the rocket car clearly wasn't the way. He had to get a real job and start making money.

He particularly wanted to be able to help his son Norman, who at sixteen was developing racing ambitions of his own. "I had never been really excited about land speed racing," says Norman, "But when my dad took me to see the movie *Grand Prix* when I was seven or eight, back in '65 when it came out, I thought to myself, *That's what I want to do*. So I always had it in my head that I wanted to race Formula cars." Craig knew that having the Breedlove name would help Norman get started. Having the Breedlove name plus money to go to racing school, however, would help even more.

Craig made his decision toward the end of 1973. He went down to the Harbor Realty office in Manhattan Beach and spoke with Mike Hubbard and was offered a job. The next step was to get a California real estate license. Like everything else Craig had undertaken in his life, he made it a crash project, doubling up on classes to complete the six-week program in just three weeks and acing the licensing exam before the end of the month. Then, like a sign that he was on the right track, he got a call from ABC offering him $25,000 to appear on the show *Superstars*, which pitted sports celebrities against each other in a multi-event competition. Craig didn't consider himself much of an athlete but there was no way he was turning down such a fat check. He threw himself into training, with Chris and Norman helping out.

He also picked up a new girlfriend, twenty-one-year-old Peggy Phillips, a petite blond beauty who worked at one of the businesses leasing space in Craig's building. They bumped into each other when Craig was training for the *Superstars* show, and it was the closest thing in Craig's life to love at first sight. They started going out and were soon living together. And when Craig headed off to Florida to tape the show, Peggy went along.

Craig acquitted himself well in the televised competition, up against the likes of Pete Rose, Roger Staubach, O. J. Simpson, and Arthur Ashe, until a sprained knee from a crash in the bike race forced him to drop out. He laughs today remembering how O.J. kept cozying up to Peggy between events. When he whispered to her, "You know, O.J. is hitting on you," Peggy refused to believe it. She said, "No, he's just being nice." Thinking about her today fills Craig with emotion. "Peggy was the most unselfish person I ever met. All she wanted to do was to be good to other people. She would buy little gifts for people. Never thought of herself. She was marvelous, and I was crazy about her."

In early 1974, armed with his brand-new license, Craig hobbled into Harbor Realty on his sprained knee to begin his career as a real estate agent. There were no volunteers at the office meeting that morning to do an open house, so he raised his hand and said, "I'll do it," not realizing that open houses were scorned as nothing but talkfests for people with no intention to buy. Then he went off and sold the house regardless. "You guys missed out," Mike Hubbard crowed to the rest of the office, delighted with his new protégé. "Craig sold the place on his first open house!"

Craig was making money from his very first day on the job. Then, three weeks later, he scored again, and this time he scored big. It happened at another open house, where he got talking to a well-to-do couple with some properties they were looking to sell. They had had some bad experiences with real estate agents and didn't want to go that route, so Craig told them about a program Harbor Realty offered whereby the company would buy qualifying properties for cash, no commission, a nice quick sale. The couple liked the idea and signed on, the deal went ahead, and Craig was stunned to earn an $80,000 commission. In less than a month he was able not only to pay off all his debts but to start investing in real estate for himself. After three months he had become the top seller at Harbor Realty and was moved into an office upstairs. After nine months he was made a full partner in the firm.

"I did really well because I worked my butt off. But you know, the thing is that I really hated selling real estate. I loved the creativity of redesigning houses and fixing up the interiors and doing all the artistic stuff, but I hated all the moneygrubbing of sales. I still feel bad to this day about the houses I sold for that couple. I mean, they were really nice people, and I'm not kidding you, they took a bath on selling those properties to Harbor Realty. I remember they asked me later what we got for their properties and I said, 'I'm not privy to that.' I didn't want to tell them that the company turned around and sold them for a lot more, and that I got 50 percent of the profit. I just didn't like the whole thing. I didn't feel ethical about it. But it got me out of the hole completely and I did really well. And then Peggy and I got married. That was a good thing. Things were very good."

Craig was well on his way to wealth by the late 1970s thanks to his success as a real estate agent and to his growing portfolio of property investments. Hard times and the loft apartment at his shop were long gone. He and

Peggy were now living in a gorgeous duplex on Hermosa Beach that they restored together, occupying the upper level and renting out the ground floor when they were done. Craig was now busy with what he calls "the best investment of my life," a pair of tennis and health clubs he developed in partnership with a group of investors. Building up the business took a lot of work but ultimately paid off, the clubs providing Craig with an income to support himself in comfort for the rest of his life.

A visitor to Craig's place back then would have seen very little evidence of his former life in racing. His shop was closed down and the *English Leather Special* and rocket car mock-up were in storage. What mementos he still possessed were packed away in boxes. The rest had been thrown away. Becoming fed up with motorsports, the selfless influence of Peggy—something had prompted him to take a long, hard look at his life. And he didn't like what he saw. "People would walk into my office and see all these awards and pictures and everything and they'd say, 'Oh my God . . .' and start looking things over. And I realized that the whole thing was just about my ego, that I'd built this monument to my ego. So I just threw it all away, gave it away. I got rid of everything."

He seemed a changed man when he was interviewed by the *New York Times* in 1976, introspective like never before, inner feelings laid bare. "I just knew I had to stop [racing]," he said. "Emotionally, I couldn't cope with the fear and pressure any longer. I had crashed going 620 miles per hour on the Flats and that shook me awake. 'What am I doing?' I asked myself. I had lost 20 good friends in 20 years of racing. At 600 miles per hour, one tiny mistake can end your life. . . . I discovered I didn't enjoy the pressure at all. Now I have a peaceful life asking myself what makes me happy and then doing it without anxiety. I love to work with my hands especially. Now and then my ego misses racing, but I put it back in its place. Slowly it's giving up. I guess it was all because I had an overwhelming desire to be successful, to do something that would make my life a part of history."

Craig was already making plans to give up real estate and use his growing wealth to start a carefree new life. He was designing a fifty-four-foot sailboat, a trimaran that would glide over the water like a bird. He and Peggy would sell the Hermosa Beach duplex and move into a trailer and spend two years building the boat and learning to sail it. Then they would head off to travel the world.

Then Peggy left.

It was Ron Irvine, the veterinarian they took their dogs to, who took her away. "It was like she tore my stomach out," Craig says of the moment Peggy told him about it. He tried to talk her into staying but she wouldn't. The fire had gone from their marriage, she said. Ron was moving north to start a new practice—in Willow Creek on the Trinity River, Bigfoot country—and she was going along. The whole thing left Craig feeling doubly sick, for he knew Ron was a notorious womanizer and the relationship wouldn't last.

It didn't. Peggy showed up five months later to say that things hadn't worked out between her and Ron and she wanted to come home if Craig would have her. When Craig said he still loved her and wanted her back, she burst into tears. At least one good thing had come from it all: Peggy now knew what she wanted to do with her life. She wanted to go to college and study to become a veterinarian. Craig said that was great. He was absolutely delighted, looking forward again to the future. So was Peggy. She returned to Willow Creek one last time to get her things and move back home.

It's still hard for Craig to talk about what happened next, the story pieced together by the police and Peggy's family of the night of May 9, 1979. During Peggy's brief return to Willow Creek, Ron Irvine asked her to accompany him to a Chamber of Commerce banquet at the local country club that he was obliged to attend. It was just to save him embarrassment, for Peggy was well known in the community by this time and everyone would be asking Ron where she was if he went alone. She therefore agreed to go.

Ron was drunk by the end of the evening. Peggy had taken the keys to the van, but when they got out to the parking lot shortly after midnight he insisted on driving and demanded that she give them back. Minutes later, heading south from the country club on Patterson Road, the van ran off the road and plunged two hundred feet into the Trinity River. The impact with the swift-running water drove Ron under the steering wheel and into the floor and instantly killed him. Peggy wasn't in the van when the police showed up. It was assumed she had gone through the shattered windshield and been swept away in the river.

Craig was frantic when he got the call. He drove through the night to Peggy's parents' house outside Sacramento and they kept a vigil for days, hoping against hope that Peggy might still be alive, that nobody had actually seen her get into the van, that maybe she had hitched a ride with someone else and would soon turn up. But she didn't. Her body washed up downstream and was discovered by campers ten days later. Her right leg was shattered. Water in her lungs indicated she had drowned.

Peggy's death hit Craig hard. "I had just a complete emotional break-down. I couldn't stop crying for a week. Finally Stan Goldstein brought in this lady, Mary, a Scientology auditor, to help me out. She drove out to my house at Hermosa Beach to do a Scientology course on 'Life Repair' that really helped me pull out of it. It got me starting to be more rational, less emotional. But it was hard. It was really hard.

"I just needed to stay busy. One thing I had been planning to do was to build Peggy a sewing room. We had restored the beach house together, made it really beautiful together, but she still wanted a sewing room. I had a strong feeling that her spirit was still around, so I went ahead and built it on the third floor, a loft with this great view of the ocean."

Craig sold the place not long after completing the sewing room. It held too many memories. He rented an apartment in Redondo Beach and bought a fifty-foot sailboat, trying to go ahead with the dream he and Peggy had had of sailing the world. He ran the boat into an offshore oil pipeline and wrecked it. He drifted into another marriage to a girl he met at the tennis club, twenty-one-year-old Jocelyn Ciniero. It didn't work out. "Boy, you sure can pick 'em," Walt Sheehan quipped after the breakup. By all outward appearances Craig seemed to be happy, hanging out at marinas and making plenty of money and playing with sailboats. Inwardly, however, he was struggling with feelings of emptiness. His life no longer seemed to have any purpose. He would later admit that for several years after Peggy's death he was "lost."

Craig moved up the coast to Oxnard in the mid-1980s and lived for a
time at Channel Islands Harbor Marina on a sailboat named *Wannago*.
He was single again. It was just him, a Siamese cat, and a fiercely loyal
German shepherd named Star. A young man named Don Baumea showed
up after a while and ended up staying with Craig for a year, helping out
around the place and living in an old camper parked outside the shop.
Star's snarling "scared the crap" out of Don when he first arrived but they
soon became friends. "She was the smartest dog I ever encountered," he
says. "I swear she understood what we were talking about. And she was
so loyal to Craig. She took care of Craig. Star was one of the great gifts
in Craig's life."

After they'd been together for a while, Don suggested that he and
Craig take the rocket car mock-up around to local fairs and marinas
in the hopes of attracting a sponsor to get the car built. "I let Don do
that," says Craig, even though he wasn't enthusiastic about the idea.
"He could never understand why I didn't want to go along and talk to
people and get the exposure. But I don't like doing that shit. It's counterproductive. People hang around and you end up wasting your time.
When I did go I wouldn't let on that I was Craig Breedlove. Somebody
would ask me a question and I'd answer in the third person. Don got
a big kick out of that."

Craig left Southern California toward the end of 1988. He sold his
sailboat and the shop in Torrance and bought a pair of mobile home
parks and Snug Harbor Marina and RV Park an hour outside Sacramento in Northern California. He moved into the owner's residence at
Snug Harbor, then started looking around for a warehouse to rent where
he could store all his equipment and tools.

He eventually stumbled on a promising property in the nearby town
of Rio Vista, a spacious building at 200 North Front Street on the banks
of the Sacramento River. It had been built in 1913 as a Ford and Lincoln
dealership and more recently had served as a tractor sales and servicing center. Now it was a boarded-up, derelict mess. The brickwork was
crumbling in places, the roof trusses were sagging, the windows were
broken, and a buildup of ancient grease lay caked on the floor. It was
in even worse shape than the space at the Perkins Machine Company

that Craig had sweated so hard to clean up almost three decades before, back when he was trying to build his original *Spirit*.

Maybe that's what stirred something in him. As he walked around the property, taking stock of all the repairs that were needed, Craig started to see not just storage space but a functioning workshop, a place to build a new land speed racer. It could be fabricated here, on a jig bolted to the floor, in the light flooding in through those windows. The lathe and the drill press could go there, the band saw there, the drafting tables against the wall over there. Just thinking about the possibilities gave him the kind of thrill he hadn't felt in years, that old feeling of excitement that came with a new project, and that gave a driving sense of purpose to life.

He went over to the local real estate office listed on the sign and bought the North Front Street property on the spot.

19

SONIC ARROW

THE REVIVAL OF CRAIG'S LAND SPEED AMBITIONS had its beginnings in 1983, when Englishman Richard Noble was vying for the record in his jet car *Thrust2*. Noble had been flooded out at Bonneville the previous year and was forced to look elsewhere for a course. It turned out to be a stroke of luck, for in his desperation he found a place that was even better, Black Rock Desert in northwest Nevada. The surface there was perfect, miles and miles of dry lakebed known as "playa" that was so naturally flat and smooth it did not need to be dragged. All that was required was to survey a track, defod it, and a lay down a line. "I knew that we'd struck a gold mine," Richard would write in his autobiography *Thrust*, recalling his first glimpse of Black Rock. He had stumbled on what would become the new mecca for ultimate speed.

Richard failed to break the LSR at Black Rock in 1982. His return in '83 was his last chance, for his sponsors had made it clear there would be no more funding. The season began with promise, Richard quickly building up to speeds of just over 600 mph. Then he hit a wall. Had *Thrust2* reached its peak potential? Was it maxing out just a few miles an hour short of Gary Gabelich's record of 622?

Craig was following Richard's progress from his boat at Redondo Beach. He was hoping Noble would succeed, because having the British claim the LSR would give it new meaning. It would make the game once again not just about personal ambition but also about American pride, like it had been back in the early 1960s, which in turn made for a more compelling sponsorship pitch. "But they were just stalled out there," says Craig. "They were not getting through the record. So I went up there to Black Rock to give them a hand."

After looking over the *Thrust2* jet car—it was a longer version of Art Arfons's *Green Monster*, double tailfins, sidesaddle cockpits on either side of the engine—Craig examined the tracks the solid metal wheels had left in the dirt. They were deep. It looked like they were plowing into the playa, an indication of too much downforce, too much drag. That could be what was robbing the Brits of that last twenty-odd miles an hour they needed.

Craig took his suspicions to team leader Ken Norris and project engineer John Ackroyd. How much downforce was the car experiencing at max speed, he asked, trying to be discreet, not wanting to tread on toes. John confided that the figure was around 13,000 pounds.

"How's that distributed on the wheels?" said Craig.

"Oh, that's just on the front wheels."

Craig's eyes grew wide. "Oh my God! You've got to get the loading off the front end, change the angle of attack. . . . When I ran *Sonic I*, do you know how much weight we had on the two front wheels?" He held up his thumb and forefinger, making a zero. "That much."

Craig had in fact just stepped into an area of tension on the British crew. Norris and Ackroyd had been telling Richard they needed to adjust the nose of the car slightly upward to increase lift and reduce drag and thus give it more speed. Richard was resisting, fearful that the flat underside of the car would catch the wind and send him flying into the air on a jet ride to the morgue.

At Ken Norris's request, Craig had a talk with Richard, telling him about his own experience going 600 mph in *Sonic I*. If Richard wanted the LSR, Craig said, if he really wanted to grab it, he would have to flirt with flying. Somewhere between the car's full weight of 6,500 pounds and zero—that was where he would find the world land speed record.

Richard relented. He agreed to have the racer's front end raised. The adjustment was tiny, a fraction of a degree, moving *Thrust2* from dead level to an ever-so-slight upward angle. But it was enough. On October 4, 1983, he streaked to a new LSR with a two-way average of 633 mph.

Some years later Richard was doing wind tunnel analysis with a model of *Thrust2*, preparing for his new land speed project, when he discovered something alarming. He rang up Craig. "Craig," he said, "you almost got me killed!"

Craig was taken aback. "What do you mean?"

"Well, we took a look at *Thrust2*, and, at the rate the lift was increasing, if I'd gone another 7 or 8 mph faster I'd have been going up at 50 Gs!"

Craig started laughing. "See Richard, there is a God!"

———————

With the LSR now in British hands, Craig tried to get something going with his *Sonic II* rocket car plans from more than a decade before. He had a logo designed, started contacting potential sponsors, and hauled the mock-up out of storage for a photo shoot with his son Norman, both of them posing in cool racing outfits. "I was racing Formula cars at the time," says Norman, then in his mid-twenties, "so my dad got me involved as driver mainly to help out my career. Ultimately, though, I think he would have driven the car himself through the sound barrier. We got Coors interested. They sent us a letter of intent to sponsor the car and we were going to call it the *Silver Bullet*. But then Coors sponsored Al Unser Jr.'s car for Indy instead and it ended up being called the *Silver Bullet*. So that was kind of a disappointment."

Craig's rocket car idea received a death blow not long thereafter when the US government made it illegal for civilians to transport hydrazine, the fuel that was to power the engine. You could still buy it and use it, but you couldn't move it. The new law therefore amounted to an outright ban on the stuff. A law would be subsequently passed limiting the potency of hydrogen peroxide as well, the rocket fuel used in *Pollution Packer*, *Courage of Australia*, and *Blue Flame*. Discouraged by this mounting government regulation, Craig gave up on rockets altogether and started thinking again about jets. He envisioned a whole new car powered by a J-79, the same engine as in *Sonic I*, now sitting in the Indianapolis Motor Speedway Museum. He was confident that with a newer, more powerful version of the jet and a more sophisticated aerodynamic design, he could not only reclaim the record but push it up to 700 mph and then to Mach 1.

The new car that emerged was a reflection of Craig's deep experience and sense of aesthetics. "It's just designed by eye," he would say, "based on whatever experience I gained from the two previous cars. I eyed it and packaged it the way I thought it should be." The design, completed in November 1990, marked a return to the tricycle configuration Craig had pioneered with his original *Spirit*, which he considered the most stable, with the rear wheels projecting eight and a half feet out from the sides and enclosed in sleek fairings. Instead of a single nose wheel, however, which made steering problematic, it had not two but three wheels up front, set a fraction of an inch apart. There would be no question this time that the racer qualified as a "car." The purists insisted on at least four wheels? With Craig's new design they would get five.

There was not a single large tailfin at the back like on Craig's previous LSR racers. *Sonic I*'s terrifying tendency to fly had permanently put him off big tailfins. He opted instead for six smaller vertical stabilizers resembling shark fins placed down the entire length of the car: two up front behind the cockpit and under the nose, two at the rear above and below the tailpipe, one atop each of the rear wheel outrigger fairings. The rear wheels themselves, significantly, were also positioned well back, more than a foot behind the jet engine's tailpipe. This was to eliminate any possibility of the car teeter-tottering up on its back wheels like *Sonic I* had done. The overall look of the car was sophisticated, elegant, and extremely far out—a forty-seven-foot-long, wasp-waisted arrow that Craig would drive in a semi-reclining position in the needle-nose tip, his butt less than a foot off the ground. To differentiate it from his now-abandoned rocket car *Sonic II*, he came up with a new name, inspired by Henry Ford's *Arrow* racer that had brought the LSR to America for the first time back in 1904. In the corner of his drawings Craig penciled "Spirit of America-Sonic Arrow."

This was the car taking shape in Craig's mind when he moved to Northern California and bought the derelict tractor dealership in Rio Vista. He gutted the building and turned it into a workshop, painting the outside a delicate, somewhat incongruous pink. Then he converted the former showroom and office into living quarters for himself and his new wife, Marilyn Taylor. They had met through Marilyn's ten-year-old son, when he broke a window on a barge moored at Craig's Snug Harbor Marina and RV Park. Marilyn says the boy was playing baseball with his friend. Craig says he was throwing rocks. "So I went over and said I'd like to pay for the window," says Marilyn. "Craig invited me in and we talked. Then he asked me out and we ended up getting married three weeks later. It was a whirlwind romance." It was Craig's fifth marriage. The family would come to include dogs Muffin and Jenny, who came into Craig's life after Star died, and a stray cat named Bambi that he and Marilyn nursed back to health after it was hit by a car.

The first concrete step Craig took toward making *Sonic Arrow* a reality was to acquire a pair of jet engines, a main and a backup. He had assumed this would be easy, the J-79 having been around now for decades, but he was mistaken. Finally, after months of searching, Craig learned of an auction being held at the Naval Air Station North Island in San Diego that included a large number of surplus J-79-8Ds out of the Phantom F-4. He put bids in on three lots but didn't get any. The entire auction was bought out by a large surplus dealer instead. Hoping that he might still have a chance of buying two of the engines, Craig tracked down the dealer, Elmo Iadevaia, and gave him a call.

"You don't remember who I am, do you?" Elmo said after Craig introduced himself and explained his problem.

Craig was at a loss. "Well no, I don't."

"I'm the guy who sold you the afterburner for *Sonic I*."

Craig had just caught a lucky break. Elmo, for old time's sake, agreed to sell him two engines of his choice for the bargain price of $5,000 apiece, plus provide him with spare parts in exchange for getting his company's name on the car. It was *Sonic Arrow*'s first sponsorship deal. Craig took Walt Sheehan down to Elmo's and together they picked the two best-looking engines, checking the insides with a borescope to make sure they were undamaged.

———————

Out in Utah on the Bonneville Salt Flats, Art Arfons was making a remarkable return to land speed competition. He was in his mid-sixties now but as tenacious as ever, intent on reclaiming the LSR with a new jet-powered *Green Monster*, number 27, a tiny, waist-high racer weighing just 1,800 pounds. "I had to call Breedlove for help when I was building it," he told author Harvey Shapiro. "I couldn't figure out the linkage steering. Craig had used it on his three-wheeler. He sent me a diagram. It's his steering in the thing. It worked good." Art crashed at 350 mph on his first trip to Bonneville with *Green Monster* number 27 in 1989. Undeterred, he repaired the damage, turned it into a four-wheeler, and returned in 1990 to try again.

Craig flew out to watch. What he saw disturbed him. Art, the iron man of land speed, was struggling. The old strength and willpower had faded. The violence of extreme speed was too much. Craig never dreamed of giving Art advice back in the 1960s. "Art knew what he wanted to do and it would have been presumptuous," he said. But that's what he did now. "I saw an old friend who was visibly shaken. It's the first time I'd ever seen him without an air of confidence about what he was doing. I thought about it before I did it and I told him what I thought. That's all."

"Craig just told me to feel out the car," said Art, "take it easy, don't do anything foolish. He said I'd been away from this kind of stuff for a long time, get accustomed to it, don't get discouraged. I really appreciated his advice."

Art made one more run after that, hitting 338 mph. Then, after a brief struggle with himself, he packed it in. "I just think it was a real good decision," said Craig. "I'm glad he got to build his car, bring it out. He found out something. Now he can retire knowing that he came out and gave it a try. I think that's fine. I'm very happy that he's safe. I love the guy and don't want to see him get hurt."

Richard Noble had also gone out to Bonneville to watch Art's record attempt. He crossed paths with Craig out on the salt flats and Craig mentioned that he was putting a new land speed project together himself. "Say, Richard, I've decided to build another car," Noble remembers him saying. "I've just come from purchasing two J-79 8 series engines. I'm committed." This was the first Noble had heard of Craig's intention of returning to LSR competition. It got him thinking. "I'd wanted to keep going after *Thrust2* and build *Thrust3*, but we found that nobody seemed remotely interested in backing us to break our own record. Now Craig's surprise announcement changed everything. As far as I was concerned, the next chapter in the land-speed history book was ready to be written: a contest between Britain and America. It was a fabulous concept, guaranteed to stir the old patriotic juices."

Noble returned to England and launched a new land speed project. His goal wasn't just to better his own record or even to reach 700 mph. He wanted to be the first to Mach 1. To make his intentions clear, he christened his planned racer *Thrust-SuperSonic Car*, a.k.a. *ThrustSSC*.

The first thing Craig did after completing his *Sonic Arrow* design was to have a model made to show potential sponsors. This was done in fiberglass by Tom Trefethen in 1991. Craig would paint the four-foot-long model in various colors and apply different decals over the next several years, starting with a Ford paint and logo scheme, which failed to attract backing from the car giant. Tom and his sister Tina Trefethen, employees of race car builder Mike McCluskey in Torrance and experts in the latest fabrication techniques using composite materials, became the first two official members of the *Sonic Arrow* team and would go on to play a crucial role in construction.

That began in 1992, after Craig moved to Rio Vista and sold Snug Harbor to raise funds to get started. The $2 million he banked was twenty times more than he had needed to build his original *Spirit* and *Sonic I*. But times had changed and costs had risen. Bringing *Sonic Arrow* to completion would eat up the whole sum and much more.

The aerodynamics of the design were not tested before Craig began fabrication. Using a wind tunnel to verify the configuration wouldn't have been of much use. A tunnel without a moving ground plane was apt to give bad data, which was worse than no data, and the few that did have a moving ground plane couldn't be run at high-enough speeds. An emerging alternative was to do computer testing, conducting something called a computational fluid dynamics study. That required massive amounts of computing time back in the early 1990s, however, or hours on a Cray supercomputer, neither of which Craig could afford. Testing a model on a rocket sled was out of the question for the same reason: it was just too expensive. There would be testing, but as with *Sonic I* it would come later, when the car was actually run. "We're going to have lots of sensors," Craig said, explaining his approach. "The plan essentially is to build the speed incrementally and evaluate the data. Once we get to seven hundred we'll switch over to an unmanned test programme and put it through the sound barrier to confirm the design."

Construction got under way in 1993, the chromoly chassis taking shape on a frame bolted to the shop floor, the Stars and Stripes waving from a seventy-six-foot-high flagpole outside. Craig proceeded slowly and carefully, making sure that every weld was perfect. He was assisted by a team of volunteers that came and went over the next two years, names like Dennis Craig and Pete Ogden, old friends of Craig's from the '60s, and several civilian employees from Travis Air Force Base nearby. Nye Frank, still married to Craig's ex-wife Lee, declined to join the project when Craig phoned him up. Finding skilled workers in fact would be an ongoing challenge, for there was no large talent pool around Rio Vista as there had been in L.A.

Down in Torrance, Tom and Tina Trefethen set to work making the air ducts that would hug either side of the racer, building them up in molds from multiple laminated layers of graphite bonded together with epoxy and resin. The finished ducts, heat treated, painted, and buffed to a high gloss, were incredibly strong. Tom and Tina would build the cockpit capsule the same way, using laminated layers of fiberglass and graphite in a Kevlar skin to create a virtually indestructible shell. Craig had originally envisioned a capsule that could be ejected away from the car and had included this in his design for *Sonic II* going back to 1969. Now, facing the challenges and costs of actual construction, he went with the simpler option of an ultra-strong cocoon to save himself in the event of a crash.

Hopefully it wouldn't come to that. Craig had designed *Sonic Arrow* with superior aerodynamics to keep it on the ground through Mach 1 and had developed a braking system to get safely stopped that was much more effective than anything he had had on his earlier cars. The ribbon chutes, manufactured by Syndex Recovery Systems, were good for speeds up to 800 mph and the brakes themselves were an entirely new concept that Craig invented himself. Rather than rely on traditional disc brakes, which could melt from the heat of friction at speeds over 300 mph, he came up with a foot-like skid pad beneath the cockpit that pressed into the ground by means of a hydraulic ram. The concept reminded the Trefethens of Tina's days as a downhill skateboard racer on L.A.'s Signal Hill in the '70s, when the quickest way to stop was to put down your feet. It was this skateboard connection that gave the brake its nickname. It came to be known as Craig's "Fred Flintstone" brake.

Craig also came up with a revolutionary design for the wheels, as inflated tires were no longer a viable option for the speeds he would be going. The obvious alternative was to use solid metal wheels like on Richard Noble's *Thrust2*, but Craig didn't like that idea. Solid discs were aesthetically unpleasing and also wouldn't hold up to extremely high speeds. As Tina Trefethen explains, "When you get a three-foot-diameter wheel going 1,000 mph, no aluminum made will survive. It would literally disintegrate. The metal's just not strong enough, no matter what alloy you cast." Building on his experience designing *Sonic I*'s wheels, Craig therefore developed something entirely new: an aluminum wheel with an outer covering of wound graphite filaments that not only had the look and the traction of a tire but also served to hold the wheel together. It worked because the graphite "tire" responded in the opposite way to centrifugal force, squeezing inward the faster the wheel turned to counter the mounting outward strain as the metal wheel tried to pull itself apart. Of the many things Craig has done in his life, this wheel he designed for *Sonic Arrow*, rated for speeds up to 850 mph, outward and inward strains perfectly balanced, remains one of his proudest achievements.

Sonic Arrow's two J-79s were in the meantime being overhauled by Harry Weiser, Ken Thomas, Todd Warren, and Ed Sellnow, jet engine specialists from Travis who volunteered their time after work. After completing the overhaul, Harry and the guys essentially hot-rodded the 79s to boost their power well above design specs. This was done by replacing the variable-width rear nozzle with a smaller, lighter, fixed-diameter tailpipe, and by running it on gasoline rather than jet fuel. The result was a hotter operating temperature and higher-velocity exhaust blasting out the back, creating 20,000 pounds of static thrust "easy," says Harry, and as much as 24,000 pounds when the car was going at high speed. Putting such a modified jet engine into a Lockheed Starfighter or F-4 Phantom was definitely not recommended. It would overheat and melt after just a few minutes. But this was not a concern in land speed racing. Craig's jet would run for not much more than a minute at a stretch, so it could burn hot.

Craig had *Sonic Arrow*'s fundamental structure complete by late 1994. It was time to give the racer some skin. He acquired a load of aluminum and hired a tin bender to shape it. The guy struggled with the job for six months—so long that it became clear he was going to need help. It was at this point that a British aluminum shaper named Alex Prosser turned up, looking for work in the States. Alex had excellent credentials and a solid recommendation from race car builder Mike McCluskey, so Craig hired him and put him in charge, then fired the first guy when he took his demotion badly. As Alex got down to the job, he discovered that most of the work that had been done was substandard and had to be scrapped. For Craig, it was $85,000 down the drain. Fortunately, Alex proved to be a master of his craft and completed the job in only three months.

Across the continent and on the other side of the Atlantic, Richard Noble was pushing ahead with his own rekindled LSR ambitions. His *ThrustSSC*

would be a speed monster like never before, a twin-engine machine powered by two Rolls-Royce Spey jets out of the British version of the F-4
Phantom. The two engines together, blasting in full afterburner, would be
capable of generating 50,000 pounds of thrust. That roughly correlated to
110,000 horsepower. Go to a large shopping mall at Christmas, take the
engine out of every car in the sprawling parking lot, and cram them into
a single racer, and you might end up with comparable juice.

The design for *ThrustSSC* that had emerged by this time had the
same basic tricycle configuration as *Sonic Arrow*. Because it had two
engines, however, Noble was able to use the configuration in reverse,
placing two fixed wheels spaced widely apart in the front, one under
each engine, and two steerable wheels on the centerline in the rear. The
advantage of this, Noble explains in his autobiography *Thrust*, was stability. "Imagine a loaded wheelbarrow with a single, central front wheel. Lift
it, and it tips easily to either side. Now imagine a barrow with two front
wheels, one on either side. It's much harder to tilt. The same principle
holds good with a high-speed car. The [Breedlove-type] tricycle layout
makes a car unstable, liable to tumble if upset by a bump. The resistance
to roll is much better if the front wheels are spread wide apart."

This increased stability, however, came at a price—the aerodynamic
price of increased frontal area and in turn increased drag. Noble was
convinced that this wouldn't matter for *ThrustSSC*, because the massive power of its twin engines was enough to overcome any additional
drag and smash its way to Mach 1. It was a brute-force approach to
the LSR and differed fundamentally from what Craig was doing in Rio
Vista. Craig, with a one-engine racer and half the power, was planning
to finesse his way through the sound barrier, piercing it with the low-
drag tip of his *Sonic Arrow*.

Fabrication of *ThrustSSC* began in the south of England in late
1994, after Noble confirmed his design with both a computational fluid
dynamics study and rocket sled testing. He was now in a race with
Craig to get his car built, for the first to reach Mach 1 would not only
reap all the glory but also likely knock the other out of competition
by killing any chance of him raising additional funds. The sponsorship
money would dry up after the historic mark was achieved. It was the

sense of urgency arising from this realization that led Noble to decide not to drive the racer himself. "In order to get *ThrustSSC* operational as soon as practically possible," he wrote later, "we had to go through one hell of a build operation. If we didn't, Craig Breedlove would beat us. I knew that managing it and finding the funding was going to be a tremendous undertaking on its own."

Noble was so effective at raising money and pushing the project forward that by mid-1995 he had almost caught up to Craig. By this time Royal Air Force fighter pilot Andy Green had been selected as the driver after an exhaustive competition. Green hadn't been particularly impressed with his first glimpse of the car, a drawing in a newspaper article alongside a photo of Craig's sleek *Arrow*. "Breedlove looked as if he had exactly the right design," he said, whereas *ThrustSSC* "seemed the wrong way to go." He nevertheless committed himself completely to the project, training in a modified flight simulator and initially being "absolutely overawed by the speed." Driving at Mach 1 down on the ground was an entirely different experience from flying at Mach 1 high up in the air.

Back in Rio Vista, Craig was running out of money, the proceeds from the sale of Snug Harbor almost used up. He had been trying since the start of the decade to land a major sponsor but was met with rejection everywhere he turned—including at his old sponsor Shell, which was spending most of its sports sponsorship budget on McLaren Formula One race cars. The company had recently declined a proposal from McLaren owner Ron Dennis for a land speed car called the *Maverick* and it didn't want to show favoritism by backing Craig.

Then, out of the blue, Craig got a call from actor Craig T. Nelson, best known for his hit TV sitcom *Coach* but also an accomplished race car driver with his Screaming Eagles Racing team on the International Motor Sports Association (IMSA) circuit. "I heard you were building a new car," Nelson said, "and about the trouble you've been having getting funding. I thought maybe I could help."

"Great!" said Craig. "I can use all the help I can get. What did you have in mind?"

"Well, I'd like to buy the film rights to your life story. I want to make a movie about you."

Nelson flew up to Rio Vista a few days later. "Craig had this brand-new *Spirit of America* sitting like a rocket ship in his garage," he remembers. "I thought it was emblematic of the entrepreneurial spirit, a kind of pioneering that you don't encounter anymore. Here was a guy who was not only trying to do something that was almost impossible, he was actually doing it. He'd been doing it for many years and was still pursuing the dream. It was pretty inspiring. I thought, *Jeez, this is something I want to participate in.* I just really admired Craig for his courage and his willingness to commit to an idea that many of us would have given up on a long time ago. And especially the way he approached it all, with such a great sense of humor, coupled with seriousness and intelligence. He was just a lot of fun to be around."

Nelson offered Craig $250,000 for the film rights to his story, enough to keep the project moving forward. He also helped Craig promote the car in the ongoing hunt for sponsors—starting with IMSA owner Charlie Slater, who offered to do the timing for *Sonic Arrow*'s LSR bid for the sum of one dollar. It was a huge gift and Craig quickly accepted. The cost of hiring USAC to officiate at a record attempt had risen so astronomically in the past three decades that he had been worried about whether he could afford to get timers at all. Slater subsequently helped Craig get substantial sponsorship from car parts retailer AutoZone as well.

And then more good news: McLaren owner Ron Dennis broke with Shell and the oil company shifted its Formula One sponsorship to Ferrari. With Ron and his *Maverick* now out of the picture—the car would never be built—Craig resubmitted his proposal to Shell and this time got lucky. When company president Jim Morgan made a personal visit to Rio Vista to look over the project, Craig had the shop immaculate and the racer looking great and the *Sonic Arrow* model repainted with the Shell logo and colors. Morgan was impressed and a deal was made.

Craig now just barely had enough funds to hire a team, complete fabrication, and mount a shoestring bid for the record. The car would use 92-octane premium Shell gasoline and henceforth would be frequently referred to by the biggest sponsor name painted on its side, *Formula Shell.*

"Man, you got the hammer," Craig remembers old-time drag racer Denis Manning exclaiming the first time he saw the racer in all its shark-finned, space-age glory.

Craig: "What do you mean, 'the hammer'?"

Denis: "The hammer, man. Lucifer's hammer. You're gonna clobber England!"

20

TURBULENCE

It was really going to happen. Craig, a grandfather of five, coming up to his fifty-ninth birthday, was returning to land speed competition after three decades. He wasn't just going to complete *Sonic Arrow*, he was going to do the driving himself. The decision was due in part—maybe a big part—to personal ambition. The rest was to keep his sponsors happy. They were backing the idea of *Spirit of America* with Craig Breedlove himself at the wheel.

To ensure that his aging body wouldn't let him down, Craig started jogging and working out with weights and exercise equipment set up in a loft at the back of the shop. At Craig T. Nelson's suggestion he also hired personal trainer and physical therapist Alyson Kimball, who had worked with Nelson's Screaming Eagles Racing team. "Alyson worked out with me every day for six months," says Craig. "That was a real great benefit. She got me into excellent physical shape."

There was also a big mental component in preparing for a return to land speed competition: Craig had to hone his concentration. It was essential for driving a car to the record and could not simply be turned on like a tap. Craig had to build up to it in the preceding months, nurturing his confidence and reducing distractions to direct his attention to what lay ahead. It was why a competent crew chief was so important, someone who could take on much of the burden of leading the team.

It was only now, as Craig struggled to get himself ready, that he came to fully appreciate how good he had had it back in the '60s. Shell and Goodyear with their full financial support had spared him the necessity of rounding up and appeasing dozens of smaller sponsors and had generally kept him under their sheltering wing. They took care of marketing and media requests, they arranged Craig's travel schedule and assigned handlers to assist him, they helped him find technical expertise, booked the salt flats and USAC timers, found Craig a PR firm when he got famous, and even helped him invest his money. All that was gone now. Craig was no longer being taken care of. He was totally exposed to everything, to all the distractions—starting with the infuriating, trumped-up lawsuits.

It went back to 1993, when Craig parted ways with a small marketing firm that had been trying to find sponsors for the car. It had come up empty so Craig turned elsewhere, to an outfit in Detroit that would hopefully get some results. It did, negotiating deals with companies like Chevrolet and Mr. Gasket. Then it kept the money for itself. When Craig realized he had been robbed and demanded the money, the Detroit firm, caught red-handed, responded with lawyers. In the end Craig had little choice but to write the theft off, heeding his lawyer's advice that seeking restitution through the courts would eat up anything he might gain.

It was just the start of a series of wrangles that would consume Craig when he needed to focus on his upcoming record attempt. Up next was a lawsuit from the first marketing firm, the one that Craig had fired after it failed to find any sponsors. Its owner, a woman named Susie, claimed that she had a verbal agreement with Craig to act as *Spirit of America*'s exclusive marketing representative and was now seeking damages of $2 million. Craig claimed that there had been no such agreement, verbal or otherwise. He prepared to fight Susie in court.

The mess with Susie was still working its way through the system when an even bigger storm blew up between Craig and a Salt Lake City coatings company that Susie had brought to Craig as a potential sponsor.

"This coatings guy, his name was Jeff, he showed up at the shop with this big spiel and a bunch of beautiful samples of coatings on different things," says Craig. "He said he had worked at one time coating J-79 blades for the navy and that he could get the finish on the engine parts within so many mils tolerance and that it would improve the engine's performance. He said, 'I'll give you $25,000 if you let me coat the engines, and I'll guarantee you that they'll run better. It'll improve your compressor performance.'

"Walt Sheehan wasn't too keen on doing the coatings. I didn't really think we needed it either, but I did need the sponsorship money, so I agreed to have Jeff's company coat one of the engines. We totally disassembled it, numbered all the compressor pieces so we could get the blades back in the right spot, and sent everything off to be coated. And they botched it. Their coating product wasn't mixed right and they put it on thick and lumpy. When we got the parts back, God, the orange peel on the blades was terrible. Walt said the whole thing was toast. Mel Marks [a retired GE engineer who was helping the project] said, 'Oh man, those coatings have screwed up your compressor. We'll have to run the other engine and keep this one as backup, maybe figure out how to get the coatings off.' So the other engine, the one we didn't get coated, that's the one we ended up putting in the car. It was just a screamer. But the coated engine, it was pretty well ruined."

Craig was still prepared to put Jeff's company logo on the car in return for the agreed-upon $25,000 to salvage something out of the fiasco. But Jeff wouldn't sign the sponsorship contract and come up with the money. And when Craig phoned him to find out what was happening, he wouldn't take Craig's calls. Finally Craig wrote him off and made a sponsorship deal with a different coatings company, an outfit in North Carolina that was prepared to sign a contract and cut a check. It was only then that Jeff responded—with a lawsuit. He claimed that he had made a verbal agreement with Craig for a no-money sponsorship to get his company on the car in return for doing the coating. Where had they made this verbal agreement whose existence Craig vehemently denied? At a dinner that Craig attended, Jeff claimed, presumably during the few minutes when Jeff's wife went to the washroom and was absent from the table, for she would later testify that she had no recollection of any such talk. Someone else was present, however, who had a clear memory of the alleged conversation. That someone was none other than the marketer Susie who was suing Craig for $2 million. She was going to testify in Jeff's lawsuit that he had a verbal agreement with Craig and Jeff was going to reciprocate by testifying in Susie's lawsuit that she did too. The same Salt Lake City lawyer was representing them both.

Craig's shop in the meantime had become a beehive of activity, a team coalescing around *Sonic Arrow* to kick the build into high gear. A few members lived within commuting distance of Rio Vista but most had been pulled in from farther afield and lived at the shop. Craig housed them in three trailers and a big mobile home parked out in the yard, and in the loft bedroom inside. There was also a cot in the open loft at the back where Craig had his exercise equipment.

Alex Prosser, Craig's original crew chief, had by this time moved on. Sticking to the build schedule, liaising with sponsors, dealing with sometimes difficult team personalities, including the team's combative female PR representative, who challenged him to a fistfight—it all pushed Alex to the breaking point and he resigned. "Undertaking a project of this magnitude with limited resources is unbelievably stressful," says Craig. "It's far more difficult than what meets the eye."

The team was now headed by an intense, hyperactive, late-twenties force of nature named Dezsö Molnar. Dezsö's background included stints as a rocket technician on a privately funded manned rocket project, as a flight engineer in the Air Force, and as the bass player, vocalist, and songwriter for a punk rock band he formed called Rocket Science, which had just come out with the album *Wide Screen Edition* ("*Send a doctor, send a nurse / Send a casket, send a hearse / He's frying like bacon, there ain't no mistaking—Lobster Head!*"). Dezsö also liked to fool around with jets and had built a jet-powered go-cart that he drove onstage with an avant-garde performance group in San Francisco called Survival Research Laboratories. The shows SRL put on, with names like

Illusions of Shameless Abundance and *Calculated Forecast of Ultimate Doom*, were extreme and controversial, featuring flame-spewing robots, ripped-apart cow carcasses and giant mechanical monsters, explosions and destruction, and a lot of mayhem—so much that they were occasionally shut down by the San Francisco Fire Department. Dezsö fit right in.

Dezsö (pronounced "Dez-shur") first approached Craig in January 1996, after seeing an item on the local TV news about *Sonic Arrow*. "They showed the new car," he recalls, "and said the plan was to run that year, but it appeared to me a long way from finished. After watching the segment, I told our [SRL] manager that I would find the car and run the team. The sound barrier on land was attractive as the last natural hurdle before going to Mars." Dezsö drove out to Rio Vista, met Craig, and got hired, starting at the bottom at $5 an hour. The car, he discovered, was advancing at a "glacial" pace. "The work was agonizingly slow. But once I had a solid grip on the order of operations to complete the parts, I scrambled ahead." Craig soon started taking more notice of Dezsö. His get-it-done energy was what the project needed. He was also in some ways a kindred spirit, unafraid to dream big and make things happen with tremendous drive. It might even be said that in Dezsö Craig had come face-to-face with a younger version of himself, an eccentric version of the 1960s Craig Breedlove. The young man became an unstoppable whirlwind when Craig promoted him to crew chief after Alex Prosser's departure. "I cut loose to fix every item I had seen from the trenches to push the project into warp drive," he says.

Dezsö recruited several new team members after taking the helm. Among them were Travis Air Force Base civilian employees Terry Hendrickson and David Veno, former coworkers of Dezsö's from his time in the service, and machinists Liisa Pine and Kevin Binkert from the Survival Research Laboratories performance group. "I had built a special effects machine that broke the sound barrier with a braided cable," says Kevin of his SRL work. "It made a little sonic boom. It was the reason I got asked to come out to Rio Vista. They wanted to build a spinning machine to spin the wheels and do a supersonic test of them, and Dezsö said, 'I know a guy who has a similar machine.' So they called me up. They decided not to build that machine but they needed a machinist, so

I stayed out there and, man, I fell in deep. I went pretty well overnight from stopping by to check the place out to working full time, putting in sometimes sixteen-hour days. It was all consuming. And I just loved it. I would have done it for nothing."

Ed Ballinger, who had worked for Craig going back to the *English Leather* rocket dragster, joined the team too, living in the trailer across from Dezsö. He remembers chasing down stock parts to put in the car, "an alternator and other stuff off a Corvette, power steering off of something else, the list goes on and on." Chris Rossi was brought in from Philadelphia to do the electrical wiring, and Harry Weiser and Ed Sellnow, out of Travis AFB, worked on the jet engine. Tina Trefethen, who had fabricated the cockpit and air ducts with her brother Tom, was liaising with companies to get the 36-inch-diameter wheels built. A big carrot for Tina, who had extensive experience racing airplanes, was that she would be named backup driver for the car.

Old-time fabricator Dennis Craig, who had been with the project from nearly the start, was now in a paid position, working full time and living in one of the trailers. He was one of those guys typically referred to as a "character." "Man, Dennis could put it away," recalls Kevin Binkert. "You wouldn't think somebody could even hold that much booze. But Dennis could, then he'd be up and already working on the car the next morning when I'd get there. I'd be thinking, *Dennis, how in the world do you do that?*" Alyson Kimball, trying to sleep in the loft bedroom, remembers Dennis too. "He'd get up real early and be downstairs in the shop at five o'clock every morning, grinding away and making all kinds of noise. So I started getting up early too and ended up doing a lot of light power-tool work on the car."

While the team experienced its share of friction—"I don't know what you've got without that," says Ed Ballinger. "Girl Scouts, I guess."—it also had its share of fun. There were jam sessions to unwind after marathon work sessions, Alyson on her saxophone and Dezsö on his bass, and trips out to local restaurants where the question would be, *What would Craig leave behind this time?*

"Part of my job was to check the table to make sure Craig didn't forget his glasses, or his wallet, or his car keys," remembers the team's new PR representative Cherié Danson. "It was standard procedure. Craig would get up and walk out and you'd be picking something up that he forgot. If you didn't, the restaurants would be calling the shop the next day, 'Hey, we've got Craig's wallet' or 'We've got Craig's glasses.' It wasn't memory loss or anything. It was just one of his quirks. It never took away from the confidence we all had that Craig was capable of setting the record. If anyone on the team didn't believe that, they wouldn't have been there. We *knew* he could do it."

———

Craig flew back to Salt Lake City in early May 1996 for the trial in Jeff's coatings company lawsuit. He went armed with affidavits, expert witnesses, and samples of coated blades to prove that the company had damaged his engine. It was to be a four-day trial, two days for Jeff to make his case, backed up by the testimony of marketer Susie, then two days for Craig's defense.

"So we get started. The first two days, Monday and Tuesday, Jeff and his lawyers tell their story. Then the judge lets them keep rattling on through Wednesday and Thursday and never let me testify. I didn't get to say one fucking word. And then at the end of the last day the judge calls us up to the front and says he's going to agree to increase the damages against me to something like $260,000 and he's going to triple that figure if he finds that a verbal agreement existed. Then he wags his finger at me and says, 'I suggest you settle this thing over the weekend, because if this court has to settle it for you next week, you may not like the outcome.'

"It was just completely stacked against us. Walt Sheehan was so upset that he said he was going to write a letter to the court. Anyway, we went to a restaurant across the street and my lawyer, this guy who'd been saying I should fight this thing, now he says, 'I really think you should think seriously about settling.' And I said, 'No shit!'"

Craig reached a settlement over the weekend, agreeing to pay Jeff $85,000. "I don't even like to think about it," he says of the bitter experience. "It was just so much bullshit. You get tied up in this crap just once in your life and, man, you end up so against the legal system it's unbelievable."

He returned to Rio Vista with a sinking heart, half expecting to be similarly reamed out by Susie when her case was heard. Fortunately, he caught a break when Susie's lawyer, who was representing her for free, dropped the case after discovering that she had a judgment against her from a separate legal wrangle that would consume any fees he hoped to gain from shaking down Craig. When the lawsuit went before the court the next year, Susie never showed up. By then, however, Craig had racked up more than a quarter million dollars in legal expenses. "It was money I should have been using to break the record and it ended up completely wasted. It would have been better spent taking it outside and burning it in the driveway."

It was now July 1996. The push was on to get *Sonic Arrow* finished by September. The plan was to take the racer first to Bonneville for testing, then to head out to Black Rock Desert for the record attempt. The thought of running the graphite tires on Bonneville's corrosive salt still upsets Tina Trefethen. "They weren't designed for that," she says. "The salt was just going to muck them up." Some of Craig's sponsors were insisting on it, however, for publicity photos and film of the car on that beautiful expanse of white desert. Craig wanted it too. There was no way he was returning to the LSR game without making at least a few passes at Bonneville, where he had first made his name.

Several team members were no longer around by this time. "Some people just don't work out," is how Dezsö put it. He was in fact proving to be a hard leader, at times bullying the others in his drive to finish the car. The harsh words and blowups generally took place when Craig was out of the shop, distracted by lawsuits and sponsors, so he didn't fully appreciate how different Dezsö's managerial style was from his own gentle manner. With so many worries intruding, Craig just wanted the work kept on schedule. And that's what Dezsö was doing. He was stepping on toes but he was getting things done, seemingly impervious to stress and fatigue as he drove the crew forward.

"Dezsö personally absorbed the weight of sponsorship duties and contractual things," says Chris Rossi, "and he did his best to make sure deadlines were met. He did make some enemies. I think there's a natural angst to being a team member doing your discipline and having somebody ride herd on you. But you have to have a leader at some point, somebody to get all the loose ends tied up, and Dezsö did a good job considering the pressure he was under. I don't know how the car would have met the deadline and got running without him being the leader he was. I mean, they'd been working on it for four years by that point and didn't have it anywhere near ready. Then all of a sudden it was, 'We've got to be at Bonneville!' Dezsö was pretty tough, but he got everybody working and we got the car done."

The shake-up that resulted in several people leaving the team coincided with the departure of Craig's wife Marilyn. She had been with Craig in Rio Vista from the beginning, helping him renovate the shop and decorating the living quarters out front. "You could see Marilyn all over in that apartment," recalls a team member. "We're talking mirrors on the ceiling, Grecian figures spouting water, a big hot tub, soft colors and nautilus shells. There was not a lot of Craig in there. It was not what you would expect for a jet car guy." When the car project got going, Marilyn threw herself into it body and soul, doing the paperwork, cooking meals for the crowd in the shop, and taking care of everybody. "She tried so hard," recalls Tina Trefethen. "Marilyn was so amazing, the best team mom ever."

It was the car that ultimately caused the breakup in the marriage. Craig and Marilyn both generally agree on that but disagree on the specifics. To Craig, the crux of the problem was the mounting stress and media onslaught as the project gathered momentum. Marilyn, emotionally fragile to begin with, couldn't handle it. It overwhelmed her, she started drinking, and it drove them apart. As Marilyn sees it, Craig's growing obsession with the project drove her away. "Craig was a nice guy," she says. "He means well. But he loses it with his car. The car was his baby. It came first. When he was getting close to running it, everything else around him, he just kind of tossed them aside."

Whatever happened, the result was that Marilyn moved into a rental house nearby with her now-teenage son and things spiraled downward. The boy was stopped by the police a few weeks later driving the Camaro that Craig was letting Marilyn use, the one that sponsor Chevrolet had loaned to the team. He was caught with a pound of marijuana in the trunk and the car was impounded. Craig had Marilyn's father come up to Rio Vista to help with the deteriorating situation but whatever good it did didn't last long. The end came when Craig attended a local Alcoholics Anonymous meeting and was given some blunt advice by people who'd been there. His only realistic options, he was told, were to accept his spouse's drinking or to just walk away. Craig chose the latter. He filed for divorce the next day. By then Chevy had withdrawn its sponsorship support and taken back the Camaro.

While this marital drama was playing itself out, Craig was dealing with a separate headache involving *Sonic Arrow*'s wheels. Two sets of five had been forged in aluminum by Center Line, then sent to Compositek for the winding on of the graphite filament tires. The assemblies had then been sent to a third company for precision machining and testing, and the costs suddenly went through the roof. The company gave an initial verbal estimate of $15,000, increased this to $34,000 on its written quote, then drew up a bill for a whopping $102,000 when the job was complete. When Craig said he could afford to pay only the written quote he had agreed to, the company let him have only one set of wheels and kept the second set until it received payment in full. Craig T. Nelson phoned the owner on Craig's behalf and begged him to be reasonable but it didn't do any good.

Craig would therefore have to make his record bid with only one set of wheels. If something went wrong with them, if the tires frayed or were otherwise damaged, he would not have any spares.

Richard Noble and *ThrustSSC* had now caught up to Craig and *Sonic Arrow*. Andy Green would take the ten-ton behemoth for its first test runs at the Farnborough RAF base in late September, pushing it to 200 mph on one of the runways and getting it stopped with inches to spare. He shrugged off the hair-raising experience as "a little sporty" and took the delayed response and general awkwardness of the car's rear-wheel steering in stride. But *ThrustSSC* would prove a major handful to drive. The backward-wheelbarrow analogy that Noble had used to make a point about the racer's stability might have been applied to its handling characteristics as well.

The car would next be taken to Jordan to begin shakedown runs on Al Jafr Desert. It was exceptionally dry there, so a land speed attempt could be made year-round. This gave the Brits, weather-wise, the luxury of time. They would be able to run *ThrustSSC* on into the winter, long after the Bonneville Salt Flats and Black Rock were flooded and Craig and his *Sonic Arrow* had been forced to go home.

21

BREEDLOVE'S BACK

CRAIG ARRIVED AT BONNEVILLE ON SEPTEMBER 14, 1996, to begin his campaign to reclaim the world land speed record. As he watched *Sonic Arrow* being lifted off its trailer and set onto the salt, the flood of emotion that washed over him was almost more than he could contain. It had been thirty-one years since he set his 600 mph record here in *Sonic I* in 1965, thirty-one years of struggle and frustration . . . and now he was back. "There was a lot of emotional drag there for Craig that day," remembers Ed Ballinger, who would be handling the chutes. "I mean, he damn near broke into tears when the car's tires touched the ground, out of the truck." Stan Goldstein, temporarily filling in as operations manager, was equally moved. At the motel in Wendover he had taped a sign on his door: WE'RE BACK!

The crew got to work setting up an awning and workshop where the car would be prepped for its first run. Crew chief Dezsö Molnar, stalking about in pith helmet and sunglasses, looked especially harried. "We have very limited time to do our ramp-up to higher speeds," he had said before leaving Rio Vista, "so we've got to be awake; we've got to be fast on our feet. We've got to turn wrenches. It's going to be intense." He was the epitome of intensity now; "wound up tight," observed a writer from *Speak* magazine, "crackling with nervous energy."

"Dez is a godsend," said Craig, looking relaxed as he held court with journalists in the shade of the team Winnebago. "He's got incredible ethics, and ah, I love him dearly. I mean I really, really love him a lot. . . . I truly think he is the best crew chief we've ever had."

The team worked on the car through the afternoon and into the evening. The laborious prep continued on into the next day, and then into the day after that. Finally, on September 17, *Sonic Arrow* was ready to go. But it had rained in the night, leaving the course too wet for running. And so they waited, counting the days as the salt slowly dried.

Behind the scenes, meanwhile, trouble had arisen. Although Craig's heart lay on the Bonneville Salt Flats, he wasn't intending to make his record attempt there. There just wasn't enough space. Decades of phosphate mining had reduced the expanse of white desert and the recent rain had reduced the usable portion of what remained even more. The plan therefore was to use Bonneville for initial testing of the car and for taking publicity photos and filming the commercials as required by the sponsors, then to move to Black Rock for the record attempt. All the required hoops had been jumped through to gain permission to run on the playa—environmental impact study, $30,000 application filing with the Bureau of Land Management, the works—and a permit had been secured. But then, on the eve of departure from Rio Vista, Craig was notified that an environmental group calling itself the Coalition for the High Rock / Black Rock National Conservation Area was opposed to him running a jet car on the playa and had filed a motion to block him. It was yet another round of legal trouble. His permit, and with it the whole project, was now tied up in the courts.

"I was just stunned. I called up the BLM and they told me this group had written a letter objecting to them granting us a permit. I said, 'So, someone writes a letter and buys a thirty-cent stamp, and all of a sudden there's a multimillion-dollar operation that's ground to a complete halt?' And he says, 'Yeah, that's about it.' So I said, 'What's it going to take to salvage this?'"

There was nothing Craig could do. The coalition's objection had set legal wheels in motion that could not be stopped. Because Black Rock was federal land, their motion now had to go before a federal judge, who had to make a ruling. And that could take months. Even if the ruling was in Craig's favor, the weather window at Black Rock would have long since closed. *Spirit of America* would be shut down for the season.

Craig did the only thing he could think of. He sent a letter to the judge explaining his predicament and asking for an expedited ruling. Then he prayed.

The salt finally dried enough to provide a few miles of usable course. With his Black Rock permit on hold and his record attempt for 1996 looking doubtful, Craig started testing *Sonic Arrow*. His first run, with the engine in idle, did not exceed 100 mph. The car handled well and his "Fred Flintstone" brake worked like a charm. Over the next two weeks he made around a dozen runs altogether, working his way up to 200 mph, then 300, then 375, the crew making adjustments and fixes as the inevitable problems presented themselves. This was the shakedown process that every experimental vehicle built from scratch had to be put through. All in all, the racer performed remarkably well.

Of the various issues that were identified during this period of testing, two would remain a source of ongoing concern. The first was the ribbon chutes. They had been fabricated by John Campbell, whose background was in braking systems for relatively light weapons systems at high altitude, where the air is much thinner, not in heavy dragsters down on the ground. "With the chutes we use on cars," explains Craig, "if you don't have enough porosity—in other words, if you don't let enough air go through—it has too solid a retarding effect. It puts such a strain on the canopy that it turns it sideways to let the air spill out. It'll spill out one side, then the chute, because it's not symmetrical anymore, it goes way around to the side and tows the back of the car over, or it'll go way up into the air and lift the back of the car. It can wander all over the place because it can't handle the pressure. At Bonneville, where the salt was wet and slippery, it was dragging the car around. It was like I was on a sheet of ice and the chute pulls the car, and Jesus, the next thing I know I'm going sideways."

The solution was to remove ribbons from the chutes. This would be an ongoing process, John Campbell and Ed Ballinger cutting away more and more of the Kevlar-strengthened strips until only half remained. "John almost couldn't believe that we had to open that much air out of the chutes," recalls Craig.

The second problem concerned the strain gauges that had been installed on the wheels to measure the aerodynamic forces at work on the car. Was *Sonic Arrow* experiencing increasing downforce as it went faster, its wheels pressing harder and harder into the ground, creating speed-robbing drag? Or was the pressure on the wheels getting lighter, indicating that aerodynamic lift was being generated, that the car wanted to fly? For a reason the crew could not fathom, the gauges would not give a meaningful reading. They were recording downforce as hovering around zero, virtually no fluctuation, which clearly wasn't right. The problem, which would take a full two years to solve, was that the gauges had been incorrectly installed, "basically 90 degrees off," says Craig, "to read torque rather than bending moment on the rear spindles. How does that stuff happen? God only knows. The government does it on huge projects with hundreds of engineers looking at the stuff. People make mistakes."

Back in Wendover after a day of testing, Craig took his three dogs, Muffin, Jenny, and a German shepherd puppy named Midnight, out for a walk. He didn't have them on leashes. It didn't seem necessary in such a sleepy town, alongside a road that wasn't much traveled. As they strolled along, Muffin and Jenny spotted another dog across the road and ran toward it to visit, Midnight trying to keep up behind. The two older dogs made it across the road. Midnight didn't. He was hit by a car.

"It was probably the only car on the highway," says Craig. "This guy was really zooming, speeding through the center of Wendover, and he got Midnight. Killed him right on the spot and didn't even stop. He just kept on going. I ran out and Midnight was all broken up. I don't think he knew what hit him. God, it just broke my heart. But life goes on."

As September gave way to October, Craig and the crew finished up what testing they could do on the salt flats and hauled *Sonic Arrow* back to Rio Vista for a thorough strip-down and cleaning. The Bonneville sojourn had been murder on the car. The wet, slushy salt had sprayed into every nook and cranny and compacted so tightly in the fairings that the wheels had almost seized up.

Craig was now desperate about his Black Rock permit, still held up in federal court. He needed a break. And on October 8 he got it. The judge considering the matter expedited the case as Craig had requested and found in his favor. The playa was at last open for his record attempt. By now, however, nearly a month of Craig's permitted time was gone. A sense of urgency thus gripped the team. They had to get the car to Black Rock and run it for the record before the weather window closed and the rains of autumn set in.

Bill Breedlove, a race car driver and distant cousin of Craig's who had recently taken over as operations manager for the team, had gone on ahead to set up the course. This would be a big job, surveying an expanse of desert thirteen miles long and football field–wide. The extreme width was to provide space for multiple lanes, necessary due to the nature of the dirt at Black Rock. "The best way to describe the alkali surface," explains Bill, "is that it's like running on an M&M candy. There's a crust on the outside that's only about three-quarters to an inch thick, and then you have this dusty, softer compound underneath. As you roll along, you break through the crust and you release all this dust and it ruts. So if you try to drive the car on it again, it'll rut-steer. A wheel can follow a rut and actually move the car around." This was not much of a problem on the Bonneville Salt Flats. The harder surface there meant that a single-lane course could be used multiple times. The course Bill laid out at Black Rock, conversely, consisted of eight side-by-side lanes, each forty-five feet wide, enough to provide Craig with plenty of undisturbed dirt. This entire expanse would have to be defodded by the crew and team volunteers, every foot walked to pick up stones and debris.

Craig and the main body of the *Sonic Arrow* crew arrived at Black Rock on October 21. They put up in the nearby town of Gerlach, Nevada, population three hundred, at a funky roadside motel and casino called Bruno's

Country Club—WHERE THE PAVEMENT ENDS AND THE WEST BEGINS according to the sign posted outside. Walt Sheehan, involved in both previous *Spirit* racers going back to 1961, had come along too. He was getting on in years and sick with cancer but was still game. Craig was glad to have him there, and not just for sentimental reasons. Nobody was better at crunching the numbers than Walt.

Base camp was set up a few miles away at the south end of the playa—motor homes, a prefab sheet metal building and attached awning to shelter the car, a pair of tractor-trailers, one of them the old galley trailer that Craig had used in the 1960s. The team was confident that they would bag the record. The car had performed well in the Bonneville testing and the acceleration data indicated that 850 mph was a "slam dunk." Craig had also proved himself ready for the challenge, his strength, reflexes, and skill as a driver undiminished despite the passage of years.

They were going to have to hurry, however. This late in the season, the weather window would not stay open much longer. One good downpour could leave the playa a muddy, unusable mess. And then there was the matter of finances. Sponsorship backing was tapped out. And so was Craig. "We were out of money," he says. "My American Express was totally maxed. And I owed money to guys on the crew. It was really difficult."

The plan was to start running the car the next day, Craig taking an initial pass in the 400 mph range, then a second one at over 500. These would serve to further test *Sonic Arrow* and to acclimate Craig to high speeds. They would also qualify the car for an official record attempt, as FIA rules specified that two runs had to be made between 400 and 500 mph to gain sanction for an attempt to break Richard Noble's 633 mph mark.

The timing would be done by the International Motor Sports Association for the sum of one dollar. Association president Charlie Slater, who had generously made the offer, subsequently sold IMSA in early 1996 but his promise carried over to the new owners. And they honored it. They sent IMSA representative Bruce Clarke out to Black Rock to time Craig's runs.

Clarke's arrival on the playa left Craig aghast. He had expected a sizable IMSA contingent, a dozen officials with lots of equipment, the kind of elaborate setup that USAC employed. "Bruce Clarke showed up all by himself with everything piled inside a rented van," Craig says. "I had no course stewards, no people to record the wind, no timing shack, no way to communicate from the car down to the timing area. I had one guy with a bunch of old wire and a set of Chrondek clocks. He's sitting out there on a wire spool with the timer, and all this dilapidated wire held together with tape and what have you. I still have two boxes of it, literally bare copper wire just twisted together."

So now the clocks became one more thing to worry about. If they failed, it wouldn't matter how fast Craig went, the run wouldn't count. And what about the lack of communication? All the *Sonic Arrow* crew had with them were walkie-talkies, line-of-sight units good over only a few miles. How would they coordinate up and down the many miles of desert that Craig would traverse? How would they ensure that the course was clear? How would they keep track of wind speeds, which could be so erratic at Black Rock, the air calm at one end of the course and blustery at the other?

Craig's longtime friend Chuck Lyford and Chuck's son Charlie stepped in with a stopgap solution. They would use the radio aboard the twin-engine Aerostar aircraft they had flown out to the playa to relay walkie-talkie messages up and down the course as they circled overhead. To communicate from the measured mile to the start line, for example, Bruce Clarke would talk to Charlie in the plane and Charlie would pass his message on to the start line, where Craig would pick it up via the headphones in his helmet.

The next day was a washout. Too much wind. It could be brutal at Black Rock, whipping up tremendous clouds of dust from where vehicles had broken through the crust, releasing the powdery stuff underneath. "When the wind comes on," says Craig, "you can't even see in the dust clouds. There's no way you could find your way off the playa. You just need to park and sit, because you can't see past the end of the hood of the car."

It wasn't until October 23 that Craig was able to make his first run, a 448 mph pass late in the day. He stopped without using his chutes, hoping to expedite the turnaround so he could get in a second run while there was still daylight. But it was too late. By the time the car was ready to go the desert was dark.

"It doesn't seem like thirty years," Craig said afterward. "I'm actually kind of amazed. I don't feel any apprehension about the car. I feel extremely comfortable. Frankly, it seems easy to me."

John Ackroyd, who had joined the team as a consultant, was somewhat more guarded. "It gets the ball rolling. It opens the door. Now, we have to go through the door.... You have to get the man right, the machine right, the course right, the weather right and your luck right . . . all on one day . . . for two runs. The game still has a few rounds to play."

It rained that night. The plan to knock off a 500 mph run the next morning had to be postponed. The crew hung around Gerlach for three days, waiting for the playa to dry, anxiety building that they would run out of season, that the campaign would grind to a halt as the last dollar was spent.

Finally, on October 27, Craig took *Spirit* out for his second run, this time hitting 563 mph. "It's a very harsh environment," he would say, describing the experience of 500-plus on the playa. "It's a very, in many respects, violent environment. The car has enormous horsepower, and you have to give total respect to it. It is unforgiving, and there can be no mistakes. It is very close to the ground, so in relation to the velocity that you travel, it's very acute. It's a very harsh ride, and it vibrates to the point where it blurs your vision. I breathe through a mechanical apparatus. My body is harnessed down to a steel frame, and I'm very close to the front wheels—they run a few inches from my back. The ride is one of precision, and when you come onto the power, it feels like some giant object has put its hand on your chest and just driven you into the seat. This car accelerates so hard you almost can't breathe. When the parachute opens, the G's go as high as 10, depending on the velocity that you release the chute. You have to have a light touch, but a decisive touch."

This only begins to describe the hairiness of Craig's run that morning. During the acceleration phase, his breathing difficulties were compounded by the fact that the airflow through his mask had been cut off. The problem had occurred during his first run. This time it was worse. "Somehow, the G forces are shutting off my air supply," he said back at Bruno's over steak and eggs. "I had to take the mask off to get air to breathe. Here you are in the middle of a 500 mph run, you're trying to get a mask off your face, driving a car with one hand, trying to watch the instruments. . . . I'm in a quandary because we don't have much time. We were using an Air Force regulator . . . we changed it [to a firefighter's regulator] because it didn't give me enough air. Given the choice of little air or no air, I'll take a little air."

And then there was the drama when Craig released the chutes coming out of the mile. The canopy jerked the back of the car up off the ground, slewed it around, and dug the nose into the dirt. "I had it pretty sideways. It's not scary, it just does a lot of damage to the car. It's scary from the idea it's dangerous. But when you're in there you're just trying to keep it from tipping over. Hard left, hard right . . . I gathered it up and it was all right."

Faulty air mask, troublesome chutes—in the challenging game of land speed racing these were mere glitches, problems to be worked around as you kept moving forward. "The car is working fine and it handles very well," Craig concluded. "I feel very confident and have been waiting for this day for thirty years."

Out on the playa at base camp, the crew worked into the night repairing the Arrow's damaged front end. Ed Ballinger cut more ribbons out of the chutes, increasing porosity still further to eliminate the lingering instability problem. Both the car and the chutes would be ready to go again in the morning. As for the air mask, Craig would just have to gut it out.

Back at Bruno's, Craig met with the rest of the crew and decided to go for the record the next day, as early as possible in the morning, before the weather front that was forecast rolled in. This seemed like rushing things after just two test runs, but Craig insisted that he was ready. The car was handling well and he felt great, physically strong from six months of training and already mentally acclimated to high speed. It had come back to him with remarkable ease. "I figured I could break Noble's record standing on my head," is how he puts it today.

The plan he and Walt Sheehan worked out was to position the car three miles out from the measured mile and to use minimum afterburner. The target: 650 mph. That would beat Richard Noble's record without venturing into the transonic zone that began somewhere in the high 600s. The failure of the rear wheel load sensors to produce meaningful readings had left Craig especially wary of going transonic, for he had no idea from his two test runs what his racer was doing.

Was *Sonic Arrow* experiencing heavy downforce? Was it in the sweet spot? Or did it want to fly?

22

WORLD'S FASTEST CAR CRASH

MONDAY, OCTOBER 28, 1996. Craig was up before dawn. He went for a jog with his dog Muffin—no breakfast; just coffee—then drove out to the playa as the sun crept over the hills. He was nervous but had it well under control, his mind focused on the task at hand, what he needed to do to win back the record. He had to do it today, before noon, for the weather window was closing. His permit to use the playa was also about to expire and all his money was spent. The plan was to grab the LSR in the morning with a two-way average of around 650 mph, then to fly to Las Vegas for Shell's national sales convention, which Craig had committed to attend, and personally deliver the good news to the company brass. He would then hit them up for more funding, while they were all smiling and happy, to keep the project alive into the next year for the assault on 700 mph and Mach 1 beyond.

The crew headed out from base camp and up the course in two groups, Craig in the lead with the start cart and a gaggle of reporters, Dezsö Molnar and Walt Sheehan presiding over a second group farther back, towing *Sonic Arrow* on its dolly. Craig continued on past the one- and two-mile markers and stopped at the three. This was the start line that he and Walt had decided on the evening before. From here he would have a three-mile run-up to Bruce Clarke's clocks at the start of the measured mile at the six-mile marker.

Craig got out of the truck. He waited for his racer and the rest of the crew to arrive.

Fifteen minutes passed. He was still waiting.

Finally he realized that something was wrong. He drove back down the course and saw to his surprise that *Sonic Arrow* had been unloaded off its dolly at the two-mile marker, four miles out from the clocks.

"Why are you guys stopped here?" he asked.

"That's what we decided on," said Walt.

"No, we decided on the three-mile, remember? We worked it out last night."

A look of confusion came over Walt's face. There had been a mix-up. Not wanting to embarrass his old friend and spend still more time moving the racer, Craig radioed ahead for the press and the rest of the crew to come back. "Walt recalculated it," he said. "We've decided to go with a four-mile approach." By the time the confusion was sorted out the better part of an hour was gone.

The run was disappointing when Craig finally got away at nine forty-five, *Sonic Arrow* being clocked through the mile at only 470 mph. The afterburner hadn't lit. At least the chutes weren't a problem. They deployed properly and didn't jerk up the back of the car. The morning was now more than half-gone, the racer at the north end of the course. Craig had yet to make the first of the two runs for his record attempt.

It was decided to stick with a four-mile approach for the run back down the course. As part of the prep, Alyson Kimball, the smallest member of the crew, crawled into one of the air ducts to check for debris. This was done before every run to make sure that nothing—a pebble, a stray bolt—got sucked into the compressor when the J-79 was fired up. That could ruin the engine. Another crew member crawled under the racer and adjusted the stop on the throttle to give Craig more power, enough to light the burner and get him to 650. There were no gradations or markings to guide this procedure. It had to be done pretty much by guesswork, by loosening the stop, sliding it a little farther along the linkage, and tightening it back up.

Craig, waiting for the car to be prepped, was feeling increasing pressure as he watched the weather. Clouds were rolling in overhead, the first sign of the forecasted storm. And dust was starting to blow around, erratic gusts picking it up from where the playa crust had been broken.

It was after eleven o'clock before the car was ready. As launch time approached, Chuck Lyford took off in his Aerostar to facilitate communications along the thirteen-mile-long course. Ed Ballinger, his pre-run work done on the chutes, was already down at the south end to monitor wind conditions. Craig T. Nelson was with him. Bill Breedlove and John Ackroyd had gone to the start of the measured mile. They would watch from there.

Sonic Arrow was sitting at the north end of the course, needle nose pointing south, fueled and set. Craig squeezed back into the cockpit. The fit was so tight that every inch counted. To give himself a fraction more space for his feet, he wore ultra-light kickboxing shoes that were a half size too small.

Alyson Kimball handed Craig his helmet, then helped him with his harness and snapped on his oxygen mask—the mask that had shut off Craig's airflow the previous day. It had been tinkered on during the night to alleviate the problem. The canopy was lowered and locked.

Craig waited.

Overhead, the Aerostar circled at one thousand feet.

Craig waited. The cockpit grew hotter. His view of the desert through the tinted canopy windshield grew darker as black clouds rolled in.

The headphones in his helmet crackled. It was Charlie Lyford in the Aerostar. "Your wind's at one-point-five," radioed Charlie, relaying the wind speed report from Bruce Clarke at the mile. One-point-five knots was fine, well below the five-knot maximum considered safe for running the car. The wind seemed to be holding.

Another relayed message from Charlie, this one from the team volunteers making sure there were no vehicles or spectators near the course: "Your course is clear. Ingress and egress are blocked."

Craig, via the mike in his helmet: "OK, I'm on my way."

He looked out at the crew—Dezsö Molnar out front and to the right, Chris Rossi at the exterior instrument panel just over Craig's head, Harry

Weiser farther back alongside the engine. He gave them a thumbs-up and started the pre-launch checklist, Dezsö indicating each step in turn with outstretched fingers.

The *Arrow*'s jet engine whined to life. The whine rose to a howl as Craig advanced the throttle. The ski brake, raising the nose of the car two inches when fully deployed, began to slide. Final step: release the brake and slam the accelerator pedal to the floor.

"Hold it, hold it, hold it, hold it!" It was Charlie's frantic voice on the radio. A message had just come in from Bruce at the mile. "The clocks are down! The clocks are down! Shut it down! Shut it off!"

It was a broken wire somewhere in the Chrondek clocks setup. Bruce would have to locate it and fix it before Craig made his run or there would be no official time.

Craig killed the engine. The J-79 slowly subsided. He sat motionless in the excruciatingly cramped cockpit. Waiting. His neck was starting to hurt.

Ten minutes passed as Bruce Clarke and Bill Breedlove hunted for the break in the wire, *Sonic Arrow*'s cockpit getting hotter and hotter.

Twenty minutes passed. Finally Craig couldn't stand it anymore. He threw open the canopy and wriggled out.

Eleven thirty. The sun, nearly at its zenith, was invisible now behind the clouds. The predicted storm front was moving in. The wind was picking up too, occasional gusts kicking dust into the air. Craig started anxiously pacing. "I'm thinking, *Shit, it's going to start blowing and we've still got to make an hour turnaround run.*"

The wind eased. The dust subsided. Finally the call came in from Charlie circling overhead. The break in the wire was fixed. The clocks were working again.

Craig climbed back into the cockpit and got strapped in. Fighting the urge to hurry, he began the start-up procedures again, Dezsö walking him through it, holding up fingers. *Main power—ON. Fuel—ON. Radio—CHECK.*

Chris Rossi, looming just outside the canopy glass, hit the "Fuel Arm" button, then closed and secured the access door to the instrument panel. He gave Craig a thumbs-up and stepped back.

Charlie Lyford on the radio: "Your course is clear. Ingress and egress are blocked."

Nobody on the track. Craig was good to go. More finger signals from Dezsö.

Fire suppression—ARM. Brake—ON.

Harry Weiser turned on the start cart, attached to the side of the car by an umbilical cord. A blast of compressed air started turning the J-79 jet engine's compressor.

A final check to make sure the area behind the car was cleared for a distance of three hundred feet.

Ed Ballinger and Craig T. Nelson were standing beside Ed's truck at the south end of the course, extraction equipment at the ready in case something went wrong and Craig had to be pried from the wreckage. An air ambulance was also on hand.

There was dust in the air. It was windy down at this end, blowing at 15 knots according to the wind gauge Nelson was holding, with occasional gusts to 25. Some of the guys standing around said that it was too windy, that maybe *Sonic Arrow* shouldn't be running at all.

"We've got one-five knots down here," Ed radioed up to Charlie Lyford in the Aerostar overhead. "One-five knots." Ed was ex-navy, at home on an aircraft carrier flight deck. "I said it like that," he remembers. "'One-five knots.' An aviation sort of thing."

Charlie relayed the message to the start line, where the air was still fairly calm. Craig would be the only one there to hear it.

The whining of *Sonic Arrow*'s engine rose to a scream. Craig watched the RPMs build to 8 percent. Ten.

Ignition—ON. He advanced the throttle to idle. Outside the car, Harry Weiser kept his eye on the engine temperature gauge, watching it build.

"Craig, your wind's at one-five."

Craig heard Charlie Lyford's report through his headphones. The wind had been at 1.5 knots on the aborted run less than an hour before and also on the earlier run when the burner didn't light. Now, hearing "one-five" from Charlie, and wanting, *needing*, for the air to be still, Craig assumed that the wind speed was unchanged, still at 1.5 knots, still within the margin of safety.

He was wrong.

He continued with the launch procedures. The crew outside the cockpit didn't stop him. Their walkie-talkies didn't receive the aircraft channel, so they hadn't heard Charlie's "one-five" message. Only Craig's helmet headphones and mike were set to the Aerostar's channel.

Ignition—OFF. Parachute—ARMED. Data Acquisition—ON.

Harry disconnected the start cart umbilical. The cart was towed out of the way.

Craig locked his gloved hands on the motorcycle-style steering yoke.

He released the ski brake.

He stomped on the accelerator pedal, pushing it right to the floor.

Kevin Binkert, who had been running the start cart with Harry, shielded his eyes from the blowing dust as he watched the racer disappear down the playa. It was an impressive takeoff, "like Craig was shot out of a cannon," Kevin remembers. "He really left in a hurry."

Kevin ran for the team's minivan and got behind the wheel. Chris, Dezsö, and Alyson got in with him. They started racing down the course after Craig, Harry following behind, towing the start cart.

"OK, the car's rolling. He's on his way."

Bill Breedlove, positioned in the observation area a half mile back from the start of the mile, heard the message over his walkie-talkie. He turned to look up the course, waiting for the dust plume to appear in the distance.

A pause. Then . . . there it was.

"So I see it coming," Bill remembers. "And all of a sudden I get a strong breeze right in my face, probably 25 miles an hour. And I remember thinking, *Holy shit.* Craig's coming in at peak velocity to the mile, I get this blast of wind and, I mean, my skin just perked right up.

"So now I'm concerned."

———————

"The thing took off like an absolute rocket ship," says Craig. "And I'm thinking, *Holy cow, I've got way too much wick.* It was going 400 in nothing flat."

Sonic Arrow wasn't in first-stage afterburner as planned. It was in third-stage judging from the kick in the pants he was getting—three rings of nozzles spraying gasoline into the white-hot exhaust blast. *Way too much power.* On the speedometer, which Craig could barely see now through the vibration, the number was soaring. The throttle linkage had been advanced too far.

"I had to get out of burner or I'd be going 800 before I got to the traps. All I was trying to do was break Richard's 633 mph record. So I back out of burner and drive along in military power for a while. But I can't see the lights yet so I decided I'd go back into burner. So I put my foot down again, relight the engine, and it takes off like a screaming banshee. I still can't see the lights and I'm up to 600 already, and I'm thinking, *Jesus, where the hell's the mile?* So I back out of throttle again."

Craig rocketed down the course, straining to see the markers, visibility poor. The combination of heavily tinted windshield and dark clouds overhead had reduced the desert to twilight. Finally, after what seemed an eternity but was in fact thirty-five seconds, he saw the start of the measured mile where Bruce had his clocks.

"Finally I see the lights. So I roll into burner again and it takes off like a scalded ape. I look down at the speedometer just as I'm entering the measured mile and I'm at 675 miles an hour, and I'm thinking, *Shit, I'm gonna come out the other end of this thing at 800.*"

Craig was just seconds away from blowing through the sound barrier and possibly right off the planet.

———————

A thousand feet overhead, Chuck Lyford had brought the Aerostar around and was heading back down the course, his son Charlie filming out the window with a mini-camcorder.

Whoom!

Sonic Arrow shot past them below, making the Aerostar's top speed of 260 mph seem like nothing. Charlie kept filming, Craig's dust plume racing ahead at phenomenal speed.

Suddenly the plume was veering off to the right. It was turning, turning, the car pitched on its side. "It looked like a dog peeing," says Chuck, "with the right fairing up in the air."

Chuck banked the Aerostar hard to the right and started down for an emergency landing. Charlie stopped filming and set the camcorder aside, his eyes glued to the drama unfolding below.

Inside the cockpit the horizon had suddenly tilted up at a sickening angle. A gust of wind had smacked *Sonic Arrow* onto its side.

"There are mountain ranges on both sides of the playa," says Craig, "and you have canyons that go up through on each side. Just before I entered the timing traps, there's a canyon both on the left and the right, so what happens is you get like a wind river that comes across the course there that's considerably faster, a lot stronger than the surrounding environment."

The blast, the "wind river," hit the car from the left and tipped it up on its side, its full weight thrown onto the rear wheel at 675 mph, Mach 0.9, alkali desert tearing at the dragging fairing and aluminum skin. "The car just came out from under me. It happened *so* fast, an absolute millisecond and it was on its side. I'd never experienced anything like that."

The cockpit, enveloped in dirt, went totally black. Craig couldn't see a thing. He took his foot off the accelerator and killed the engine. He did not release the chutes. That would have been a panicked response and likely fatal with the car on its side. "I don't do emotional things," he says when pressed about his feelings at this point during the crash. "No, the first reaction is, 'Oh shit. . . .' I mean, it happened that fast. And then you want to know where the hell you're at, and what the next thing to do is, when you absolutely have no clue what's going on."

He braced for a barrel roll or end-over-end tumble. The centrifugal forces alone at this speed would be enough to tear his body to pieces. He would be literally spun apart inside the cockpit, like Glenn Leasher had been back in 1962. *This is it, pal,* he was thinking. *You're done.*

The horrific rending inside tumbling wreckage—it didn't come. *Sonic Arrow* just stayed there, up on its side, as it screamed off course at over 600.

One second.

A wobble. The windshield cleared for an instant, giving Craig a glimpse ahead before darkness descended again.

Two seconds.

The *Arrow* hung there, perched on the edge of oblivion, the cockpit shrouded in blackness.

Three seconds.

Craig stared into the abyss.

———————

Bill Breedlove, at the start to the mile: "I'm studying the car. As it comes into the mile I notice it takes a pitch. It almost wheelbarrels, like somebody picked it up by the back end. It rolled to its right side, Craig made a corrective turn, and then it went over onto its left side. And he's off course."

Craig was in big trouble. Bill ran to his truck.

———————

Chris Rossi, in the minivan following Craig from the start line: "I'll never forget it. It was just the sinking-est feeling that the car was coming apart. I was looking out the windshield at this plume of dust veering to the right, crossing our path, and I'm thinking, *Oh my God, this is it*. My first thought was that Craig couldn't be alive."

In the backseat, Alyson Kimball started saying the Lord's Prayer. It looked like Craig was going to smash into the mountains.

Craig T. Nelson, at the south end of the course: "From our vantage point we could see his plume of dust coming up off the lakebed, and it wasn't straight. The wind was pushing it over. Then it started veering. I remember one of the guys saying, 'Oh my God, he's off course.'

"So we got in the crew truck and we raced down. We had quite a bit of ground to cover before we got there, so I had a lot of time to think about what could have happened. It seemed like forever."

Nelson, like everyone else racing toward *Sonic Arrow*, was expecting the worst.

The car, after what seemed an eternity, dropped back down onto all its wheels. With the left fairing no longer dragging, the dirt obscuring the windshield cleared in an instant, giving Craig his first clear view ahead. He saw that he was bearing down on a motor home . . . at 500 mph.

He turned right as hard as he dared, his mind in overdrive, processing the information that was now flooding in. *Clear the motor home. . . . Get around the spectator area. . . . Avoid the rock outcrop extending out onto the playa.* He cranked the steering yoke all the way over, putting the front wheels into their maximum 2 degree turn. Given his speed, it was so sharp that the car's outboard wheels started to lift up.

Finally, with the spectator area cleared and the rock outcrop avoided, Craig released the primary chute. The Kevlar-reinforced canopy deployed with a bang, throwing him forward against his harness.

The numbers on the speedometer quickly ticked down. Three hundred. Two hundred. One hundred. Craig deployed the ski brake. It dug into the playa, throwing up dust.

The racer ground to a halt two miles off course, facing north back the way it had come. It had done a complete U-turn. The whine of the jet engine continued to subside until all that remained was the ticking of the blades in the slowly rotating compressor. Craig sat there for a moment, collecting himself, trying to figure out what had happened. The wind had hit him from the left ... and he had rolled onto his left side. That didn't make sense.

"The car had rolled *into* the crosswind instead of away from the crosswind. That just blew my mind. I kept trying to figure out why in the hell it would do that. In any normal situation, the wind would blow you over in the direction the wind was moving, not *into* the wind. I mean, I was doing just perfect, and one-millionth of a second later, I was riding on my side. It happened that fast. I just knew it was a really odd occurrence."

———————

Bill Breedlove, roaring up in his truck, was first on the scene.

"I pull up, and I'm panicked. I'm thinking, *Oh my God ... this might not be good.* I run up to the car, expecting the worst, that Craig might be injured inside or whatever. I come up and I get the canopy off and I look down, and there's panic in my voice. I say, 'Craig, are you OK ...?' And he pulls his helmet off and looks up at me and he says, 'Yeah, yeah, I'm fine.' Cool as a cucumber, after sliding along on his side at 675 miles an hour. That was such a relief. I have to tell you, this is when I took total pride in this guy. I developed a whole new respect for him under that adversity. He stayed just so cool."

Bill helped Craig wriggle out of the cockpit. "You sure you're OK?" he asked again, hardly able to believe that Craig could have escaped unscathed from such a spectacular crash.

"Oh yeah," said Craig, like he was brushing off a stumble on the sidewalk. "I'm fine."

They started examining the car. It looked to Bill like the left fairing had been ground down by a giant belt sander.

The Aerostar came in for an emergency landing and skidded to a stop. The door was flung open. Chuck and Charlie Lyford came tumbling out in their fire suits, headsets still on, and raced forward. Doria Nelson, who had gone along for the ride, followed them out of the plane, Charlie's camcorder in hand. She started filming.

"So we come up," says Charlie, "and we're huffing and puffing, cables hanging off our headsets and everything. It was kind of a funny scene. And Craig says, 'Looks like I've got some work to do.' Then he looks at us and says, 'You guys want to go to lunch?' I could not believe it. There must have been a time a decade or two earlier when he just ran out of adrenaline, because he wasn't worked up. It was amazing."

The minivan with Chris Rossi, Kevin Binkert, Dezsö Molnar, and Alyson Kimball arrived a few moments later. They were all similarly struck by Craig's calmness. "When we got there," Alyson recalls, "Craig was already out of the vehicle. He was walking around it with his hands on his head, like he was studying the thing. And he was OK. I couldn't believe it. He just wanted to know what happened to his vehicle. It was like a guy with his prize sports car. It was like, 'Wow . . . is my car OK?'"

Here were Ed Ballinger and Craig T. Nelson arriving from the south end. "By the time we got there Craig was already out of the cockpit," says Nelson. "He was laughing, giggling like a high school kid. I was just dumbfounded. And then I started laughing. I was in shock, to tell you the truth." Nelson gave Craig a relieved hug and quipped, "It turns right real well."

Spectators and press, initially kept away, were now descending on the crash site. "I looked to the horizon," recalls Chuck Lyford, "and I see these little dots on it, coming toward us. It was like in a *Mad Max* movie. There were all these cars and trucks and all this dust, all coming in our direction, coming over the curvature of the Earth. It was quite a scene."

Reporters rushed forward with questions, Craig remaining almost blasé throughout. "I know now that we have enough power to go supersonic," he said, trying to look on the bright side.

Weren't you terrified? Didn't the experience shake you?

Craig shrugged. "You run these things, it's your job. I'm standing here. It's no big deal."

Sonic Arrow, scraped and battered, was loaded onto its truck. Craig, facing an uncertain future, drove back into Gerlach for lunch.

––––––––––

Craig flew down to Las Vegas later that afternoon to attend the Shell convention. It was only then, in the privacy of Chuck Lyford's plane, that the emotional impact of the crash caught up. "He didn't get shaky or anything," remembers Alyson Kimball, who accompanied him on the trip. "He just got a bit glassy-eyed, a bit teary, when his mind had a chance to process what happened. Once he had time to think about it, that's when he was like, 'Oh my God, that was close.'"

Craig arrived at the convention not as a conquering hero but to break the news that he had crashed *Sonic Arrow* and needed at least $1 million to rebuild. Whatever relief he felt at having walked away from what should have been a fatal wreck was tempered by disappointment over the opportunity that had been missed. Noble's record had been an easy target, what Craig calls "low-hanging fruit." And he had failed to grab it.

He put in his Vegas appearance and made his pitch to Shell for more money. And Shell came through. It provided another financial injection, just barely enough to keep the project afloat so that Craig could make another assault on the record the following season.

This time he would not be competing alone on the playa. In 1997 it would be *Sonic Arrow* versus *ThrustSSC*.

23

THE BOOM

SONIC ARROW WAS IN PRETTY BAD SHAPE as it was eased into the shop in Rio Vista following the crash. Its whole left side was scraped up and the left air duct was ground down and needed rebuilding. The prognosis then got worse when the crew took the aluminum skin off and discovered that the chassis was also bent. Straightening it out was going to be a huge job. On the plus side, the composite capsule containing the cockpit remained sound and needed only a fresh coat of paint. "Man, that capsule proved itself," says Tina Trefethen proudly. "It was just a miracle. It saved Craig's life." Even more surprising was that the J-79 jet engine was OK. A vast amount of dirt must have been sucked through it as the car careened down the desert, but the inside of the compressor remained miraculously unscathed.

Craig was still puzzling over what had happened out on the playa. The wind of course had been the immediate cause of the crash. But why had *Sonic Arrow* rolled onto its side *into* the wind? His first thought was that he had gotten into the transonic zone where weird things could happen as supersonic airflow started to have an uneven effect on different parts of the car. "The only thing I could think of was that the lower ventral fin at the back was dividing the airflow under the car into two channels, left and right. When the wind hit the side of the car, the airflow in one channel went supersonic while it was still subsonic in the other channel, and so that shock-chocked the air in that channel and lifted up that side of the car." To remedy this, Craig would remove the lower rear fin and relocate the parachute compartment above the tail-pipe. This would allow unobstructed, undivided airflow under the rear of the car. The rear wheel fairings would also be subtly reconfigured to tweak the car's aerodynamics and lock the rear end on the ground.

There was something else about the crash, however, that continued to bother him. The stunning speed at which *Sonic Arrow* tipped over indicated that a tremendous amount of energy had been released, energy that Craig suspected went beyond what would have been generated by uneven supersonic airflow. Confirmation of this would come the following year in Richard Noble's book *Thrust*, where the real reason for *ThrustSSC's* rear-wheel steering was revealed. "Glynne Bowsher, their engineering guy, did a gyroscopic analysis of the wheels rotating so fast," says Craig, "and figured out that if they turned the wheels so many degrees it would roll that twelve-foot-wide beast on its side. That's why they went with the rear steering. And I thought, *Holy shit, I wonder if that had something to do with my car rolling on its side into the wind.*"

The phenomenon, which Craig would subsequently explore with Don Baumea, was known as gyroscopic precession torque (GPT). Viewed through the lens of GPT, when the wind at Black Rock hit the side of *Sonic Arrow*, the sudden leftward pressure on the vehicle, coupled with the energy in the heavy front wheels rotating at high speed, caused it to tip over in the direction of the wheels' rotation. "Glynne figured it out," says Craig, "but he figured it wrong. You don't need rear-wheel steering because steering's got nothing to do with it. You can't steer a car fast enough to have a problem with gyroscopic torque. The car's got to be snapped sideways really fast, a really quick rate change in yaw, like when a gust of wind hits it. That's when you get enough energy to roll the car over. It's an odd phenomenon, and a serious deal. We feel we really learned something that's very critical to high-speed cars. Anybody that wants to go really fast better be sure their car's not going to yaw. And don't run in the wind, that's for shit-sure."

At least Craig now knew that *Sonic Arrow* could take him to Mach 1. This was confirmed by the printout of the onboard instrumentation data from the last run, which showed a speed buildup to 675 mph followed by a sudden drop-off to zero. The stunning thing about the line on the graph was that it rose to a sharp, straight point at the top, indicating that there had been no loss of acceleration right up to the forty-five-second mark when the car crashed. According to Walt Sheehan's calculations, had Craig kept going he would have blown through Mach 1 in another five seconds and topped out at 920 mph.

Craig wanted to start rebuilding the car as soon as it was wheeled back into the shop. But he was exhausted and so was everyone else. Dezsö Molnar in particular was burned out and adamant that he needed a break. Repairs therefore didn't begin until January 1997, starting with the preparation of a detailed work schedule. It revealed that there wasn't going to be enough time to get everything done before the planned return to Black Rock in September.

"I was really over a barrel," says Craig. "I called John Ackroyd and he came over from England to help us get organized and get more stuff done, but we had a really difficult time getting the car ready. And another problem was that we didn't have enough money. We'd calculated that to get the car repaired from the crash and go out and run it was going to cost $1.1 million, but with all our sponsors chipping in we ended up with a budget of only $700,000. So that added a whole bunch of extra stress to the project, having to get everything done on an absolute shoestring."

John Ackroyd recruited three new team members to help with the rebuild: fabricator Vernon Rich and tin benders Brian Ball and Phil Gross, veterans of Richard Noble's *Thrust2*. Another team newcomer was Dave Schmidt, "Decal Dave," a local mechanic with a ZZ Top beard and an eye for symmetry that got him the exacting job of applying sponsor decals to the car.

The work proceeded, the crew putting in long days trying to get everything done. Straightening out the chassis was a particularly tough job. "That was a giant undertaking," says Vernon Rich. "We put concrete anchors into the floor of the shop and painstakingly built a frame jig and got it exactly flat and parallel, like to within ten-thousandths of an inch, so we could figure out where the car was off and start straightening it out. And then we had a frigging earthquake. It shifted the engine and it just fucked it all up. So we had to redo the whole goddamn thing. We were just sick."

The British, meanwhile, had given up on Al Jafr Desert in Jordan. The course that had been prepared there was proving too rough, crisscrossed by Bedouin camels and trucks that the team couldn't keep away. The surrounding terrain was also dangerously stony. If *ThrustSSC* ran off the cleared course, all the rocks lying around would possibly cause a crash and almost certainly wreck the engines. The car made its last runs on Al Jafr in June 1997, hitting a top speed of 540 mph and enduring a terrible pounding that damaged the suspension. The crew packed it in after that. The hazards were just too great to continue.

Andy Green wasn't sorry to leave. He had been going through a private hell trying to keep *ThrustSSC* running in a straight line with the rear-wheel steering. The back end would start to slowly weave back and forth when he got going, then the zigzags would speed up the faster he went until he was out of control. It was like trying to fly a fighter jet with the computer-controlled stabilizing systems shut off, almost impossible to do with any precision. "By most technical definitions *ThrustSSC* was undrivable," Andy would later admit. "Test pilots have a scale in which one is fabulous and ten is uncontrollable, like trying to hold wet spaghetti vertical. *SSC* was up in the seven or eight territory." Andy came very close to telling Richard Noble he couldn't drive the car and they would have to find somebody else. But he didn't. He kept his concerns to himself and figured out a way to manage the zigzags, making major steering corrections before they were needed and twitching the wheel for minor corrections in between. It was an incredibly difficult way to drive a car, but it worked.

The plan now was to take *ThrustSSC* to Black Rock Desert. Richard Noble secured a Bureau of Land Management permit to use the playa and sent an advance party to prepare a course parallel to the one being laid down for Craig. He then tackled the seemingly impossible task of raising £600,000 in two months to get the car and the team out to Black Rock to run for the record. By appealing to sponsors, taking out loans, and connecting directly with the public through the nascent technology of the internet, Noble somehow succeeded. At the beginning of September, a giant Antonov 124 cargo aircraft took off from the RAF base at Farnborough with *ThrustSSC* in its cavernous belly. It banked west and headed out across the Atlantic, en route to Reno, Nevada.

———

There was no Bonneville sojourn for Craig in 1997. He went straight to Black Rock in the first week of September, his twelve-person crew settling into rooms at Bruno's Country Club and in a camper and Airstream trailer outside. IMSA wouldn't be doing his timing this year. Craig had hired the Sports Car Club of America instead. After the previous year's communications fiasco he also made arrangements to provide his own radio setup. A high antenna was erected and repeater station set up to give the crew's walkie-talkies a fifteen-mile range, enough to maintain radio contact down the entire length of the course and to connect base camp with the old post office building back in Gerlach, where the *Spirit of America* media center and souvenir shop were located. The little house behind the post office had also been rented for overflow accommodation, mostly for team volunteers.

The British team arrived a few days later, wheeling *ThrustSSC* into an inflatable hangar that they erected on the playa in just a few hours. It sparked some envy when Craig and his crew went over to greet them, for they had struggled for days piecing together the used prefab structure that housed *Sonic Arrow*, creaking metal sheets on a frame held together with thousands of bolts. The size and efficiency of the British camp was in fact intimidating: a thirty-three-member team that included a number of military personnel and all kinds of experts, an equal number of volunteers, two spare engines for the car, two microlight airplanes, two six-wheel-drive all-terrain vehicles, and a heavy forklift. They had come well prepared for what was being hyped as "the duel in the desert." Craig remembers overhearing a quip passing between two Shell representatives who tagged along: "Do you think we backed the wrong team?"

Craig stepped into the yellow hangar and took his first in-person look at *ThrustSSC*. The pictures he had seen had not prepared him for its hulking mass, two huge engines sticking out on either side like a brick wall, twenty thousand pounds of weight sinking the wheels three inches into the dirt. It seemed like the antithesis of *Sonic Arrow* right down to its paint job, carbon black versus the *Arrow*'s virginal white. "It was the damndest thing I ever saw," says Craig. "That car was built stronger than a battleship. It actually had an I-beam in it. The Rio Vista Bridge doesn't have anything in it that strong. It was built for stormy weather, I'm telling you, man."

Dave Veno and Terry Hendrickson, who were there as well, remember being particularly impressed with the way the *Thrust* crew climbed all over the car without the least worry of doing damage. "They walked on top of that thing the way we would walk on the wings of a C-5," says Dave, referring to the US military's largest transport aircraft. "When we asked if we could take a look in the cockpit, they said, 'Sure, just climb up on it.' And we're like, 'Really?'"

And then there was the rear-wheel steering. "I went to Richard," Craig continues, "and said, 'Why did you go with this rear-wheel steering?' And he said, 'Well, there wasn't enough room under the wheel fairings to make the front wheels steer.' But that wasn't true. They had the front wheels off the car when I was there and I got on a creeper and slid under the car and it was just a cavern in there. You could have put a cow inside. So I'm thinking, *What the hell is Richard talking about? He's got enough room in here to make the front wheels steer.*

"Anyway, I was giddy. I couldn't believe that they had built something with so much drag. I thought I was going to blow them away like they were tied to a telephone pole. I was so excited because I was going to beat them by a hundred miles an hour."

Craig began testing *Sonic Arrow* on September 6, the first day of his BLM permit. There was a bad omen right from the start. When he lowered the canopy prior to making his first run he noticed that the hinge bolts securing it to the chassis were loose. Deeply disconcerted, he killed the engine and waved Dezsö over.

"I know what you're thinking," said Dezsö as he tightened the hinges. "If we don't even have the canopy bolted down right, what else is wrong that we can't see?"

"That's *exactly* what I'm thinking," said Craig.

Problem fixed, Craig started making slow runs in idle, taking the car up to 227 mph, checking everything out. Some time off for adjustments and he resumed testing on September 8, the day the British started running *SSC*. The two teams started the practice of tossing a coin to determine when they would use the desert, the winner getting the prime morning hours, the loser the afternoon, when the wind tended to pick up and dust started blowing around. The dust was especially bad this year due to the extreme dryness of the playa.

Craig won the toss and got the morning. His plan was to make three runs in the 300, 400, and 500 mph ranges. The first came off without a hitch, Craig using his "Fred Flintstone" brake to stop. *Sonic Arrow* had only one chute loaded—more were being couriered out from the manufacturer—and he wanted to save it for his return pass at 400. The car was turned around and prepped for the next run.

Alyson Kimball was standing by to wriggle into the air duct to check for debris. "It was a regular thing," she remembers. "I'd found stuff before—screws, pebbles, things like that—so this was an important task. They would shove me in there before a run, and after a run to make sure everything was OK for next time. But this time Dezsö said, 'No, it's OK. I think we're OK.' I don't know why he said that. We were in a competition with the British now, so maybe we couldn't afford to lose any time when it was our turn to run."

The J-79 was restarted. Craig advanced the throttle. The whine rose to a shriek, then it started making a strange rattling sound.

Craig hit the shutoff switch, killing the engine. He pushed open the canopy and said to the crew, "Did you hear that?"

It hadn't been Craig's imagination. The engine didn't sound right. They tried starting it again but heard the same thing, a rattling vibration that indicated something was wrong.

Craig hit the kill-switch and Harry Weiser peered into the air duct. His flashlight revealed a disaster inside the compressor. "There was a tremendous slice in the leading edge of the blades all the way through," says Harry, "seventeen stages of these things, thousands of blades, each one of them hit. There was no way that engine was ever going to run again with that kind of damage. Whatever went through there just destroyed it."

He pulled his head out of the duct and delivered the bad news: "The engine's been fodded."

Craig couldn't believe it. In all his years using jets he had never fodded an engine. But when he scrambled out of the cockpit and looked for himself he saw it was true. An examination of the indentations left in the blades would later reveal that the culprit had been a small bolt.

The incident remains to this day a source of suspicion and speculation for some of the crew. While it would never be openly discussed, the possibility of sabotage privately occurred to several members—sabotage by someone on their own team, a bolt surreptitiously tossed into the air duct to scupper the project. Such feelings were perhaps inevitable considering the tension that existed that year on the team, which was about to get even worse. Even Craig admits to having harbored dark thoughts. The conclusion he came to, however, was that the fodding was likely nothing more than a screwup, the sort of thing that happens when people are tired and under too much pressure. "It was probably just a spare bolt that was dropped, that fell down somewhere inside the car during prep. It got left behind and somehow worked its way into the engine."

Sonic Arrow was loaded into its trailer and hauled back to Rio Vista for the engine to be replaced. Craig kept up an optimistic front but he knew the project had been dealt a likely fatal blow. His backup J-79 was the one that had received the disastrous coating treatment and remained a stinker despite the endless hours of sanding that had been done to remove the orange peel from the blades. It was all the team had, however, so they set to work tuning it up and installing it in the car. For Craig had to keep going. He had invested too much to give up now. Carrying on was also what everyone was expecting, starting with the TV channel Speedvision, which was sponsoring *Sonic Arrow* and wanted a show.

Back at Black Rock, the British were gaining momentum. Andy Green hit 517 mph in *ThrustSSC* after just three days of testing, then pushed into the low 600s before mechanical trouble and high winds sent the car back to its shelter. The team was in high spirits as they fixed the problems and waited for better conditions, confident that when they got going again they would set a new speed record. But that wasn't their ultimate goal. "Getting the record does not interest us," Richard Noble boldly stated, tempting fate. "Going 700 mph does not interest us. We are here to go Mach 1."

Through round-the-clock effort and frantic fundraising, Craig got *Sonic Arrow* back to the playa on September 16, the crew exhausted, his credit cards maxed. Crew chief Dezsö Molnar was now really starting to show the strain. He shocked Craig by coming to his motel room and telling him he wanted to quit. "He said he couldn't take it," says Craig, "that it was too much stress. I said, 'Man, what a time to blow out. If you do this, you're just totally blowing me away.' Anyway, he agreed not to leave. But that really became a problem." Alyson Kimball, who shared a room with Dezsö when accommodation at Bruno's was tight, recalls him banging his head against the headboard during the night. "It was like what a kid would do, like you can't get rid of whatever's inside your brain. I remember getting up and putting pillows behind his head so he wouldn't hurt himself and calming him down. It was intense."

Craig got down to work running the car, shaking out the problems, and trying to build up his speed. It didn't go well. The replacement engine, as expected, lacked the power of *Sonic Arrow*'s original J-79. "It wasn't worth a shit," says Craig. "We had some other problems with the car too. It started worming around, these weird handling problems, and I'm thinking, 'What the hell is going on with this thing?'"

Then the vibrations started. The problem was due to a buildup of dirt between the front wheels. This hadn't occurred the previous year because the playa had contained more moisture and the surface had held together like clay. Not so in '97. The bone-dry dirt was powdering when

Sonic Arrow passed over and getting up through the tiny gap between the three front wheels. Craig suspected that something like this was happening to cause the vibrations. He could feel the wheels out of balance up through the steering column battering his knees. He wanted them taken off to investigate, but that was a big job and the crew resisted. It was impossible to imagine that anything significant could get through such a small gap and work its way up inside.

"I don't know what it was," says Craig, "but for some reason the crew didn't want to take the wheels off to check them out, which wasn't simple to do. I guess they thought I was off my rocker. They just wanted to wash down between the wheels, use an air compressor, stuff like that. And God, I just made any number of runs where I'd get up over 300 mph and the thing would shake so bad that I couldn't see the instruments. Everything would just be a big blur."

What was going on with the crew? Part of it was fatigue. The rest was demoralization. As Richard Noble would observe, reflecting on his own long experience, "When you ask people to invest their dreams in yours, and then you don't deliver, things can fall apart pretty quickly." Things were falling apart for Craig now. The frustration of trying to make the car work, coupled with the mounting sense of crisis as money ran out, was proving too much. Team cohesiveness was breaking down, with many of the cracks leading back to crew chief Dezsö. "Dezsö had been more laid back the year before," says operations manager Bill Breedlove. "But in '97 he got really irritable with the crew and had them almost on the verge of mutiny. A bunch of people wanted to quit. We'd had setbacks, it was getting tedious, and people were fed up with the tantrums."

One person who quit was Walt Sheehan, very ill now with cancer. "I couldn't watch it anymore," he said. "The kid [Dezsö] doesn't have any idea what he is doing which leaves the rest of them pretty lost." The fodding of the engine had particularly annoyed him. "I saw it coming when they would scoop up the spent parachutes off the playa and stuff them into the inlet."

Craig kept making runs into the last week of September, gutting out the vibrations to push *Sonic Arrow* up past 500 mph. Finally the car couldn't take any more. "The shaking got so bad," he says, "that it broke one of the ¾-inch bolts on the wheel control arms, just sheared it right off. Fortunately it didn't cause an accident. I got the thing stopped. So finally the crew lifted up the front of the car and dropped the wheels out the bottom and took them apart, and there's this *huge* buildup of dirt inside the wheel chambers. I was absolutely amazed that so much dirt could get through such a tiny slot. It was like having five potatoes inside there. It was just throwing the whole front end out of balance, like a washing machine load when all the clothes get over to one side."

Craig and most of the crew had already returned to Gerlach when Bill Breedlove and Dezsö Molnar got the front wheels separated and started scraping handfuls of dirt off the inside rims. There was no doubt this was the source of the problem. "So Dezsö and I are looking at these big clumps of dirt," says Bill, "and I said, 'We ought to remove the center wheel. The other two are way strong enough to handle the weight of the car. And that way we'll have access to clean the wheels and there'll be fewer problems because the dirt won't get trapped.' But Dezsö didn't seem to like that idea. Maybe he thought I was stepping into what he thought was his area.

"What happened next . . . look, I'm going to take some blame for this. Maybe I shouldn't have said anything. But I got on the radio to Craig and I said, 'I think I got it figured out here.' Dezsö had just sort of disappeared by this point. I got the impression right after that he had jumped into his car and was driving back into Gerlach. Anyway, Dezsö heard me start to say something to Craig about the wheel problem and he started swearing and talking gibberish over the radio, 'You son of a bitch, you motherfucker,' stuff like that, trying to drown me out. Maybe he thought I was going to say something sensitive that he didn't want the British or anybody to hear, or maybe he wanted to talk to Craig first, I don't know. But he just lost it. He started into this crazy rant-like thing and I'm trying to stop him, 'Dezsö, stop, stop,' but he just keeps going. He just went completely Daffy Duck. It was crazy."

Dezsö's outburst went out over the airwaves. The British heard it at their base camp and were astounded. Spectators heard it at the course overlook on Highway 34, where radios were kept tuned to the frequencies the two teams were using. A Shell representative who had just flown out to Black Rock that day heard it too. And he wasn't happy about it.

———————

Craig was still struggling with the vibration problem when the British team blew the land speed record away. On September 25 Andy Green pushed *ThrustSSC* to a fantastic new record of 714 mph, the biggest jump in LSR history. He did it with such calm efficiency that he made it look easy. But it wasn't, not by a long shot. As Craig himself is the first to point out, what Andy accomplished was extraordinary.

"I saw the in-car footage of Andy driving that thing and he was going lock to lock trying to control that rear-wheel steering. I never had to steer my car like that. Ever. *ThrustSSC* was probably the evilest-handling LSR car ever built. I wouldn't have driven it myself. But Andy had a sense of duty and he figured out how to do it. He knew that when it got to a certain place he had to start turning right or left before it needed it, that he had to do this and do that at different speed ranges. He was so smart that he was able to anticipate what that car was going to do and react before it did it. I'll tell you what, the British wouldn't have got that record if it wasn't for Andy Green. Period. He absolutely was *the* driver for the job."

Craig was there watching. He drove down to the end of the course afterward and congratulated Andy and Richard Noble and the rest of the team with a smile. If he had to lose, he would do it with grace, like Donald Campbell. But it was tough, a huge disappointment. He had not just missed the opportunity of setting a new record in the mid-600s; he had been denied the chance of adding "First to 700" to his long list of achievements. The only thing left was Mach 1. And with the way *Sonic Arrow* was performing that seemed beyond reach.

Dezső's radio outburst, in the meantime, had not been forgotten. The Shell representative who overheard it reported the incident to head office, and the top brass was equally disturbed. The fallout was that company president Jim Morgan sent a letter to Craig at Black Rock informing him that if he expected to keep his primary sponsor, Dezső had to go.

Craig hated confrontation. He tried to avoid unpleasant scenes but this time he had no choice. He sat down with Dezsö out behind the rented house in Gerlach and told him as gently as he could that he was sending him home. Team volunteer Richard Parks watched from a distance.

"Craig was out back with Dezsö," recalls Richard. "They were under a tree and Dezsö was crying because Craig was letting him go. Craig was sitting there consoling this young man, he was acting like a caring father, and right there I saw his humanity, that he was a very gentle person. Dezsö was sobbing away and Craig was so gentle with him, and so kind, and so patient. He seemed to have the right words for the situation. I was very, very impressed.

"I watched for quite some time. It just affected me some way. I could see the tragedy of everything, but I could see also the redemptive features that were starting to play out. And I started to see Dezsö in a different way too. Nobody thought that stress even bothered Dezsö. He seemed like a Teutonic giant. What we didn't realize was that he had been dying inside trying to keep this thing going. He couldn't cope with being in a situation where failure had become the only outcome. He was just so driven. I think that's what drew Craig to him."

It was about a week later that the boom came.

To give Andy Green and the *ThrustSSC* crew full credit, they unequivocally broke the sound barrier for the first time on October 13. The sonic booms were widely heard but the record wasn't considered official, the team having gone fifty seconds over the allowed time of one hour in completing their two runs. It was a crushing disappointment, for the Brits had made a tremendous effort and the car had endured a huge pounding and couldn't take much more. Undeterred, they got to work patching up the racer to try again.

Craig had the playa to himself the next day. He was timed doing 558 and 583 mph through the mile and hit a top speed of 636 mph according to *Sonic Arrow*'s onboard data recorder. This might have sparked

some hope a few weeks before, but not now, not with Andy's new Big
Number posted on the USA-vs.-UK scoreboard outside the Black Rock
Saloon. The *Arrow* also had nothing left. The backup engine was a dud,
the graphite tires were nearly shot, and the car's handling problem, its
tendency to "worm around," was becoming acute, Craig having to battle
a hard pull to the right. He almost lost it on the last run. "Something
is really haywire," he said, walking off the close call. "She almost came
around when I shut down the engine." The tracks the car had left in the
dirt were subsequently found to be out of line by a whole foot.

Sonic Arrow was towed back to base camp. The next day, October
15, the playa belonged to *ThrustSSC*. Craig joined Richard Noble in
the British command post that morning, a quarter mile back from the
USAC timing shack facing the mile. He heard Andy Green's girlfriend
Jayne Millington calmly say on the radio, "SSC with firechase is rolling.
Clear supersonic. Clear supersonic." And he clearly heard the boom that
followed a half minute later. "There was a definite *ba-boom* sound when
the car went supersonic. The shock wave was very prominent. You could
actually feel the concussion in the air."

Andy broke the speed barrier one way, then turned around and did
it again to make the record official, two runs within the allotted hour
for a new land speed record of 763.035 mph—Mach 1.02. "It was one
hell of a moment," Richard Noble would write of the celebrations that
followed, Craig joining in. "I remembered what Donald Campbell had
said when he broke the [wheel-driven] land speed record back in 1964:
'I'm just glad we've got the bastard.' At that moment I knew exactly
what he meant. All I could say at first was, 'We bloody did it! Thank
God it's over.'"

Sonic Arrow crew member Chris Rossi was on the other side of the
course with a 500 millimeter lens on his Nikon camera and the morning
sun to his back. He captured an amazing photo as *ThrustSSC* streaked
past, going supersonic, four distinct shock waves angling off the top of
the car and distorting the distant mountains like folds in the air. Down
at *Sonic Arrow* base camp at the south end of the course, Ed Ballinger
was working in the metal shelter when somebody said, "Here he comes!"
Ed started toward the big metal doors to go out and watch. "I was just

reaching for the door when the sonic boom hit. It blew the doors in about a foot and hit my fist. . . . We were happy for Andy. He did it and survived. But then we turned around and looked at our car and our team and everything, and we were just ticked off, just sort of deflated."

The British were done. They packed up and went home. They had achieved what they came for and had pushed *ThrustSSC* to the very limit of its speed potential. "When I spoke to their chief aerodynamicist Ron Ayers about it," says Craig, "he told me that even if they had used the more powerful Spey 205 engines they had brought along as backups, they'd have been lucky to get another three to seven miles an hour out of that car under the best conditions. They had hit an absolute stone wall in drag when it went Mach 1. It was just not capable of going any faster."

The *Sonic Arrow* team, left alone on the playa, soldiered on into November, chasing the fantastically high number of 763. But it was hopeless. The *Arrow's* sole set of tires were coming apart after two seasons, the weather was deteriorating, and the project was sputtering on financial fumes, relying on donations from the public and T-shirt sales to keep going. Breaking the land speed record was as much about luck as anything else and Craig just didn't have it this year. The stars had aligned for the British instead.

The end came in the middle of November. Bill Breedlove, out at dawn every morning to check the state of the course, saw it first. He returned to Gerlach and got Craig and they drove back out to the desert together. The playa was its usual tan color as they proceeded down a used lane. Then, around the measured mile, a change in contrast became visible up ahead, a strip two hundred feet wide that was noticeably darker. It was like a river of moisture running across the course, the first sign that the water table was reaching the surface. And sure enough, when they got to it, the truck tires began to sink in.

They stopped and got out and Craig felt the wet dirt. He looked at the snow on the mountains, felt the cold breeze on his face. The loss of calm air in the morning—that was another harbinger of winter. Soon the desert would be flooded, bringing the season to a close.

"OK," he said, heaving a sigh of surrender. "Let's tell everybody to pack it up. We're going home."

EPILOGUE

CRAIG LEFT BLACK ROCK IN November 1997 emotionally shattered and $100,000 in debt. "It's been like the summer from hell," he told the *Reno Gazette-Journal* before heading home. "I'm really disappointed about not getting the record and I feel bad. There were so many people supporting me and I feel like I let them down."

It was when *Sonic Arrow* was being wheeled back into the shop that he discovered the cause of one of his problems. "I was in the office when I heard this loud crash. I ran out and saw the whole rear end of the car had collapsed onto the floor. What had happened was, the car was being rolled into the shop and the front end slid off the dolly when it hit the expansion joint in the floor. The nose dropped down onto the concrete and the whole car just snapped." It seemed an inexplicable amount of damage for a fall of less than a foot. What was going on? Craig examined the welds that had parted, the ones joining the rear axles to the frame, and saw to his horror that they had never been completed. In the rush to get the car rebuilt after the '96 crash, only the outside part of the axle mounts had been welded back on to the frame. The hard-to-see inside had been entirely missed. He suddenly understood why *Sonic Arrow* had had that strange "worming around" feeling: the join between the axles and the frame had been tearing apart. The whole time Craig was running out on the playa, he had been one good jolt away from destruction.

Craig quickly got over his disappointment as he had so many times before and began preparing for another crack at the record. Richard Noble and Andy Green had raised the bar very high but he was still confident that he could do better, that *Sonic Arrow* was capable of 800 mph if he got it working right. "Going 8 in 98!" was how he concluded his Christmas newsletter to *Spirit of America* supporters at the end of the year. He began rebuilding the car with a scaled-down team headed by Vernon Rich, who succeeded Dezsö Molnar as crew chief, but he couldn't get the necessary sponsorship for a return to Black Rock the next season. Prospects looked better for 1999 but ultimately that fell apart too, as Craig ended up raising less than half the million dollars he needed. After that the project slowly subsided. In 2000 the team was down to media relations manager Cherié Danson and mechanic Dave Schmidt, who continued to work on the car as a volunteer after the funding dried up. Things just petered out after that. By the end of the year *Sonic Arrow* was effectively mothballed.

Craig was inducted into the International Motorsports Hall of Fame in the summer of 2000. Accompanying him to the induction ceremony at Talladega was one of the last things Cherié did before leaving. As they sat at the banquet table with inductees A. J. Foyt, Don Prudhomme, Mario Andretti, and others, Cherié was surprised to see that Craig was hardly touching his meal. After decades of ultimate speed adrenaline and being in the spotlight, he still had butterflies in his stomach and was unable to eat. He delivered his acceptance speech without a hitch just the same. And when the audience applauded he flashed the old Breedlove smile, his face craggy but still handsome at age sixty-three.

A man came up afterward, pushing through the crowd of fans getting autographs and taking photos, and seized Craig by the hand. "Mr. Breedlove," he said, "I met you back in 1965 when I was only ten and have followed your career ever since. I just can't express how your efforts and determination have impacted my life, and I couldn't leave here tonight without telling you that."

The expiration of Craig's Shell contract at the end of 2005 snuffed out any lingering hopes he had of reviving *Sonic Arrow* for another record attempt. He put the word out that he was willing to sell the racer, which had been sitting idle in his shop now for going on eight years.

It was Dezsö Molnar who brought him a buyer. Billionaire adventurer Steve Fossett, whose many records included the first solo nonstop flight around the world in an airplane, wanted the LSR and believed *Sonic Arrow* could get it. Craig's asking price was a firm $2 million, the amount he had personally put into the car.

"Steve was a really good businessman," says Craig. "With the car, what he would do was he'd agree to my price and start trying to pick up a lot of extras, then we'd get right down to closing the deal and he'd say, 'OK, there's just one more thing to talk about. This $2 million you're asking for, that's too much.' And so we'd go right back to where we started. Steve did that twice in person, then he did it a third time, called me up when I was down in Mexico. This time I said, 'Look, Steve, I'm not going to sell the car. Just forget it.' And he just blew up on the phone and started yelling at me. So I hung up. We eventually sorted it out and Steve agreed to pay the two million. Then, right at the end, when we're sitting at the table and he's about to write out the check, he tried it a *fourth* time. So I said, 'You know what, Steve, I think I'll just *give* you the car and have you teach me how to negotiate.' We had a laugh about it, and Steve wrote out the check."

Craig was back down in Mexico when the Fossett crew subsequently showed up in Rio Vista with a big truck. They loaded up the car, the frame jig, the design drawings, and everything else Craig had set out for them and hauled it away, leaving a big empty space in the shop.

Craig got a call from Fossett's lead engineer a few days later. The man was agitated. "Where are the rest of the drawings?" he asked.

Craig didn't know what the guy was talking about. As far as he knew all the drawings he had made had been picked up along with the car. "Well, how many drawings did you get?" he said.

The engineer leafed through what he had. "I've got maybe twenty sketches here and a couple blueprints. That's it."

"Well, you got everything, then."

"Come on, for something like this—there's got to be hundreds of drawings. We want them."

Craig didn't have hundreds of drawings. He never did. He explained to the incredulous engineer that that handful of sketches and blueprints was everything he had put down on paper. It was how he worked, going all the way back to his first *Spirit*. "When I'm building a car, everything I want to do is in my head. I know every nut and bolt, every little piece. I've designed the whole thing down to the smallest detail, every single component, and I just don't need a lot of engineering drawings because I'm in the shop working on the car alongside the guys."

Sonic Arrow was extensively modified for Steve Fossett. The car was left looking radically different; most notably, its distinctive shark-fin stabilizers were cut off to reduce drag. Craig thought the changes were counterproductive but doesn't like saying too much. Fossett bought the car fair and square and could do what he liked. Original *Sonic Arrow* team member Tina Trefethen is more outspoken. "I was totally heartbroken when I saw how they had butchered it and hacked it up," she says. "That car should have been put on a pedestal in a museum and never touched. Every piece on it was spectacular. It was one of the most gorgeous things ever built." How the altered racer might have performed remains a matter of speculation, for Fossett never got a chance to run it. He died in September 2007 when the small plane he was piloting crashed in the mountains west of Nevada's Great Basin Desert. He had been scouting locations for his LSR bid.

Craig had remarried by this time, to a young Mexican woman named Yadira Figueroa Gracian. It was his sixth marriage, not counting the annulled Las Vegas union he stumbled into in the late 1960s. After clearing his remaining debts from *Sonic Arrow*, he settled into a laid-back life with Yadi, dividing his time between Rio Vista and his ocean-view house in the Mexican town of San Carlos, with regular stops in L.A. for business and side trips to Nevada to visit his two surviving kids, Norman and Dawn. His eldest child, daughter Chris, succumbed to cancer in 2008. Craig was a grandfather now with five grown grandkids: Norman's daughter Brook, Dawn's children Thomas and Leona, and Chris's daughters Stephanie and Tara. None of them inherited his obsession with speed.

"I'm really content in my situation and my life," he told me when I interviewed him for my book *Speed Duel* in 2009. "I've been successful in business and I'm comfortable financially and I've got a beautiful home in Mexico where I'm sitting right now with my dachshund in my lap. I'm happily married and things are good."

Half a world away in Britain, Richard Noble was formulating plans for a new land speed racer, an even faster successor to *ThrustSSC*. He made it official at a press conference in October 2008, announcing his intentions to build a next-generation vehicle called *Bloodhound* that would be driven once again by Andy Green. Their goal this time: 1,000 mph, well beyond the velocity of most bullets. At that speed four football fields would flash by in one second.

The design for *Bloodhound* that was subsequently revealed adhered to the tricycle configuration that Craig favored, with two front wheels close together inside the chassis and two rear wheels spaced apart on outriggers. There would be small winglets on either side of the nose, like on *Sonic I*, to keep the car on the ground, and driver Andy Green would sit well forward in the position Craig favored. The planned propulsion system, however, was very different from Craig's way of thinking. It would be a hybrid system consisting of a jet engine and a hydrogen peroxide rocket stacked one atop the other and working together. There would be a car engine as well, a supercharged V8 to drive the rocket's oxidizer pump.

It was reading about Noble's new car that rekindled Craig's interest in land speed. It started slowly with musings on *Bloodhound*'s shortcomings—his main concern was that its hybrid propulsion system was too complex—and the inevitable question: *How could it be done better?* A couple years passed and Craig continued to play around with ideas, attracted by the challenge and excitement of a possible new project but at the same time cautious about wading in too deep. He was in his early seventies, after all. Didn't that make him too old for chasing the record?

The answer was no. By 2012 Craig had moved beyond idle thinking and casual sketches to serious design work on a new *Spirit of America* racer. Ironically, just as *Bloodhound* showed influences from Craig's earlier LSR cars, Craig's new *Spirit* showed the influence of *ThrustSSC* in its use of twin jets. He initially planned on using two late-model engines, something from the 1970s or '80s. He discovered, however, that newer engines in the power range he wanted were designed for maximum performance at high altitude, where the air was thin. For use in dense air down on the ground, the reliable old J-79, that tried-and-true workhorse, was still the best choice.

The project had taken hold of Craig by 2014. "I just got a wild hair and decided to go after it," he told *Hot Rod* that year. "It seemed like a good idea at the time and we'll see what happens." He purchased two working J-79s—no easy feat, for the military was now in the practice of cutting holes in discarded engines before dumping them on the surplus market—and began assembling a team, starting with engineer Neil Roberts, who turned Craig's drawings into an evolving series of 3-D renderings on a computer. Roberts in turn brought Lockheed Martin flight test engineer Mark Zweig on board as the driver. Craig's old friend Stan Goldstein, the same age as Craig but still going strong, was tapped as manager of operations. What was needed now was a whole lot of money, for the cost of building and running an ultimate LSR car had gone through the roof. This was by far the biggest hurdle that Craig had to clear on his way to reclaiming the record. He was faced with raising well over $20 million.

Craig started approaching sponsors with a proposal and model. In his pitch he outlined a three-year plan to build two identical *Spirit of America* racers. This would make it easier to show the car at sponsor events and ensure program continuity in the event of a crash. Yes, he admitted, the *Bloodhound* team had some impressive engineering and a big head start, "but I think our design is more straightforward. [Our car] has a much lower center of gravity. It doesn't have the engines stacked vertically. They have basically three powerplants in the car to coordinate and talk to each other. My experience has always been that you have to be able to not high-tech yourself out of business. . . . I think our approach is more straightforward, simpler, and probably more reliable."

No major sponsorship deals were forthcoming. As the rejections mounted, Craig started thinking about alternate approaches, more cost-effective ways to challenge the record . . . and his mind kept going back to the rocket car he had designed back in 1969 using Jerry Elverum's Apollo lunar descent engine. A rocket just made so much sense—massive power from a motor a fraction the size of a jet, no need for air ducts, certain to work every time if hypergolic fuels were used. It also allowed for the ultimate low-drag racer configuration, long and low and narrow, like an arrow.

Hydrazine and nitrogen tetroxide, the hypergolic fuels Craig had used in the *English Leather Special* rocket dragster, were out of the question. They had been labeled hazardous and strictly regulated since the late 1980s. As Craig puts it, "You've got to be practically the vice president of the United States to even look at that stuff today." So what were all the private rocket companies that were now out there using? The rise of ventures like SpaceX, Virgin Galactic, and Blue Origin suggested that something had changed. Maybe there was another way forward.

There was. In mid-2016 Craig paid a visit to Jerry Elverum, now eighty-nine years old, and learned that there were other hypergolic rocket fuels readily available on the market that were effective, cheap, and ecologically friendly. "Jerry told me about a fuel and oxidizer called furfuryl alcohol and white fuming nitric acid (WFNA)," says Craig with rising excitement. "They're used in industry and I can go out and buy them no problem. They aren't quite as powerful as hydrazine and NTO but they're hypergolic and will work just fine with Jerry's pintle injector. They're really just about perfect for an LSR car."

The *Spirit of America* project suddenly took a big turn, Craig scrapping his plans for a twin-engine jet car and updating his old rocket car design. He also revived his strategy from the early 1970s of running a scaled-down rocket dragster as a first step toward building a full-sized LSR car. What rocket dragster? Craig's very own *English Leather Special*, which had recently come up for sale after sitting abandoned in a field.

Craig reacquired it at the end of 2016 and is now fixing it up as a test vehicle for his new fuels.

Craig turned eighty-one on March 23, 2018. He recently sold his home in Mexico and bought a place in Oxnard west of L.A. to be near Maxwell Industries, where the new car will be built. He continues to lead a semi-nomadic existence, driving back and forth between Rio Vista and Oxnard with Yadi and their two dogs, a rotund little dachshund named Matilda and a high-strung mongrel named Abby that Craig found abandoned in Mexico. He currently has three projects on the go: the rebuild of the rocket dragster; the restoration of his original *Spirit of America* three-wheeler, which the Museum of Science and Industry in Chicago returned to him in early 2016; and his ultimate speed monster, his new rocket car. "Wait till you see this thing," he says, sounding like he's still in his twenties. "This new car is so slick it's unbelievable. And it'll be faster and less expensive to build."

Who will do the driving? That remains to be decided—although Craig concedes it won't be him.

Well, probably not.

SOURCES & NOTES

MY MAIN SOURCE IN WRITING this book was Craig Breedlove. I first interviewed Craig for my previous land speed book, *Speed Duel: The Inside Story of the Land Speed Record in the Sixties* (Firefly, 2010), a total of about three hours of recorded conversations between July 2009 and February 2010. We stayed in touch after the book came out and subsequently spent several days together in L.A. in March 2014, when Craig showed me his plans for his twin-engine LSR jet car. By this time he had broached the idea of my writing his biography. I began work on the project in the spring of 2016.

Between June 2016 and September 2017 I recorded more than twenty hours of interviews with Craig over the phone covering the whole of his life. I also spent several days with him in Rio Vista, California, in October 2016. I recorded five more hours of reminiscences during my visit and was granted access to the dozens of boxes of photographs and documents Craig has stored in his shop. Craig also allowed me to read an unpublished autobiography entitled "Speedlove: The Spirit of America Story" that he wrote in 2004 with his old Igniters buddy Marvin Gelbart.

I was also fortunate to interview the following people involved in Craig's life:

- **Nick Arias**: Screwdrivers member and drag rival in the 1950s; died in 2017 (May 21, 2016)

- **Ed Ballinger**: Involved with the *English Leather Special* rocket dragster in the early 1970s; member of the *Sonic Arrow* team, 1996–1997 (July 5, 2016, and March 21, 2017)
- **Don Baumea**: Longtime friend; lived with Craig in the late 1980s (interviewed July 2, 2016; email correspondence June 27–August 18, 2016)
- **Kevin Binkert**: *Sonic Arrow* team member, 1996–1997 (July 5, 2016)
- **George Boskoff**: *Spirit of America* and *Sonic I* fabricator and crew member, 1962–1965 (March 11 and 20 and April 1, 9, and 13, 2017)
- **Cynthia Bowman**: Craig's half sister from his mother's second marriage (June 18, 2009)
- **Portia Bowman**: Craig's mother; died in 2009 (June 23, 2009)
- **Bill Breedlove**: *Sonic Arrow* manager of operations, 1996–1997; he and Craig call themselves distant cousins but their exact relationship is unknown (September 17–18, 2016)
- **Norman Breedlove**: Craig's only son (June 8, 2016, and April 28, 2017)
- **Georgia Breedlove-Egger**: Craig's half sister from his father's second marriage (email correspondence July 25, 2016)
- **Allan "Buzzy" Buskirk**: *Spirit of America* team member, 1962–1964 (interviewed May 31, 2016; email correspondence June 2, 2016)
- **Michael Chernik**: Son of Harvey Chernik, who manned the counter at Quincy Automotive where Craig worked in the 1950s (June 24, 2016)
- **Ron Christensen**: Wendover resident in the 1950s and early 1960s; *Sonic Arrow* team volunteer, 1996–1997 (interviewed June 22, 2016; email correspondence February 10–11, 2017)
- **Carl Cruz**: Igniters member in the 1950s (June 14, 2016)
- **Bob Davids**: *Spirit of America* and *Sonic I* team member, 1961–1965 (interviewed June 18, 2009, and February 6 and March 10, 2017; email correspondence March 9–11, 2017)
- **Jerry Elverum**: Designed the rocket motor for Craig's LSR rocket car and rocket dragster in the early 1970s, based on his design for the Apollo Lunar Excursion Module rocket motor (March 21, 2017)
- **Richard Faulkner**: Elementary and high school friend; son-in-law of Ed Perkins, Craig's first sponsor (June 8, 2016)

- **Lee Frank:** Née Lee Roberts; Craig's second wife (July 22, 2009)
- **Mike Freebairn:** High school friend in the 1950s; involved with original *Spirit of America* jet car (June 2, 2009, and July 22, 2016)
- **Marvin Gelbart:** Igniters member in the 1950s (interviewed May 26, 2016; email correspondence June 1, 2016)
- **Gale Reed Gilbert:** California highway patrolman who visited Craig's shop when *Sonic I* was being built in 1965; eyewitness to the start of the Watts riots (August 21, 2016)
- **Stan Goldstein:** Friend since the early 1950s; involved in all of Craig's LSR projects from 1960 to present (May 27 and June 15, 2009, July 29 and October 30, 2016, and March 12, 2017)
- **Tom Hanna:** *Sonic I* team member, 1965 (May 21, 2009)
- **Donald Heath:** Son of Western Motel owner Earl Heath; expert on the subject of Wendover in the 1960s (July 9, 2016)
- **Terry Hendrickson:** *Sonic Arrow* team member, 1996–1997 (October 23, 2016)
- **Marge Kastler:** Née Marge Toombs; Craig's first wife (September 1, 2016)
- **Alyson Kimball:** *Sonic Arrow* team member, 1996–1997 (July 8, 2016, and April 28, 2017)
- **George Klass:** *Sonic I* team member, 1965; employed by Craig for *Sonic I* tour and in Goodyear drag tire business, 1966–1967 (May 4 and October 14, 2009, and June 29, 2016)
- **Bob Koken:** General Electric J-79 specialist assigned to *Sonic I* crew in 1965; died in 2012 (May 19, 2009)
- **Charlie Lyford:** Eyewitness to *Sonic Arrow* crash in 1996 (September 20, 2016)
- **Chuck Lyford:** Friend of Craig's since the late 1960s; eyewitness to *Sonic Arrow* crash in 1996; killed in a racing accident in 2017 (September 28, 2016)
- **Lamar Melville:** Utah highway patrolman based in Wendover in the 1960s; present at Bonneville for most land speed attempts at the time (November 5, 2009)
- **Rexford Metz:** Cameraman on the movies *Spirit of America*, 1962–1963, and *The Wildest Ride*, 1964 (May 18, 2009)

- **Cherié Miller**: Formerly Cherié Danson; *Sonic Arrow* team member, 1996–2000 (September 20, 2016)
- **Dezsö Molnar**: *Sonic Arrow* crew chief, 1996–1997 (email correspondence September 23, 2016–July 5, 2017)
- **Bill Moore**: Lifelong friend from kindergarten until Bill's death in 2010 (July 28, 2009)
- **Craig T. Nelson**: Friend and *Sonic Arrow* supporter, 1995–1997; purchased the film rights to Craig's life story in 1995; eyewitness to *Sonic Arrow* crash in 1996 (October 3, 2016)
- **Richard Parks**: *Sonic Arrow* team volunteer, 1997; son of National Hot Rod Association founder and president Wally Parks (August 21, 2016)
- **Nick Perkins**: Son of Ed Perkins, Craig's first sponsor (June 20, 2016)
- **Liisa Pine Schoonmaker**: *Sonic Arrow* team member, 1996 (July 10, 2016)
- **Vernon Rich**: *Sonic Arrow* team member, 1997; *Sonic Arrow* crew chief, 1998 (August 24, 2016)
- **Neil Roberts**: Design engineer involved in Craig's twin-engine jet car project in the 2010s (March 20, 2014)
- **Chris Rossi**: *Sonic Arrow* team member, 1996–1997 (interviewed September 19, 2016; email correspondence April 27, 2017)
- **Bard Rudder**: Worked at Craig's Goodyear store in the late 1960s (June 22, 2016)
- **Art Russell**: Lifelong friend since high school; involved in *Spirit of America* and *Sonic I* projects, 1962–1965 (June 17, 2009, and July 7, 2017)
- **Doug Sarian**: Igniters member in the 1950s (June 4, 2016)
- **Rod Schapel**: *Spirit of America* team member, 1961–1963 (June 10 and July 29, 2009)
- **Robin Sipe**: J-79 jet engine specialist; involved in Craig's twin-engine jet car project in the 2010s (email correspondence June 2, 2016)
- **Marilyn Taylor**: Craig's fifth wife (August 29, 2016)
- **Ken Thomas**: J-79 jet engine specialist; *Sonic Arrow* team member, 1996–1997 (July 9, 2016)

- **Tina Trefethen**: *Sonic Arrow* team member, 1990–1996 (interviewed September 2 and 12, 2016; letter correspondence November 2016)
- **Dave Veno**: *Sonic Arrow* team member, 1996–1997 (October 23, 2016)
- **Fritz Voigt**: Mickey Thompson's partner in *Challenger* LSR car in the late 1950s and early 1960s; died in 2014 (July 17, 2009)
- **Harry Weiser**: J-79 jet engine specialist; *Sonic Arrow* team member, 1996–1997 (June 19 and July 9, 2016)
- **Humpy Wheeler**: Sales manager in Firestone's racing division in the 1960s (August 4, 2009)

Here are additional sources and supplementary notes for each chapter:

1. Igniter

US census records for 1920, 1930, and 1940, and Canadian census records for 1916, all at ancestry.com; *Los Angeles City Directory*, volumes for 1920–1939 (Los Angeles Public Library collection at rescarta.lapl.org); *Louisville Courier-Journal*, December 30, 1908 (Craig's grandparents Gorman and Florence Breedlove in Kentucky). Don Baumea put me on to the importance of Craig's childhood involvement with model airplanes. Harvey Chernik's son Michael told me the bootlegger story. Other sources: S. Ravi Tam, *Distant Vistas: Exploring the Historical Neighborhoods of Mar Vista* (Mar Vista Historical Society, 2013), 75 (on Craig's childhood home at 3940 Marcasel); *Long Beach (CA) Independent*, October 3, 1943 (article on Norm Breedlove); Craig Breedlove and Bill Neely, *Spirit of America* (Chicago: Henry Regnery Co., 1971), chapters 1–3 (Craig driving Adair's dragster at Saugus on pp. 18–19); Marvin Gelbart, *The Igniters* (Bloomington, IN: AuthorHouse, 2008), passim (firecracker episode on pp. 207–9); *Drag News*, July 27, 1957, 7 (Quincy Speed Shop ad); Samuel Hawley, *Speed Duel: The Inside Story of the Land Speed Record in the Sixties* (Richmond Hill, ON: Firefly, 2010), 10–13.

Norm Breedlove's long career as a special effects technician in the movies and on TV included a stint on the show *The Rebel* in the late 1950s, where he designed the sawed-off shotgun nicknamed "Troubleshooter" used by his friend Nick Adams, who starred as Johnny Yuma. According to Craig, Norm was also involved in the creation of the sawed-off Winchester rifle that Steve McQueen used in his hit TV series *Wanted: Dead or Alive*.

2. Through the Roof

"Bombs over Bonneville," *Hot Rod*, September 1954, 36 (photos of "Craig Bow-man" and his racer); "They Went This-a-Way at Bonneville," *Hot Rod*, Decem-ber 1954, 43 (Craig's coupe listed under the name "Quincy Speed Shop"); Helen V. Hutchings, "Many a Dad Shopped at Quincy's," *Old Cars*, May 24, 2000, 39; *The Gondolier*, 1955 (Venice High School yearbook; Craig, unlike most of his classmates, did not participate in any extracurricular activities, and his graduation photo on page 26 is captioned simply "Craig Bowman, Industrial Arts"); "Never Scrap a Coupe," *Hot Rod*, September 1960 (about Craig's '34 coupe); *Los Angeles Times*, June 12, 1964 (sports columnist Jim Murray gives details on Craig's early life, including his Culver Boulevard crash), and December 5, 1965 ("Everybody said it was a tricky course"); Breedlove and Neely, *Spirit of America*, 20–38; Haw-ley, *Speed Duel*, 9–10 and 13–14; *Spirit of America*, documentary coproduced by Goodyear and Shell in 1963 (footage of Craig in his teens running his coupe at Bonneville and El Mirage).

3. Belly Tank Racer

Motoracing and Economy Car News, August 9–16, 1963, 7 (Craig recalling the beginnings of his LSR plans); *Los Angeles Times*, December 5, 1965 (Craig on his stint as a fireman); *Spirit of America*, 1963 film (footage of Craig running the belly tank racer at Bonneville); Breedlove and Neely, *Spirit of America*, 39–47; Hawley, *Speed Duel*, 14–15. During this period when Craig was struggling to support his family, his dad Norm tried without success to get him a job as an assistant camera-man at a Hollywood studio.

4. The Jet Car Idea

Los Angeles Times, December 5, 1965 ("It was hard for people"); *Los Angeles Herald-Examiner*, September 27, 1964 ("If you had the world's fastest elephant"); Breedlove and Neely, *Spirit of America*, 47–64; Harvey Shapiro, *Man Against the Salt* (Lon-don: Minerva Press, 1997), 206–10; Hawley, *Speed Duel*, 19–22. According to Fritz Voigt, Mickey Thompson went the four-engine route with *Challenger* rather than using a pair of more powerful Allison V-12s because he wanted to get sponsorship from a US car manufacturer. "It was all about sponsorship. Allison or somebody would never have given us any money" (interview with the author, July 17, 2009).

The coincidence of Art Russell and Bill Moore both winning the Fisher Body Craftsman's Guild contest would become even greater in 1963, when Bob Davids won as well. That three of the guys involved in the *Spirit* project won this prestigious national contest is an indication of the caliber of young men Craig had on his team.

5. Spirit Is Born

Breedlove and Neely, *Spirit of America*, 65–76; Hawley, *Speed Duel*, 52–59; *Spirit of America*, 1963 film (footage of *Spirit* model being tested and car under construction in Craig's dad's garage and at Epperly's shop); Louise Noeth, "The Science of Speed," *Goodguys Goodtimes Gazette*, October 2008, 14–15 (Walt Sheehan's involvement with Craig); Mickey Thompson with Griffith Borgeson, *Challenger: Mickey Thompson's Own Story of His Life of Speed* (Englewood Cliffs, NJ: Prentice-Hall, 1964), 174 ("When Judy and Fritz"). See Hawley, *Speed Duel*, for the full story of Athol Graham, Nathan Ostich, Mickey Thompson, Donald Campbell, and Art Arfons at Bonneville in 1960. Bob Davids went on to achieve great success in business, starting several companies employing thousands of people. He shared his thoughts with me on the subject of leadership and Craig's helming of the *Spirit of America* project.

6. Black Line Zigzag

Los Angeles Times, July 8 and August 5 (*Spirit* unveiled at Wilshire Country Club), 1962; *Spirit of America*, 1963 film (includes Spotlite Newsreel film "Jet Car Unveiled" and footage of the car running at Bonneville in 1962); Breedlove and Neely, *Spirit of America*, 77–93; Hawley, *Speed Duel*, 83–91. Craig and Lee (full name Leota Ann Roberts) were married on June 10, 1962. Craig drew a salary of $400 a month (equal to his pay at the fire department) while completing *Spirit* after Shell came on board. According to Allan Buskirk, Shell provided a Ford F-850 truck with a big box on the back to tow *Spirit* around on its dolly. This "banana truck," as the crew called it, was considered inadequate because the box obscured the driver's view of the racer towing behind. The crew therefore used Craig's F-150 pickup to tow *Spirit*.

7. Bringing It Back

Bill Lawler's letter to *Spirit* crew, July 17, 1963 (courtesy Bob Davids); "Spirit of America" media brochure, Shell Oil, 1964 (technical specs); *Deseret News*, July 31–August 6, 1963 (most thorough newspaper coverage); *Los Angeles Times*, August

3 and 6, 1963; Breedlove and Neely, *Spirit of America*, chap. 10; Craig Breedlove, "Driving a World's Record 407 Miles per Hour," *Popular Mechanics*, November 1963, 87–92ff. (lots of details on *Spirit*; vivid description by Craig of speed run); J. G. Anthony, "The Fastest Thing on Wheels!" *Car Life*, November 1963, 25–30; Devon Francis, "Can They Hit 500 m.p.h.?" *Popular Science*, August 1964, 70–73ff.; "407.45 mph!" *Motoracing and Economy Car News*, August 9–16, 1963 (Ben Torres dialogue); Hays Gorey, "Cool Run for an Old Hot Rodder," *Sports Illustrated*, August 19, 1963, 46–51; Hawley, *Speed Duel*, chap. 10; "Assault on the Salt," *Measure* (Hewlett-Packard company magazine), October 1968, 8–10 (details on USAC timing system). Lee Bible story: *Ludington Daily News* ("Garage Mechanic to Drive Triplex Against Record") and *Brooklyn Standard Union*, March 13, 1929; *Sarasota Herald*, *Brooklyn Daily Eagle*, and *Montreal Gazette*, March 14, 1929; magazine section, *St. Petersburg Times*, December 12, 1937, 5.

8. American Hero

Craig's scrapbooks of congratulatory telegrams and newspaper clippings; *New York Times*, August 6, 1963 ("He's a remarkable salesman"); Breedlove and Neely, *Spirit of America*, 102–15; Cyril Posthumus, *Land Speed Record: A Complete History of World Record-Breaking Cars from 39.24 to 600+ mph* (New York: Crown Publishers, 1971), 177 ("Who the hell . . ."); David Tremayne, *Donald Campbell: The Man Behind the Mask* (London: Bantam Books, 2004), 263–84 (Breedlove on Campbell; British press hoping for "fireworks"); *Los Angeles Times*, May 25, 1964 (plans for Breedlove movie); *Palos Verdes News*, March 3, 1966 (details about Craig's new house at 29443 Whitley Collins in Palos Verdes). Additional sources on *Spirit II*: George Klass, forum posting, April 18, 2015, jalopyjournal.com ("I guess they didn't have . . ."); George Klass, email correspondence with author, January 25, 2017; Phil Burgess, "Breedlove's Sleek Slingshot," March 23, 2013, www.nhra.com.

9. Speed War

Breedlove and Neely, *Spirit of America*, 110–22; Hawley, *Speed Duel*, 168–84; *Spirit of America*, Shell and Goodyear promotional film, 1963 (Craig on corrosiveness of salt: "It powders up"); Craig Breedlove, "My Nightmare Ride at 540 mph—and No Brakes!" *Family Weekly*, December 13, 1964 (Craig writing notes to his kids). The best newspaper source for the 1964 Bonneville season is the *Deseret News*, October 1–14, 1964. Also: *Akron Beacon Journal*, October 4, 6, 12 (George Koehne crash photo), and 14, 1964, and *New York Times*, October 14, 1964 ("We're going to stay").

A great unpublished source on Walt and Art Arfons is the candid audio recordings made by writer Jack Olsen for his two *Sports Illustrated* articles on the estranged half brothers in 1965, Jack Olsen Papers, series 7: Sound Recordings, University of Oregon Libraries, Special Collections. Used for this chapter: box 12, reel 94, side A ("all-out blood-stinkin' war") and box 13, reel 102, side B ("He parked his bus").

10. Roll the Ambulance

"Spirit of America: Organization and Operations on the Salt," 3–4, and "Turn-Around and Starting" (typewritten instructions issued to the SOA crew), July 17, 1963, provided to me by Bob Davids. USAC field telephone communications and background chatter were taken verbatim from Jim Economides's audio recording featured in *Breedlove 500+* (1964 Capitol Records LP) and *The Wildest Ride* (1964 Goodyear and Shell movie). Published sources: *Deseret News*, October 15 and 16, 1964; *Salt Lake Tribune* (*Tribune* reporter Marion Dunn was with Norm Breedlove at the USAC shack); *Akron Beacon Journal* and *New York Times*, October 16, 1964; Hays Gorey, "Fast, Wet—and Almost Dead," *Sports Illustrated*, October 26, 1964, 72–74; Breedlove, "Nightmare Ride," *Family Weekly*, December 13, 1964; Breedlove and Neely, *Spirit of America*, 123–28; Bill Neely, "For My Next Act, I'm Going to Set Myself on Fire," *Playboy*, May 1972, 136–40ff; Hawley, *Speed Duel*, 184–201; Bill Neely, *Tire Wars: Racing with Goodyear* (Tucson, AZ: Aztex, 1993), 111–12.

11. "I Almost Drowned in That Thing!"

Dialogue on the embankment was taken verbatim from Jim Economides's audio recording on the *Breedlove 500+* album and from the 1964 movie *The Wildest Ride*. See also the audio transcript in Cole Coonce, *Infinity Over Zero* (La Crescenta, CA: Kerosene Bomb Publishing, 2002), 69–76. Newspapers: *Deseret News*, October 16 (Hi McDonald's account of crash), October 17 (Art Arfons: "I can't quit"), and October 29, 1964 ("Boy, isn't that something"); *New York Times*, October 16, 1964; *Los Angeles Times*, June 12, 1964; *Palos Verdes News*, June 26, 1966 (Jack Carter recalls crash). Also: Breedlove, "Nightmare Ride," *Family Weekly*, December 13, 1964, 4–6; Breedlove and Neely, *Spirit of America*, 129–35 (Art Arfons: "The only way"); Neely, "For My Next Act," *Playboy*, May 1972, 181–82; Hawley, *Speed Duel*, 194–201; Neely, *Tire Wars*, 111.

12. Sonic I

Breedlove and Neely, *Spirit of America*, 137–49 (Craig's description of J-79 test on pp. 148–49); Breedlove, "750 mph . . . Here I Come," *Popular Mechanics*, September 1965, 88–92ff. (*Sonic I* technical details); *Los Angeles Times*, December 5, 1965 (Craig calls wind tunnel testing "useless"); "Supersonic Chase on Bonneville Flats," *Christian Science Monitor*, October 4, 1965. George Klass lived at Craig's Palos Verdes house for several months while *Sonic I* was being built and was subsequently employed by Craig in 1966 and '67, so he got to know him quite well. George Boskoff told me the story about Connie Swingle using his rifle on the glass sample. Quin Epperly, Nye Frank, Bob Davids, and Al Buskirk did most of the restoration work on the original *Spirit of America* prior to its trip to the Chicago museum. With *Sonic I*, Craig used the same no-risk pitch he used with Shell to get sub-sponsorship deals with Lamson & Sessions and Champion Spark Plugs, both companies agreeing to pay him $5,000 if he broke the record.

According to J-79 specialist Bob Koken, the GE technician who accompanied the *Sonic I* crew to Bonneville in 1965, "The engine Breedlove had was one of the earliest J-79s. . . . They only made about ten like it. It was considerably different from the later engines and considerably less powerful, one of the weakest of the J-79s. I'm guessing it was good for about 13,000 or 13,500 pounds of thrust at sea level. The later engines got as high as 17,000. . . . We were really proud of the J-79 at the time. It was a lot more powerful than the J-47 and used only about two-thirds the fuel" (interview with the author, May 19, 2009).

13. Back into Battle

Art Arfons's "Little shit" comment: Jack Olsen Papers, series 7: Sound Recordings, University of Oregon Libraries, Special Collections, reel 101, side A. Craig's secret course booking through M-Z Promotions was mentioned in the *Deseret News*, November 3, 1965. *Sonic I* unveiling: *Deseret News*, September 30, 1965; *Christian Science Monitor*, October 4, 1965 (mentions logo-on-tail disagreement between Craig and Goodyear). Also: Goodyear *Sonic I* press releases #11500-965 to #11504-965, September 29, 1965 (my thanks to Bob Davids for copies from his personal collection); *Deseret News*, October 2–23, 1965 (daily reports of happenings on salt flats); *Los Angeles Times*, December 5, 1965 ("Friend, when you get"); Breedlove and Neely, *Spirit of America*, 153–65 ("This run had scared me" on p. 163); Hawley, *Speed Duel*, 258–66.

I am indebted to model makers Howard Stratham and Arie Brass for sending me a draft copy of their research paper "The Various Configurations of *Spirit of America—Sonic I*" (unpublished manuscript, January 29, 2017). It helped me sort out the precise sequence of events during *Sonic I*'s run for the record in 1965.

14. Russian Roulette with Jets

Deseret News, November 2–4 and 15, 1965; *Akron Beacon Journal*, November 3, 5, 15, and 16, 1965; *New York Times*, November 3 and 16, 1965; Craig Breedlove, "600 MPH—What It's Really Like!" *Motor Trend*, March 1966, 46; Jack Olsen, "Enemies in Speedland II: Duel on the Salt," *Sports Illustrated*, December 6, 1965, 130 ("They've heard there's a cold front" and "It was not!"); Breedlove and Neely, *Spirit of America*, 160–85; Hawley, *Speed Duel*, 266–89; Jerry Kirshenbaum, "A Speed King Without a Kingdom," *Sports Illustrated*, April 27, 1970, 73 ("walking out on a limb"); Sam Low, "Six Hundred at Bonneville," www.samlow.com/speed /sixhundredatbonneville.htm ("Ask Walt if he really knows"); *Sonic I* footage in the film *Chase the Wind*, produced and directed by Al Blanchard (Allend'or Production, no date [early 1970s]); raw *Sonic I* footage at WPA Film Library (www .wpafilmlibrary.com/videos/137475) and at Getty Images (www.gettyimages.com, search term "Craig Breedlove"). In *Chase the Wind*, *Sonic I* can be seen exiting the mile with its front wheels up off the ground.

Art Arfons confirmed to USAC historian Donald Davidson some years later that his "What's going to happen here?" encounter with Craig did indeed occur. (Shapiro, *Man Against the Salt*, 146). Lee Breedlove's ultimate women's LSR was broken by Kitty O'Neill, driving a three-wheel vehicle, in 1976. Lee's mark for a four-wheel vehicle stood until 2013.

15. Cutthroat

On Craig's Goodyear store: "Breedlove Opens Shop," *Torrance (CA) Daily Breeze*, October 4, 1967. The store was located at 2475 Pacific Coast Highway on the corner of Crenshaw. On the Rod Schapel lawsuit: "Breedlove Wins Suit," *Palm Springs (CA) Desert Sun*, August 11, 1966, and *Redlands (CA) Daily Facts*, August 11, 1966. On the turbine car story: Bill Kilpatrick, "The 'Big' Engine That Almost Did," *Popular Mechanics*, August 1967, 69–71; "Shelby Withdraws Turbines from Race," *Los Angeles Times*, May 8, 1968; Bob Ottum, "Turbines and Trauma at Indy," *Sports Illustrated*, May 20, 1968, 26–27; Kirshenbaum, "Speed King," *Sports Illustrated*, April 27, 1970, 68 ("Craig is too open"); Gordon Cruikshank, "Whistling in the

Dark," *Motor Sport*, April 2006, 58–63; Anthony Granatelli, *They Call Me Mister 500* (New York: Bantam Books, 1970), 291–362 (excellent in-depth account); Rinsey Mills, *Carroll Shelby* (Minneapolis: Motorbooks, 2012), 473–74; Stephen Cox, "Stealing the 500: The Story of Carroll Shelby's 1968 Turbine-Powered Indycar," two-part article at www.sopwithmotorsports.com, August 26 and September 7, 2016.

16. Hard Times

Breedlove and Neely, *Spirit of America*, 189–204; Joe Scalzo, "Black Coffee, Battered Buick, and Broke," *Car Life*, June 1969, 26–32. *Aqua America*: "The Craig Breedlove Story—Determination," *Palos Verdes News*, March 3, 1966; "Jet Hydro Record in Contention," *Motor Boating*, February 1966, 138. Hydroplane designer Ted Jones was involved in the project. Motorboat racing on Lake Havasu: Kim Chaplin, "Too Fast for the Three Fastest," *Sports Illustrated*, December 4, 1967, 96–97 ("Let's go tell Larry"); *Reno Gazette-Journal*, November 27, 1967, and November 29, 1968; *Seattle Spokesman-Review*, November 30, 1968. Craig launched his drag chute venture with Jack Carter in June 1966 (*Palos Verdes News*, June 26, 1966). The business was based in Craig's shop at 2412 Amsler Street in Torrance. Craig ran the AMX at San Angelo, Texas, on February 14, 1968, with co-drivers Lee Breedlove and Ron Dykes and broke 106 speed and distance records. AMC made a ten-minute promotional film of the event titled *Texas Takeover* (1968). On the AMC-sponsored *American Spirit* racer: "The Name of the Game," *Hot Rod*, December 1968, 100–102; *Nevada State Journal*, November 6 and 10, 1968. *American Spirit* was 20½ feet long, 70 inches wide between the outrigger wheels, and weighed 2,000 pounds. The three engines that were to go in it were a 373-cubic-inch V8 (B class), a 296-cubic-inch V8 (C class), and a 182-cubic-inch 6-cylinder (D class). Craig's divorce: *Las Vegas Review-Journal*, November 14, 1968; Kirshenbaum, "Speed King," *Sports Illustrated*, April 27, 1970, 68 ("It's like the man said"). Snowmobile racing: "Breedlove Turns to Snowmobiles," *Daily Sitka (AK) Sentinel*, January 31, 1969.

17. Playing with Fire

Bill Neely, "For His Next Act . . . ," *Road and Track*, March 1971, 97–98; E. K. von Delden, "Breedlove's Rocket Racers," *Hot Rod*, May 1971, 112–17; Breedlove and Neely, *Spirit of America*, 207–11; Craig Breedlove rocket car interview, 1971, KUTV News Collection (A0303), J. Willard Marriott Library, University of Utah.

Craig's original design for his *Sonic II* rocket car is dated December 22, 1969. On *Blue Flame*: *Hendersonville Times-News*, October 14 and 24, 1970; George Ferguson, "The Run Was a Natural Gas," *Sports Illustrated*, November 9, 1970, 50–55 ("Plenty boss, man"); Sarah Kasprowicz, *The Reluctant Rocketman* (Waukesha, WI: GreenBean Creative Solutions, 2013). The owner of the pickup that pushed *Blue Flame* was Dana Fuller of San Francisco. The fact that the natural gas industry-sponsored racer set the record without using natural gas was kept out of the papers. Planned head-to-head race at Bonneville between Gary Gabelich and Craig: *Long Beach (CA) Press-Telegram* and *Palm Springs (CA) Desert News*, May 28, 1971; Bruce Wennerstrom, "Race of the Century!" *Mechanix Illustrated*, November 1972, 63–65ff. *Screaming Yellow Zonker*: *Denton (TX) Record-Chronicle*, May 30, 1972; *Kingsport (TN) News*, June 14, 1972. *English Leather Special*: *St. Louis Post-Dispatch*, August 2, 1973; *Los Angeles Times* and *Nevada State Journal*, August 29, 1973; *Pomona (CA) Progress-Bulletin*, September 12, 1973; *Los Angeles Herald-Examiner*, September 13, 1973; *Bellevue (WA) American*, September 20, 1973; promotional materials for the car prepared by Bob Perilla Associates of New York (in Craig's personal collection); *Rocket Man Craig Breedlove*, 1973 film of Craig at the AHRA meet in St. Louis in August 1973 ("It's safe").

Ky Michaelson, who was involved in the *Pollution Packer* hydrogen peroxide dragster, would call Craig's dragster "the scariest rocket car of all time": Ky Michaelson, *Rocketman: My Rocket-Propelled Life and High-Octane Creations* (Saint Paul, MN: Motorbooks, 2007), 107. "It's frightening," Craig would concede in August 1973. "It's absolutely terrifying. But that's the good part about it, because people come to races to see something spectacular. That's what racing's all about." He went on to point out that while his bipropellants were completely safe in their separate tanks, "with hydrogen peroxide, the stuff can go off if you get any dirt in it or anything" (*Rocket Man Craig Breedlove* film).

18. The River

Dan Gerber, "Fastest Foot in the West," *Sports Illustrated*, December 17, 1973, 51 (Craig wants to help his son); Jackie Lapin, "Breedlove: The Quest for Speed Burns Out," *New York Times*, June 29, 1976 ("I just knew I had to stop"); *Eureka (CA) Times-Standard*, May 11, 1979 (Peggy's death); David Diamond, "The Fast American Hero," *Wired*, November 1, 1996 (Craig was "lost"). Craig is still an active part-owner in the two clubs he helped develop in the late 1970s. They are the South End Racquet and Health Club and the West End Racquet and Health Club, both located in Torrance.

19. Sonic Arrow

On the short-lived revival of Craig's LSR rocket car project: "Sprit of America Team Support Personnel," January 20, 1987; fundraising ad from unidentified magazine, July 1987, selling World Speed Record Team memberships, T-shirts, and jackets, both in Craig's personal collection. For *Sonic Arrow*, Tina Trefethen sent me a treasure trove of photos, written reminiscences, and supplementary documentation, including a "Participation History in Craig Breedlove's Spirit of America Project" containing a timeline for and details on the car's fabrication. On Art Arfons and *Green Monster* number 27: Shapiro, *Man Against the Salt*, 379 ("I had to call Breedlove"), 384 ("Art knew what he wanted"), and 387 ("I just think it was a real good decision"). On *Thrust2*: Richard Noble, *Thrust: Through the Sound Barrier* (London: Partridge, 1998), 97 ("Craig, you son of a gun"). On *Thrust-SSC*: Noble, *Thrust*, 122 ("I'd wanted to keep going"), 141 ("Imagine a loaded wheelbarrow"), 155 (Craig: "It's just designed" and "We're going to have lots of sensors"), 168 ("In order to get *ThrustSSC* operational"), and 172 and 202 (Andy Green comments). Other sources: Steve Sneddon, "Breedlove's Speed Quest," *Reno Gazette-Journal*, October 12, 1993; Shav Glick, "Riding the Four-Ton Dart," *Los Angeles Times*, August 25, 1995; R. R., "Back to Black Rock," *Motor Sport*, December 1993, 1220–21; Rich Taylor, "Breaking the Sound Barrier—on Wheels!" *Popular Mechanics*, September 1995, 68–71; Arthur St. Antoine, "Mach My Day!" *Los Angeles*, August 1996, 50–52; John Ackroyd, *Jet Blast and the Hand of Fate* (Gateshead, UK: Redline Books, 2007), 193; Matt Smith, "Monsters of Drag," *SF Weekly*, August 13, 1997; "Coach Gets Caught in a Full Nelson," *New York Magazine*, October 7, 1996, 11.

Craig vigorously refutes the claim that the *Budweiser Rocket* was the first car to go supersonic on December 17, 1979. The unsanctioned record attempt, which was the subject of a TV special, consisted of a single one-way pass through timing lights set just fifty-two feet apart and ignored the rules of land speed racing. Moreover, the results from the timing lights and clocks, which might have carried some weight, were not even used. The *Budweiser Rocket* team based their supersonic claim instead on a combination of onboard instrumentation and on readings from an uncalibrated, manually aimed radar that was tracking the car. From these they came up with an estimated top speed of 739 mph. No sonic boom was heard during the run. The data used to calculate the speed were never released.

Craig subsequently spoke with Earl Flanders, who was hired to operate the clocks on the controversial run, and asked him what really happened. "All I can tell you is that the car went 666," said Earl. Craig: "You mean you clocked the car on the run?" Earl: "Yes, I did." Craig: "So what's the deal with the 739 they're claiming?" Earl: "It's a total fraud. It didn't happen." Years later Craig tracked down the actual timing paper for the *Budweiser Rocket*'s run and it confirmed what Earl had said. According to the electronic timer, the car had done 666.234 mph through the clocks. (Author interviews with Craig, October 23–24, 2016; Cole Coonce interview with Craig, *Infinity Over Zero*, 210–11. For Richard Noble's take on the *Budweiser Rocket* see *Thrust*, 106–7.)

20. Turbulence

Coatings company lawsuit: case notes from State of Utah archives. The complaint was filed in the Third District Court, Salt Lake City, on February 8, 1995, and the trial held on May 6–9, 1996. Other sources: Diamond, "Fast American Hero," *Wired*, November 1, 1996; Robert Riddell, "Fast Car," *Speak*, Spring 1997, 40–45; James Mueller, "Breedlove's First Car a Real Draw at the Museum of Science and Industry," *Chicago Tribune*, November 10, 1996; Matt Smith, "Monsters of Drag," *SF Weekly*, August 13, 1997 ("Some people just don't work out"); Mark Pauline, "SRL Banned in San Fran," *SRL News*, January 31, 2012. *ThrustSSC*: Noble, *Thrust*, 207 ("a little sporty"); Richard Noble, "How We Broke the Sound Barrier," *Motor Sport*, December 1997, 5–6; R. J. Smith, "Speed Freaks," *Spin*, January 1998, 121. My thanks to Ron Christensen for sending me a copy of Dezsö Molnar's *Rocket Science* album and a clip of the song "Lobster Head."

21. Breedlove's Back

Bill Maloney, "Craig Breedlove Unveils Speed of Sound Land Speed Record Car," *The Auto Channel*, July 12, 1996, www.theautochannel.com/news/date/19960712 /news01216.html; *Reno Gazette-Journal*, September 13 and October 9, 15, 16, and 19–28, 1996; Diamond, "Fast American Hero," *Wired*, November 1, 1996 ("We have very limited time"); Riddell, "Fast Car," *Speak*, Spring 1997, 42; D. Brian Burghart, "Three Strange Days: The World's Land Speed Record Will Come to Those Who Wait," www.pyramid.net/burghart/racers.html ("It's a very harsh environment").

Craig made a preliminary trip to Black Rock in July 1996 to test *Sonic Arrow*'s ski brake. The brake was attached to the back of a Chevy pickup and Craig sat in the truck bed, facing backward. It worked perfectly, bringing the truck to a firm stop from 60 mph. "The Bureau of Land Management was concerned that we not damage the surface of the playa with the ski brake underneath the car," Craig says.

"Which is kind of ironic, considering they now have dunes about three feet high all over Burning Man, and they were worried about this little ski."

22. World's Fastest Car Crash

Craig provided me with a copy of the printout of the onboard instrumentation data, which shows *Sonic Arrow*'s speed buildup to 675 mph in forty-five seconds. (Unlike Craig's previous *Spirit of America* racers, which measured air speed, *Arrow*'s speedometer measured actual speed through wheel rotations.) Details on *Sonic Arrow*'s start-up procedures came from a checklist, titled "Chris Rossi's checklist," that Ron Christensen found discarded at Bonneville on October 5, 1996. The five-page document lists forty-four steps for preparing the car for a run. Chris Rossi went over the steps with me to help me better understand what was involved. Other sources: newspaper reports in the *Reno Gazette-Journal* (most thorough coverage), *Deseret News*, and *New York Times*, October 29, 1996; Ackroyd, *Jet Blast*, 209–12; Coonce, *Infinity Over Zero*, 90–94. According to Charlie Lyford, the minicassette containing the video footage that he and Doria Nelson shot of the crash found its way to a TV station and was shown on the news, then disappeared.

23. The Boom

Don Baumea, "The Art of the Roll" (unpublished manuscript, revised edition, June 21, 2015), research paper on the work Don and Craig did on the phenomenon of gyroscopic precession torque as it related to Craig's crash in 1996; Craig's *Spirit of America* Christmas newsletter, December 1997. Other sources: *Reno Gazette-Journal*, May 4, July 17, August 10 and 30, September 3–October 29, and November 4, 11, and 17, 1997; *Deseret News*, September 13 and 15 and October 4, 6, and 14, 1997; Richard Hoffer, "The Great Race," *Sports Illustrated*, September 29, 1997, 60–66; Kevin Wilson, "The Long Wait," *Autoweek*, October 13, 1997, 14–16; Burghart, "Three Strange Days," www.pyramid.net/burghart/racers.html; Smith, "Speed Freaks," *Spin*, January 1998, 94–97ff; Coonce, *Infinity Over Zero*, 212 ("Getting the record does not interest us"); Ackroyd, *Jet Blast*, 224–35; Noble, *Thrust*, 85 ("When you ask people"), 88–89 (Black Rock map showing British and American camps and course layout), 158 (real reason for *ThrustSSC*'s rear steering), 233 ("By most technical definitions"), and 286–87 ("It was one hell of a moment"); Louise Noeth, "The Science of Speed: How Walt Sheehan Made Craig Breedlove a Household Name," *Goodguys Goodtimes Gazette*, October 2008, 14

("The kid doesn't have any idea"; Walt Sheehan died in December 1997, just two months after leaving the playa). Cherié Miller also provided me with a series of press releases she wrote when she was in charge of public relations for *Spirit of America* from late 1996 to 2000.

Sonic Arrow's fodded J-79 was subsequently purchased by Robin Sipe, owner of S&S Turbine Services in Fort St. John, British Columbia, where it was refurbished to pump natural gas. It is currently being used for that purpose at the Aliso Canyon natural gas compression facility in the L.A. suburb of Northridge, just a few miles from where Craig grew up. (Robin Sipe email to author, June 2, 2016.)

Epilogue

Craig's attempts to mount an LSR bid in 1998–1999: *Reno Gazette-Journal*, March 19, May 21, and June 18, 1998, and March 26 and August 3, 1999. Craig's IMSHF induction in 2000: Cherié Miller, "Dream Warriors," *Spirit of America* press release, undated (2000). Also: Michael Mattis, "Craig Breedlove," *Salon*, July 31, 1999, www.salon.com/people/rewind/1999/07/31/breedlove. Craig's plan for a twin-engine jet car: Brad Stanhope, "Breedlove Guns for 1,000-mph Car," *Fairfield-Suisan (CA) Daily Republic*, August 18, 2013; Mark Vaughn, "Breedlove's Back!" *Autoweek*, May 7, 2014, www.autoweek.com/article/car-news/breedloves-back; Neil Roberts, "Spirit of America Announced," May 8, 2014, www.thinkfastengineering .com/2014/05/spirit-america-announced; Rob Kinnan, "Craig Breedlove: Interview with America's 600-mph Man," *Hot Rod Network*, August 10, 2014, www.hotrod .com/news/craig-breedlove-americas-600-mph-man ("our design is more straight-forward"); Ted Sillanpaa, "Legendary Driver Craig Breedlove Built the Fastest Car on Earth, and He Could Do It Again," *Maxim*, October 2014; *Spirit of America* website, www.soa1000.com, set up by Neil Roberts in 2015. The best source of information on *Bloodhound* is the team's website www.bloodhoundssc.com.

INDEX